FREE Test Taking Tips DVD Offer

To help us better serve you, we have developed a Test Taking Tips DVD that we would like to give you for FREE. **This DVD covers world-class test taking tips that you can use to be even more successful when you are taking your test.**

All that we ask is that you email us your feedback about your study guide. Please let us know what you thought about it – whether that is good, bad or indifferent.

To get your **FREE Test Taking Tips DVD**, email freedvd@studyguideteam.com with "FREE DVD" in the subject line and the following information in the body of the email:

    a. The title of your study guide.

    b. Your product rating on a scale of 1-5, with 5 being the highest rating.

    c. Your feedback about the study guide. What did you think of it?

    d. Your full name and shipping address to send your free DVD.

If you have any questions or concerns, please don't hesitate to contact us at freedvd@studyguideteam.com.

Thanks again!

PSAT Prep Book 2018 & 2019 Practice Tests

Three Full-Length PSAT Practice Tests

Test Prep Books College Entrance Team

Table of Contents

Quick Overview

As you draw closer to taking your exam, effective preparation becomes more and more important. Thankfully, you have this study guide to help you get ready. Use this guide to help keep your studying on track and refer to it often.

This study guide contains several key sections that will help you be successful on your exam. The guide contains tips for what you should do the night before and the day of the test. Also included are test-taking tips. Knowing the right information is not always enough. Many well-prepared test takers struggle with exams. These tips will help equip you to accurately read, assess, and answer test questions.

A large part of the guide is devoted to showing you what content to expect on the exam and to helping you better understand that content. Near the end of this guide is a practice test so that you can see how well you have grasped the content. Then, answer explanations are provided so that you can understand why you missed certain questions.

Don't try to cram the night before you take your exam. This is not a wise strategy for a few reasons. First, your retention of the information will be low. Your time would be better used by reviewing information you already know rather than trying to learn a lot of new information. Second, you will likely become stressed as you try to gain a large amount of knowledge in a short amount of time. Third, you will be depriving yourself of sleep. So be sure to go to bed at a reasonable time the night before. Being well-rested helps you focus and remain calm.

Be sure to eat a substantial breakfast the morning of the exam. If you are taking the exam in the afternoon, be sure to have a good lunch as well. Being hungry is distracting and can make it difficult to focus. You have hopefully spent lots of time preparing for the exam. Don't let an empty stomach get in the way of success!

When travelling to the testing center, leave earlier than needed. That way, you have a buffer in case you experience any delays. This will help you remain calm and will keep you from missing your appointment time at the testing center.

Be sure to pace yourself during the exam. Don't try to rush through the exam. There is no need to risk performing poorly on the exam just so you can leave the testing center early. Allow yourself to use all of the allotted time if needed.

Remain positive while taking the exam even if you feel like you are performing poorly. Thinking about the content you should have mastered will not help you perform better on the exam.

Once the exam is complete, take some time to relax. Even if you feel that you need to take the exam again, you will be well served by some down time before you begin studying again. It's often easier to convince yourself to study if you know that it will come with a reward!

Test-Taking Strategies

1. Predicting the Answer

When you feel confident in your preparation for a multiple-choice test, try predicting the answer before reading the answer choices. This is especially useful on questions that test objective factual knowledge or that ask you to fill in a blank. By predicting the answer before reading the available choices, you eliminate the possibility that you will be distracted or led astray by an incorrect answer choice. You will feel more confident in your selection if you read the question, predict the answer, and then find your prediction among the answer choices. After using this strategy, be sure to still read all of the answer choices carefully and completely. If you feel unprepared, you should not attempt to predict the answers. This would be a waste of time and an opportunity for your mind to wander in the wrong direction.

2. Reading the Whole Question

Too often, test takers scan a multiple-choice question, recognize a few familiar words, and immediately jump to the answer choices. Test authors are aware of this common impatience, and they will sometimes prey upon it. For instance, a test author might subtly turn the question into a negative, or he or she might redirect the focus of the question right at the end. The only way to avoid falling into these traps is to read the entirety of the question carefully before reading the answer choices.

3. Looking for Wrong Answers

Long and complicated multiple-choice questions can be intimidating. One way to simplify a difficult multiple-choice question is to eliminate all of the answer choices that are clearly wrong. In most sets of answers, there will be at least one selection that can be dismissed right away. If the test is administered on paper, the test taker could draw a line through it to indicate that it may be ignored; otherwise, the test taker will have to perform this operation mentally or on scratch paper. In either case, once the obviously incorrect answers have been eliminated, the remaining choices may be considered. Sometimes identifying the clearly wrong answers will give the test taker some information about the correct answer. For instance, if one of the remaining answer choices is a direct opposite of one of the eliminated answer choices, it may well be the correct answer. The opposite of obviously wrong is obviously right! Of course, this is not always the case. Some answers are obviously incorrect simply because they are irrelevant to the question being asked. Still, identifying and eliminating some incorrect answer choices is a good way to simplify a multiple-choice question.

4. Don't Overanalyze

Anxious test takers often overanalyze questions. When you are nervous, your brain will often run wild, causing you to make associations and discover clues that don't actually exist. If you feel that this may be a problem for you, do whatever you can to slow down during the test. Try taking a deep breath or counting to ten. As you read and consider the question, restrict yourself to the particular words used by the author. Avoid thought tangents about what the author *really* meant, or what he or she was *trying* to say. The only things that matter on a multiple-choice test are the words that are actually in the question. You must avoid reading too much into a multiple-choice question, or supposing that the writer meant something other than what he or she wrote.

5. No Need for Panic

It is wise to learn as many strategies as possible before taking a multiple-choice test, but it is likely that you will come across a few questions for which you simply don't know the answer. In this situation, avoid panicking. Because most multiple-choice tests include dozens of questions, the relative value of a single wrong answer is small. Moreover, your failure on one question has no effect on your success elsewhere on the test. As much as possible, you should compartmentalize each question on a multiple-choice test. In other words, you should not allow your feelings about one question to affect your success on the others. When you find a question that you either don't understand or don't know how to answer, just take a deep breath and do your best. Read the entire question slowly and carefully. Try rephrasing the question a couple of different ways. Then, read all of the answer choices carefully. After eliminating obviously wrong answers, make a selection and move on to the next question.

6. Confusing Answer Choices

When working on a difficult multiple-choice question, there may be a tendency to focus on the answer choices that are the easiest to understand. Many people, whether consciously or not, gravitate to the answer choices that require the least concentration, knowledge, and memory. This is a mistake. When you come across an answer choice that is confusing, you should give it extra attention. A question might be confusing because you do not know the subject matter to which it refers. If this is the case, don't eliminate the answer before you have affirmatively settled on another. When you come across an answer choice of this type, set it aside as you look at the remaining choices. If you can confidently assert that one of the other choices is correct, you can leave the confusing answer aside. Otherwise, you will need to take a moment to try to better understand the confusing answer choice. Rephrasing is one way to tease out the sense of a confusing answer choice.

7. Your First Instinct

Many people struggle with multiple-choice tests because they overthink the questions. If you have studied sufficiently for the test, you should be prepared to trust your first instinct once you have carefully and completely read the question and all of the answer choices. There is a great deal of research suggesting that the mind can come to the correct conclusion very quickly once it has obtained all of the relevant information. At times, it may seem to you as if your intuition is working faster even than your reasoning mind. This may in fact be true. The knowledge you obtain while studying may be retrieved from your subconscious before you have a chance to work out the associations that support it. Verify your instinct by working out the reasons that it should be trusted.

8. Key Words

Many test takers struggle with multiple-choice questions because they have poor reading comprehension skills. Quickly reading and understanding a multiple-choice question requires a mixture of skill and experience. To help with this, try jotting down a few key words and phrases on a piece of scrap paper. Doing this concentrates the process of reading and forces the mind to weigh the relative importance of the question's parts. In selecting words and phrases to write down, the test taker thinks about the question more deeply and carefully. This is especially true for multiple-choice questions that are preceded by a long prompt.

9. Subtle Negatives

One of the oldest tricks in the multiple-choice test writer's book is to subtly reverse the meaning of a question with a word like *not* or *except*. If you are not paying attention to each word in the question, you can easily be led astray by this trick. For instance, a common question format is, "Which of the following is...?" Obviously, if the question instead is, "Which of the following is not...?," then the answer will be quite different. Even worse, the test makers are aware of the potential for this mistake and will include one answer choice that would be correct if the question were not negated or reversed. A test taker who misses the reversal will find what he or she believes to be a correct answer and will be so confident that he or she will fail to reread the question and discover the original error. The only way to avoid this is to practice a wide variety of multiple-choice questions and to pay close attention to each and every word.

10. Reading Every Answer Choice

It may seem obvious, but you should always read every one of the answer choices! Too many test takers fall into the habit of scanning the question and assuming that they understand the question because they recognize a few key words. From there, they pick the first answer choice that answers the question they believe they have read. Test takers who read all of the answer choices might discover that one of the latter answer choices is actually *more* correct. Moreover, reading all of the answer choices can remind you of facts related to the question that can help you arrive at the correct answer. Sometimes, a misstatement or incorrect detail in one of the latter answer choices will trigger your memory of the subject and will enable you to find the right answer. Failing to read all of the answer choices is like not reading all of the items on a restaurant menu: you might miss out on the perfect choice.

11. Spot the Hedges

One of the keys to success on multiple-choice tests is paying close attention to every word. This is never truer than with words like almost, most, some, and sometimes. These words are called "hedges" because they indicate that a statement is not totally true or not true in every place and time. An absolute statement will contain no hedges, but in many subjects, like literature and history, the answers are not always straightforward or absolute. There are always exceptions to the rules in these subjects. For this reason, you should favor those multiple-choice questions that contain hedging language. The presence of qualifying words indicates that the author is taking special care with his or her words, which is certainly important when composing the right answer. After all, there are many ways to be wrong, but there is only one way to be right! For this reason, it is wise to avoid answers that are absolute when taking a multiple-choice test. An absolute answer is one that says things are either all one way or all another. They often include words like *every*, *always*, *best*, and *never*. If you are taking a multiple-choice test in a subject that doesn't lend itself to absolute answers, be on your guard if you see any of these words.

12. Long Answers

In many subject areas, the answers are not simple. As already mentioned, the right answer often requires hedges. Another common feature of the answers to a complex or subjective question are qualifying clauses, which are groups of words that subtly modify the meaning of the sentence. If the question or answer choice describes a rule to which there are exceptions or the subject matter is complicated, ambiguous, or confusing, the correct answer will require many words in order to be expressed clearly and accurately. In essence, you should not be deterred by answer choices that seem excessively long. Oftentimes, the author of the text will not be able to write the correct answer without offering some qualifications and modifications. Your job is to read the answer choices thoroughly and completely and to select the one that most accurately and precisely answers the question.

13. Restating to Understand

Sometimes, a question on a multiple-choice test is difficult not because of what it asks but because of how it is written. If this is the case, restate the question or answer choice in different words. This process serves a couple of important purposes. First, it forces you to concentrate on the core of the question. In order to rephrase the question accurately, you have to understand it well. Rephrasing the question will concentrate your mind on the key words and ideas. Second, it will present the information to your mind in a fresh way. This process may trigger your memory and render some useful scrap of information picked up while studying.

14. True Statements

Sometimes an answer choice will be true in itself, but it does not answer the question. This is one of the main reasons why it is essential to read the question carefully and completely before proceeding to the answer choices. Too often, test takers skip ahead to the answer choices and look for true statements. Having found one of these, they are content to select it without reference to the question above. Obviously, this provides an easy way for test makers to play tricks. The savvy test taker will always read the entire question before turning to the answer choices. Then, having settled on a correct answer choice, he or she will refer to the original question and ensure that the selected answer is relevant. The mistake of choosing a correct-but-irrelevant answer choice is especially common on questions related to specific pieces of objective knowledge, like historical or scientific facts. A prepared test taker will have a wealth of factual knowledge at his or her disposal, and should not be careless in its application.

15. No Patterns

One of the more dangerous ideas that circulates about multiple-choice tests is that the correct answers tend to fall into patterns. These erroneous ideas range from a belief that B and C are the most common right answers, to the idea that an unprepared test-taker should answer "A-B-A-C-A-D-A-B-A." It cannot be emphasized enough that pattern-seeking of this type is exactly the WRONG way to approach a multiple-choice test. To begin with, it is highly unlikely that the test maker will plot the correct answers according to some predetermined pattern. The questions are scrambled and delivered in a random order. Furthermore, even if the test maker was following a pattern in the assignation of correct answers, there is no reason why the test taker would know which pattern he or she was using. Any attempt to discern a pattern in the answer choices is a waste of time and a distraction from the real work of taking the test. A test taker would be much better served by extra preparation before the test than by reliance on a pattern in the answers.

FREE DVD OFFER

Don't forget that doing well on your exam includes both understanding the test content and understanding how to use what you know to do well on the test. We offer a completely FREE Test Taking Tips DVD that covers world class test taking tips that you can use to be even more successful when you are taking your test.

All that we ask is that you email us your feedback about your study guide. To get your **FREE Test Taking Tips DVD**, email freedvd@studyguideteam.com with "FREE DVD" in the subject line and the following information in the body of the email:

- The title of your study guide.
- Your product rating on a scale of 1-5, with 5 being the highest rating.
- Your feedback about the study guide. What did you think of it?
- Your full name and shipping address to send your free DVD.

Introduction to the PSAT

Function of the Test

The Preliminary SAT/National Merit Scholarship Qualifying Test (PSAT/NMSQT) is an introductory version of the SAT exam. Given by the College Board with support from the National Merit Scholarship Corporation (NMSC), the PSAT is designed to help U.S. students get ready for the SAT or ACT. It also serves as a qualifying measure to identify students for college scholarships, including the National Merit Scholarship Program. Students taking the PSAT/NMSQT are automatically considered for the National Merit Scholarship Program, a contest that recognizes and awards scholars based on academic performance. About 50,000 pupils are acknowledged for extraordinary PSAT scores every year. Approximately 16,000 of these students become National Merit Semifinalists, and about half of this group is awarded scholarships.

Over 3.5 million high school students take the PSAT every year. Most are sophomore or junior high school students residing in the U.S. However, younger students may also register to take the PSAT. Students who are not U.S. citizens or residents can take the PSAT as well, by locating and contacting a local school that offers it.

Test Administration

The PSAT/NMSQT is offered on various dates in the fall at schools throughout the United States. Some schools will pay all or part of the exam registration fee for their pupils. Since the financial responsibility of the student for the exam is different for each school, it is best to consult the school's guidance department for specifics.

Tenth grade students who would like another chance to take the PSAT can take the PSAT 10 in the spring at various schools throughout the U.S. In addition to serving as a practice test for the SAT, scholarship programs use the PSAT 10 to screen for prospective students, but unlike the PSAT/NMSQT, it is not part of the National Merit Scholarship Program.

Students with documented disabilities can contact the College Board to make alternative arrangements to take the PSAT. All reasonable applications are reviewed.

Test Format

The PSAT gauges a student's proficiency in three areas: Reading, Mathematics, and Writing and Language. All the tests that fall under the SAT umbrella (including the PSAT) were redesigned in 2015. The revised PSAT is very similar to the new SAT in substance, structure, and scoring methodology, except that the PSAT does not include an essay. 1520 is the highest possible score for the PSAT.

The reading portion of the PSAT measures comprehension, requiring candidates to read multi-paragraph fiction and non-fiction segments including informational visuals, such as charts, tables and graphs, and answer questions based on this content. Three critical sectors are tested for the math section: Solving problems and analyzing data, Algebra, and complex equations and operations. The writing and language portion requires students to evaluate and edit writing and graphics to obtain an answer that correctly conveys the information given in the passage.

The PSAT contains 139 multiple-choice questions, with each section comprising over 40 questions. A different length of time is given for each section, for a total of two hours, 45 minutes.

Section	Time (In Minutes)	Number of Questions
Reading	60	47
Writing and Language	35	44
Mathematics	70	48
Total	**165**	**139**

Scoring

Scores for the newly revised PSAT are based on a scale of 320 to 1520. Scores range from 160-760 for the Math section and 160-760 for the Reading and Writing and Language combined. The PSAT also no longer penalizes for incorrect answers, as it did in the previous version. Therefore, a student's raw score is the number of correctly answered questions. Score reports also list sub-scores for math, reading and writing on a scale from 8 to 38, in order to give candidates an idea of strengths and weaknesses. Mean, or average, scores received by characteristic U.S. test-takers, are broken down by grade level.

The report ranks scores based on a percentile between 1 and 99 so students can see how they measured up to other test takers. Average (50th percentile), scores range from about 470 to 480 in each section, for a total of 940 to 960. Good scores are typically defined as higher than 50 percent. Scores of 95 percent or higher are in contention for National Merit Semifinalist and Finalist slots, but scholarships usually only go to the top one percent of 10th graders taking the PSAT.

Recent/Future Developments

A redesigned version of the PSAT was launched in October 2015. Changes include a longer total length (2 hours, 45 minutes, versus the previous time of 2 hours, 10 minutes), a total of four multiple-choice answers per question instead of five as in the past, and no guessing penalty, so students earn points based only on questions answered correctly. The revised PSAT also has more of a well-rounded emphasis on life skills and the thinking needed at a college level, incorporating concepts learned in science, history and social studies into the reading, math and writing sections. It is important to note that since the redesigned PSAT is different than in the past, scores on previous tests should not be compared to those taken in the current year.

When the PSAT was revamped, a number of new Services for Students with Disabilities (SSD) regulations occurred as well. For example, the PSAT/NMSQT printed test manual for nonstandard testers (often referred to as the "pink book") is no longer used. Instead, every candidate will use the standard exam booklet unless an alternative design (such as large print, Braille, MP3 Audio, and Assistive Technology Compatible) is requested.

There is also a new option allowing students to save time by completing classifying data prior to the exam by choosing the pre-administration option on the PSAT registration website. And starting in January 2015, the College Board forged new collaborations with five scholarship providers to expand scholarship opportunities earlier in students' high school careers.

Practice Test #1

Reading Test

Passage #1

Questions 1–6 are based on the following excerpt from the article "The Lancashire Witches 1612–2012," by Robert Poole:

Four hundred years ago, in 1612, the north-west of England was the scene of England's biggest peacetime witch trial: the trial of the Lancashire witches. Twenty people, mostly from the Pendle area of Lancashire, were imprisoned in the castle as witches. Ten were hanged, one died in gaol, one was sentenced to stand in the pillory, and eight were acquitted. The 2012 anniversary sees a small flood of commemorative events, including works of fiction by Blake Morrison, Carol Ann Duffy, and Jeanette Winterson. How did this witch trial come about, and what accounts for its enduring fame?

We know so much about the Lancashire Witches because the trial was recorded in unique detail by the clerk of the court, Thomas Potts, who published his account soon afterwards as *The Wonderful Discovery of Witches in the County of Lancaster*. I have recently published a modern-English edition of this book, together with an essay piecing together what we know of the events of 1612. It has been a fascinating exercise, revealing how Potts carefully edited the evidence, and also how the case against the "witches" was constructed and manipulated to bring about a spectacular show trial. It all began in mid-March when a pedlar from Halifax named John Law had a frightening encounter with a poor young woman, Alizon Device, in a field near Colne. He refused her request for pins and there was a brief argument during which he was seized by a fit that left him with "his head … drawn awry, his eyes and face deformed, his speech not well to be understood; his thighs and legs stark lame." We can now recognize this as a stroke, perhaps triggered by the stressful encounter. Alizon Device was sent for and surprised all by confessing to the bewitching of John Law and then begged for forgiveness.

When Alizon Device was unable to cure the pedlar, the local magistrate, Roger Nowell was called in. Characterized by Thomas Potts as "God's justice" he was alert to instances of witchcraft, which were regarded by the Lancashire's puritan-inclined authorities as part of the cultural rubble of "popery"—Roman Catholicism—long overdue to be swept away at the end of the county's very slow protestant reformation. "With weeping tears" Alizon explained that she had been led astray by her grandmother, "old Demdike," well-known in the district for her knowledge of old Catholic prayers, charms, cures, magic, and curses. Nowell quickly interviewed Alizon's grandmother and mother, as well as Demdike's supposed rival, "old Chattox" and her daughter Anne. Their panicky attempts to explain themselves and shift the blame to others eventually only ended up incriminating them, and the four were sent to Lancaster gaol in early April to await trial at the summer assizes. The initial picture revealed was of a couple of poor, marginal local families in the forest of Pendle with a longstanding reputation for magical powers, which they had occasionally used at the request of their wealthier neighbours. There had been disputes but none of these were part of ordinary village life. Not until 1612 did any of this come to the attention of the authorities.

The net was widened still further at the end of April when Alizon's younger brother James and younger sister Jennet, only nine years old, came up between them with a story about a "great meeting of witches" at their grandmother's house, known as Malkin Tower. This meeting was presumably to discuss the plight of those arrested and the threat of further arrests, but according to the evidence extracted from the children by the magistrates, a plot was hatched to blow up Lancaster castle with gunpowder, kill the gaoler, and rescue the imprisoned witches. It was, in short, a conspiracy against royal authority to rival the gunpowder plot of 1605—something to be expected in a county known for its particularly strong underground Roman Catholic presence.

Those present at the meeting were mostly family members and neighbours, but they also included Alice Nutter, described by Potts as "a rich woman [who] had a great estate, and children of good hope: in the common opinion of the world, of good temper, free from envy or malice." Her part in the affair remains mysterious, but she seems to have had Catholic family connections, and may have been one herself, providing an added motive for her to be prosecuted.

1. What's the point of this passage, and why did the author write it?
    a. The author is documenting a historic witchcraft trial while uncovering/investigating the role of suspicion and anti-Catholicism in the events.
    b. The author seeks long-overdue reparations for the ancestors of those accused and executed for witchcraft in Lancashire.
    c. The author is educating the reader about actual occult practices of the 1600s.
    d. The author argues that the Lancashire witch trials were more brutal than the infamous Salem trials.

2. Which term best captures the meaning of the author's use of "enduring" in the first paragraph?
    a. Un-original
    b. Popular
    c. Wicked
    d. Circumstantial

3. What textual information is present within the passage that most lends itself to the author's credibility?
    a. His prose is consistent with the time.
    b. This is a reflective passage; the author doesn't need to establish credibility.
    c. The author cites specific quotes.
    d. The author has published a modern account of the case and has written on the subject before.

4. What might the following excerpt suggest about the trial or, at the very least, Thomas Potts' account of the trial(s)?

"It has been a fascinating exercise, revealing how Potts carefully edited the evidence, and also how the case against the 'witches' was constructed and manipulated to bring about a spectacular show trial."

a. The events were so grand that the public was allowed access to such a spectacular set of cases.
b. Sections may have been exaggerated or stretched to create notoriety on an extraordinary case.
c. Evidence was faked, making the trial a total farce.
d. The trial was corrupt from the beginning.

5. Which statement best describes the political atmosphere of the 1600s that influenced the Alizon Device witch trial/case?

a. Fear of witches was prevalent during this period.
b. Magistrates were seeking ways to cement their power during this period of unrest.
c. In a highly superstitious culture, the Protestant church and government were highly motivated to root out any potential sources that could undermine the current regime.
d. Lancashire was originally a prominent area for pagan celebration, making the modern Protestants very weary of whispers of witchcraft and open to witch trials to resolve any potential threats to Christianity.

6. Which best describes the strongest "evidence" used in the case against Alizon and the witches?

a. Knowledge of the occult and witchcraft
b. "Spectral evidence"
c. Popular rumors of witchcraft and Catholic association
d. Self-incriminating speech

Passage #2

Questions 7–15 are based upon the following passage:

The Myth of Head Heat Loss

It has recently been brought to my attention that most people believe that 75% of your body heat is lost through your head. I had certainly heard this before, and am not going to attempt to say I didn't believe it when I first heard it. It is natural to be gullible to anything said with enough authority. But the "fact" that the majority of your body heat is lost through your head is a lie.

Let me explain. Heat loss is proportional to surface area exposed. An elephant loses a great deal more heat than an anteater, because it has a much greater surface area than an anteater. Each cell has mitochondria that produce energy in the form of heat, and it takes a lot more energy to run an elephant than an anteater.

So, each part of your body loses its proportional amount of heat in accordance with its surface area. The human torso probably loses the most heat, though the legs lose a significant amount as well. Some people have asked, "Why does it feel so much warmer when you cover your head than when you don't?" Well, that's because your head, because it is not clothed, is losing a lot of heat while the clothing on the rest of your body provides insulation. If you went outside with a hat and pants but no shirt, not only would you look stupid but your heat loss would be significantly greater because so much more of you would be exposed. So, if given the choice to cover your chest or your head in the cold, choose the chest. It could save your life.

7. The selection is told from what point of view?
    a. First
    b. Second
    c. Third
    d. Both A and B

8. What is the primary purpose of this passage?
    a. To provide evidence that disproves a myth
    b. To compare elephants and anteaters
    c. To explain why it is appropriate to wear clothes in winter
    d. To show how people are gullible

9. Which of the following best describes the main idea of the passage?
    a. It is better to wear a shirt than a hat
    b. Heat loss is proportional to surface area exposed
    c. It is natural to be gullible
    d. The human chest loses the most heat

10. Why does the author compare elephants and anteaters?
    a. To express an opinion
    b. To give an example that helps clarify the main point
    c. To show the differences between them
    d. To persuade why one is better than the other

11. The statement, "If you went outside with a hat and pants but no shirt, not only would you look stupid but your heat loss would be significantly greater because so much more of you would be exposed" is which of the following?
    a. An opinion
    b. A fact
    c. An opinion within a fact
    d. Neither

12. Which of the following best describes the tone of the passage?
    a. Harsh
    b. Angry
    c. Casual
    d. Indifferent

13. The author appeals to which branch of rhetoric to prove their case?
    a. Factual evidence
    b. Emotion
    c. Ethics and morals
    d. Author qualification

14. The selection is written in which of the following styles?
    a. Narrative
    b. Persuasive
    c. Informative
    d. Descriptive

15. Which of the following sentences provides the best evidence to support the main idea?
    a. "It is natural to be gullible to anything said with enough authority."
    b. "Each part of your body loses its proportional amount of heat in accordance with its surface area."
    c. "If given the choice to cover your chest or your head in the cold, choose the chest."
    d. "But the 'fact' that the majority of your body heat it lost through your head is a lie."

Passage #3

Questions 16–21 are based on the following passage:

When researchers and engineers undertake a large-scale scientific project, they may end up making discoveries and developing technologies that have far wider uses than originally intended. This is especially true in NASA, one of the most influential and innovative scientific organizations in America. NASA *spinoff technology* refers to innovations originally developed for NASA space projects that are now used in a wide range of different commercial fields. Many consumers are unaware that products they are buying are based on NASA research! Spinoff technology proves that it is worthwhile to invest in science research because it could enrich people's lives in unexpected ways.

The first spinoff technology worth mentioning is baby food. In space, where astronauts have limited access to fresh food and fewer options about their daily meals, malnutrition is a serious concern. Consequently, NASA researchers were looking for ways to enhance the nutritional value of astronauts' food. Scientists found that a certain type of algae could be added to food, improving the food's neurological benefits. When experts in the commercial food industry learned of this algae's potential to boost brain health, they were quick to begin their own research. The nutritional substance from algae then developed into a product called life's DHA, which can be found in over 90% of infant food sold in America.

Another intriguing example of a spinoff technology can be found in fashion. People who are always dropping their sunglasses may have invested in a pair of sunglasses with scratch resistant lenses—that is, it's impossible to scratch the glass, even if the glasses are dropped on an abrasive surface. This innovation is incredibly advantageous for people who are clumsy, but most shoppers don't know that this technology was originally developed by NASA. Scientists first created scratch resistant glass to help protect costly and crucial equipment from getting scratched in space, especially the helmet visors in space suits. However, sunglasses companies later realized that this technology could be profitable for their products, and they licensed the technology from NASA.

16. What is the main purpose of this article?
    a. To advise consumers to do more research before making a purchase
    b. To persuade readers to support NASA research
    c. To tell a narrative about the history of space technology
    d. To define and describe instances of spinoff technology

13

17. What is the organizational structure of this article?
   a. A general definition followed by more specific examples
   b. A general opinion followed by supporting arguments
   c. An important moment in history followed by chronological details
   d. A popular misconception followed by counterevidence

18. Why did NASA scientists research algae?
   a. They already knew algae was healthy for babies.
   b. They were interested in how to grow food in space.
   c. They were looking for ways to add health benefits to food.
   d. They hoped to use it to protect expensive research equipment.

19. What does the word "neurological" mean in the second paragraph?
   a. Related to the body
   b. Related to the brain
   c. Related to vitamins
   d. Related to technology

20. Why does the author mention space suit helmets?
   a. To give an example of astronaut fashion
   b. To explain where sunglasses got their shape
   c. To explain how astronauts protect their eyes
   d. To give an example of valuable space equipment

21. Which statement would the author probably NOT agree with?
   a. Consumers don't always know the history of the products they are buying.
   b. Sometimes new innovations have unexpected applications.
   c. It is difficult to make money from scientific research.
   d. Space equipment is often very expensive.

Passage #4

Questions 22–26 are based on the following passage:

Christopher Columbus is often credited for discovering America. This is incorrect. First, it is impossible to "discover" somewhere where people already live; however, Christopher Columbus did explore places in the New World that were previously untouched by Europe, so the term "explorer" would be more accurate. Another correction must be made, as well: Christopher Columbus was not the first European explorer to reach the present-day Americas! Rather, it was Leif Erikson who first came to the New World and contacted the natives, nearly five hundred years before Christopher Columbus.

Leif Erikson, the son of Erik the Red (a famous Viking outlaw and explorer in his own right), was born in either 970 or 980, depending on which historian you seek. His own family, though, did not raise Leif, which was a Viking tradition. Instead, one of Erik's prisoners taught Leif reading and writing, languages, sailing, and weaponry. At age 12,

Leif was considered a man and returned to his family. He killed a man during a dispute shortly after his return, and the council banished the Erikson clan to Greenland.

In 999, Leif left Greenland and traveled to Norway where he would serve as a guard to King Olaf Tryggvason. It was there that he became a convert to Christianity. Leif later tried to return home with the intention of taking supplies and spreading Christianity to Greenland, however his ship was blown off course and he arrived in a strange new land: present day Newfoundland, Canada.

When he finally returned to his adopted homeland Greenland, Leif consulted with a merchant who had also seen the shores of this previously unknown land we now know as Canada. The son of the legendary Viking explorer then gathered a crew of 35 men and set sail. Leif became the first European to touch foot in the New World as he explored present-day Baffin Island and Labrador, Canada. His crew called the land "Vinland," since it was plentiful with grapes.

During their time in present-day Newfoundland, Leif's expedition made contact with the natives whom they referred to as Skraelings (which translates to "wretched ones" in Norse). There are several secondhand accounts of their meetings. Some contemporaries described trade between the peoples. Other accounts describe clashes where the Skraelings defeated the Viking explorers with long spears, while still others claim the Vikings dominated the natives. Regardless of the circumstances, it seems that the Vikings made contact of some kind. This happened around 1000, nearly five hundred years before Columbus famously sailed the ocean blue.

Eventually, in 1003, Leif set sail for home and arrived at Greenland with a ship full of timber. In 1020, seventeen years later, the legendary Viking died. Many believe that Leif Erikson should receive more credit for his contributions in exploring the New World.

22. Which of the following best describes how the author generally presents the information?
    a. Chronological order
    b. Comparison-contrast
    c. Cause-effect
    d. Conclusion-premises

23. Which of the following is an opinion, rather than historical fact, expressed by the author?
    a. Leif Erikson was definitely the son of Erik the Red; however, historians debate the year of his birth.
    b. Leif Erikson's crew called the land "Vinland," since it was plentiful with grapes.
    c. Leif Erikson deserves more credit for his contributions in exploring the New World.
    d. Leif Erikson explored the Americas nearly five hundred years before Christopher Columbus.

24. Which of the following most accurately describes the author's main conclusion?
    a. Leif Erikson is a legendary Viking explorer.
    b. Leif Erikson deserves more credit for exploring America hundreds of years before Columbus.
    c. Spreading Christianity motivated Leif Erikson's expeditions more than any other factor.
    d. Leif Erikson contacted the natives nearly five hundred years before Columbus.

25. Which of the following best describes the author's intent in the passage?
    a. To entertain
    b. To inform
    c. To alert
    d. To suggest

26. Which of the following can be logically inferred from the passage?
    a. The Vikings disliked exploring the New World.
    b. Leif Erikson's banishment from Iceland led to his exploration of present-day Canada.
    c. Leif Erikson never shared his stories of exploration with the King of Norway.
    d. Historians have difficulty definitively pinpointing events in the Vikings' history.

Passage #5

Questions 27–31 are based on the following passage:

George Washington emerged out of the American Revolution as an unlikely champion of liberty. On June 14, 1775, the Second Continental Congress created the Continental Army, and John Adams, serving in the Congress, nominated Washington to be its first commander. Washington fought under the British during the French and Indian War, and his experience and prestige proved instrumental to the American war effort. Washington provided invaluable leadership, training, and strategy during the Revolutionary War. He emerged from the war as the embodiment of liberty and freedom from tyranny.

After vanquishing the heavily favored British forces, Washington could have pronounced himself as the autocratic leader of the former colonies without any opposition, but he famously refused and returned to his Mount Vernon plantation. His restraint proved his commitment to the fledgling state's republicanism. Washington was later unanimously elected as the first American president. But it is Washington's farewell address that cemented his legacy as a visionary worthy of study.

In 1796, President Washington issued his farewell address by public letter. Washington enlisted his good friend, Alexander Hamilton, in drafting his most famous address. The letter expressed Washington's faith in the Constitution and rule of law. He encouraged his fellow Americans to put aside partisan differences and establish a national union. Washington warned Americans against meddling in foreign affairs and entering military alliances. Additionally, he stated his opposition to national political parties, which he considered partisan and counterproductive.

Americans would be wise to remember Washington's farewell, especially during presidential elections when politics hits a fever pitch. They might want to question the political institutions that were not planned by the Founding Fathers, such as the nomination process and political parties themselves.

27. Which of the following statements is based on the information in the passage above?
    a. George Washington's background as a wealthy landholder directly led to his faith in equality, liberty, and democracy.
    b. George Washington would have opposed America's involvement in the Second World War.
    c. George Washington would not have been able to write as great a farewell address without the assistance of Alexander Hamilton.
    d. George Washington would probably not approve of modern political parties.

16

28. What is the purpose of this passage?
    a. To inform American voters about a Founding Father's sage advice on a contemporary issue and explain its applicability to modern times
    b. To introduce George Washington to readers as a historical figure worthy of study
    c. To note that George Washington was more than a famous military hero
    d. To convince readers that George Washington is a hero of republicanism and liberty

29. What is the tone of the passage?
    a. Informative
    b. Excited
    c. Bitter
    d. Comic

30. What does the word *meddling* mean in paragraph 3?
    a. Supporting
    b. Speaking against
    c. Interfering
    d. Gathering

31. According to the passage, what did George Washington do when he was offered a role as leader of the former colonies?
    a. He refused the offer.
    b. He accepted the offer.
    c. He became angry at the offer.
    d. He accepted the offer then regretted it later.

Passage #6

Questions 32–36 are based upon the following passage adapted from Mineralogy --- Encyclopedia International, Grolier:

Mineralogy is the science of minerals, which are the naturally occurring elements and compounds that make up the solid parts of the universe. Mineralogy is usually considered in terms of materials in the Earth, but meteorites provide samples of minerals from outside the Earth.

A mineral may be defined as a naturally occurring, homogeneous solid, inorganically formed, with a definite chemical composition and an ordered atomic arrangement. The qualification *naturally occurring* is essential because it is possible to reproduce most minerals in the laboratory. For example, evaporating a solution of sodium chloride produces crystal indistinguishable from those of the mineral halite, but such laboratory-produced crystals are not minerals.

A *homogeneous solid* is one consisting of a single kind of material that cannot be separated into simpler compounds by any physical method. The requirement that a mineral be solid eliminates gases and liquids from consideration. Thus ice is a mineral (a very common one, especially at high altitudes and latitudes) but water is not. Some mineralogists dispute this restriction and would consider both water and native mercury (also a liquid) as minerals.

The restriction of minerals to *inorganically formed* substances eliminates those homogenous solids produced by animals and plants. Thus the shell of an oyster and the pearl inside, though both consist of calcium carbonate indistinguishable chemically or physically from the mineral aragonite comma are not usually considered minerals.

The requirement of a *definite chemical composition* implies that a mineral is a chemical compound, and the composition of a chemical compound is readily expressed by a formula. Mineral formulas may be simple or complex, depending upon the number of elements present and the proportions in which they are combined.

Minerals are crystalline solids, and the presence of an *ordered atomic arrangement* is the criterion of the crystalline state. Under favorable conditions of formation the ordered atomic arrangement is expressed in the external crystal form. In fact, the presence of an ordered atomic arrangement and crystalline solids was deduced from the external regularity of crystals by a French mineralogist, Abbé R. Haüy, early in the 19th century.

32. According to the text, an object or substance must have all of the following criteria to be considered a mineral except for?
    a. Be naturally occurring
    b. Be a homogeneous solid
    c. Be organically formed
    d. Have a definite chemical composition

33. One can deduce that French mineralogist Abbé R. Haüy specialized in what field of study?
    a. Geology
    b. Psychology
    c. Biology
    d. Botany

34. What is the definition of the word "homogeneous" as it appears in the following sentence?

"A homogeneous solid is one consisting of a single kind of material that cannot be separated into simpler compounds by any physical method."
    a. Made of similar substances
    b. Differing in some areas
    c. Having a higher atomic mass
    d. Lacking necessary properties

35. The suffix -logy refers to which of the following?
    a. The properties of
    b. The chemical makeup of
    c. The study of
    d. The classification of

36. The author included the counterargument in the following passage to achieve which following effect?

The requirement that a mineral be solid eliminates gases and liquids from consideration. Thus ice is a mineral (a very common one, especially at high altitudes and latitudes) but water is not. Some mineralogists dispute this restriction and would consider both water and native mercury (also a liquid) as minerals.

    a. To complicate the subject matter

    b. To express a bias

    c. To point to the fact that there are differing opinions in the field of mineralogy concerning the characteristics necessary to determine whether a substance or material is a mineral

    d. To create a new subsection of minerals

Passage #7

Questions 37–41 are based on the following passage:

The Middle Ages were a time of great superstition and theological debate. Many beliefs were developed and practiced, while some died out or were listed as heresy. Boethianism is a Medieval theological philosophy that attributes sin to gratification and righteousness with virtue and God's providence. Boethianism holds that sin, greed, and corruption are means to attain temporary pleasure, but that they inherently harm the person's soul as well as other human beings.

In *The Canterbury Tales,* we observe more instances of bad actions punished than goodness being rewarded. This would appear to be some reflection of Boethianism. In the "Pardoner's Tale," all three thieves wind up dead, which is a result of their desire for wealth. Each wrong doer pays with their life, and they are unable to enjoy the wealth they worked to steal. Within his tales, Chaucer gives reprieve to people undergoing struggle, but also interweaves stories of contemptible individuals being cosmically punished for their wickedness. The thieves idolize physical wealth, which leads to their downfall. This same theme and ideological principle of Boethianism is repeated in the "Friar's Tale," whose summoner character attempts to gain further wealth by partnering with a demon. The summoner's refusal to repent for his avarice and corruption leads to the demon dragging his soul to Hell. Again, we see the theme of the individual who puts faith and morality aside in favor for a physical prize. The result, of course, is that the summoner loses everything.

The examples of the righteous being rewarded tend to appear in a spiritual context within the *Canterbury Tales*. However, there are a few instances where we see goodness resulting in physical reward. In the Prioress' Tale, we see corporal punishment for barbarism *and* a reward for goodness. The Jews are punished for their murder of the child, giving a sense of law and order (though racist) to the plot. While the boy does die, he is granted a lasting reward by being able to sing even after his death, a miracle that marks that the murdered youth led a pure life. Here, the miracle represents eternal favor with God.

Again, we see the theological philosophy of Boethianism in Chaucer's *The Canterbury Tales* through acts of sin and righteousness and the consequences that follow. When pleasures of the world are sought instead of God's favor, we see characters being punished in tragic ways. However, the absence of worldly lust has its own set of consequences for the characters seeking to obtain God's favor.

37. What would be a potential reward for living a good life, as described in Boethianism?
    a. A long life sustained by the good deeds one has done over a lifetime
    b. Wealth and fertility for oneself and the extension of one's family line
    c. Vengeance for those who have been persecuted by others who have a capacity for committing wrongdoing
    d. God's divine favor for one's righteousness

38. What might be the main reason why the author chose to discuss Boethianism through examining The Canterbury Tales?
    a. *The Canterbury Tales* is a well-known text.
    b. *The Canterbury Tales* is the only known fictional text that contains use of Boethianism.
    c. *The Canterbury Tales* presents a manuscript written in the medieval period that can help illustrate Boethianism through stories and show how people of the time might have responded to the idea.
    d. Within each individual tale in *The Canterbury Tales*, the reader can read about different levels of Boethianism and how each level leads to greater enlightenment.

39. What "ideological principle" is the author referring to in the middle of the second paragraph when talking about the "Friar's Tale"?
    a. The principle that the act of ravaging another's possessions is the same as ravaging one's soul.
    b. The principle that thieves who idolize physical wealth will be punished in an earthly sense as well as eternally.
    c. The principle that fraternization with a demon will result in one losing everything, including his or her life.
    d. The principle that a desire for material goods leads to moral malfeasance punishable by a higher being.

40. Which of the following words, if substituted for the word *avarice* in paragraph two, would LEAST change the meaning of the sentence?
    a. Perniciousness
    b. Pithiness
    c. Parsimoniousness
    d. Precariousness

41. Based on the passage, what view does Boethianism take on desire?
    a. Desire does not exist in the context of Boethianism
    b. Desire is a virtue and should be welcomed
    c. Having desire is evidence of demonic possession
    d. Desire for pleasure can lead toward sin

Passage #8

Questions 42–45 are based on the following passage:

Smoking tobacco products is terribly destructive. A single cigarette contains over 4,000 chemicals, including 43 known carcinogens and 400 deadly toxins. Some of the most dangerous ingredients include tar, carbon monoxide, formaldehyde, ammonia, arsenic, and DDT. Smoking can cause numerous types of cancer including throat, mouth, nasal cavity, esophagus, stomach, pancreas, kidney, bladder, and cervical.

Cigarettes contain a drug called nicotine, one of the most addictive substances known to man. Addiction is defined as a compulsion to seek the substance despite negative consequences. According to the National Institute of Drug Abuse, nearly 35 million smokers expressed a desire to quit smoking in 2015; however, more than 85 percent of those addicts will not achieve their goal. Almost all smokers regret picking up that first cigarette. You would be wise to learn from their mistake if you have not yet started smoking.

According to the U.S. Department of Health and Human Services, 16 million people in the United States presently suffer from a smoking-related condition and nearly nine million suffer from a serious smoking-related illness. According to the Centers for Disease Control and Prevention (CDC), tobacco products cause nearly six million deaths per year. This number is projected to rise to over eight million deaths by 2030. Smokers, on average, die ten years earlier than their nonsmoking peers.

In the United States, local, state, and federal governments typically tax tobacco products, which leads to high prices. Nicotine addicts sometimes pay more for a pack of cigarettes than for a few gallons of gas. Additionally, smokers tend to stink. The smell of smoke is all-consuming and creates a pervasive nastiness. Smokers also risk staining their teeth and fingers with yellow residue from the tar.

Smoking is deadly, expensive, and socially unappealing. Clearly, smoking is not worth the risks.

42. Which of the following best describes the passage?
    a. Narrative
    b. Persuasive
    c. Expository
    d. Technical

43. Which of the following statements most accurately summarizes the passage?
    a. Tobacco is less healthy than many alternatives.
    b. Tobacco is deadly, expensive, and socially unappealing, and smokers would be much better off kicking the addiction.
    c. In the United States, local, state, and federal governments typically tax tobacco products, which leads to high prices.
    d. Tobacco products shorten smokers' lives by ten years and kill more than six million people per year.

44. The author would be most likely to agree with which of the following statements?
    a. Smokers should only quit cold turkey and avoid all nicotine cessation devices.
    b. Other substances are more addictive than tobacco.
    c. Smokers should quit for whatever reason that gets them to stop smoking.
    d. People who want to continue smoking should advocate for a reduction in tobacco product taxes.

45. Which of the following represents an opinion statement on the part of the author?
a. According to the Centers for Disease Control and Prevention (CDC), tobacco products cause nearly six million deaths per year.
b. Nicotine addicts sometimes pay more for a pack of cigarettes than a few gallons of gas.
c. They also risk staining their teeth and fingers with yellow residue from the tar.
d. Additionally, smokers tend to stink. The smell of smoke is all-consuming and creates a pervasive nastiness.

Passage #9

Questions 46–52 are based on the following excerpt from a novel set in nineteenth-century France:

"Mademoiselle Eugénie is pretty—I think I remember that to be her name."

"Very pretty, or rather, very beautiful," replied Albert, "but of that style of beauty which I don't appreciate; I am an ungrateful fellow."

"Really," said Monte Cristo, lowering his voice, "you don't appear to me to be very enthusiastic on the subject of this marriage."

"Mademoiselle Danglars is too rich for me," replied Morcerf, "and that frightens me."

"Bah," exclaimed Monte Cristo, "that's a fine reason to give. Are you not rich yourself?"

"My father's income is about 50,000 francs per annum; and he will give me, perhaps, ten or twelve thousand when I marry."

"That, perhaps, might not be considered a large sum, in Paris especially," said the count; "but everything doesn't depend on wealth, and it's a fine thing to have a good name, and to occupy a high station in society. Your name is celebrated, your position magnificent; and then the Comte de Morcerf is a soldier, and it's pleasing to see the integrity of a Bayard united to the poverty of a Duguesclin; disinterestedness is the brightest ray in which a noble sword can shine. As for me, I consider the union with Mademoiselle Danglars a most suitable one; she will enrich you, and you will ennoble her."

Albert shook his head, and looked thoughtful. "There is still something else," said he.

"I confess," observed Monte Cristo, "that I have some difficulty in comprehending your objection to a young lady who is both rich and beautiful."

"Oh," said Morcerf, "this repugnance, if repugnance it may be called, isn't all on my side."

"Whence can it arise, then? for you told me your father desired the marriage."

"It's my mother who dissents; she has a clear and penetrating judgment, and doesn't smile on the proposed union. I cannot account for it, but she seems to entertain some prejudice against the Danglars."

"Ah," said the count, in a somewhat forced tone, "that may be easily explained; the Comtesse de Morcerf, who is aristocracy and refinement itself, doesn't relish the idea of being allied by your marriage with one of ignoble birth; that is natural enough."

46. The meaning of the word "repugnance" is closest to which of the following?
    a. Strong resemblance
    b. Strong dislike
    c. Extreme shyness
    d. Extreme dissimilarity

47. What can be inferred about Albert's family?
    a. Their finances are uncertain.
    b. Albert is the only son in his family.
    c. Their name is more respected than the Danglars'.
    d. Albert's mother and father both agree on their decisions.

48. What is Albert's attitude towards his impending marriage?
    a. Pragmatic
    b. Romantic
    c. Indifferent
    d. Apprehensive

49. What is the best description of the Count's relationship with Albert?
    a. He's like a strict parent, criticizing Albert's choices.
    b. He's like a wise uncle, giving practical advice to Albert.
    c. He's like a close friend, supporting all of Albert's opinions.
    d. He's like a suspicious investigator, asking many probing questions.

50. Which sentence is true of Albert's mother?
    a. She belongs to a noble family.
    b. She often makes poor choices.
    c. She is primarily occupied with money.
    d. She is unconcerned about her son's future.

51. Based on this passage, what is probably NOT true about French society in the 1800s?
    a. Children often received money from their parents.
    b. Marriages were sometimes arranged between families.
    c. The richest people in society were also the most respected.
    d. People were often expected to marry within their same social class.

52. Why is the Count puzzled by Albert's attitude toward his marriage?
    a. He seems reluctant to marry Eugénie, despite her wealth and beauty.
    b. He is marrying against his father's wishes, despite usually following his advice.
    c. He appears excited to marry someone he doesn't love, despite being a hopeless romantic.
    d. He expresses reverence towards Eugénie, despite being from a higher social class than her.

Writing and Language Test

Questions 1–9 are based on the following passage:

While all dogs (1) descend through gray wolves, it's easy to notice that dog breeds come in a variety of shapes and sizes. With such a (2) drastic range of traits, appearances and body types dogs are one of the most variable and adaptable species on the planet. (3) But why so many

23

differences. The answer is that humans have actually played a major role in altering the biology of dogs. (4) This was done through a process called selective breeding.

(5) Selective breeding which is also called artificial selection is the processes in which animals with desired traits are bred in order to produce offspring that share the same traits. In natural selection, (6) animals must adapt to their environments increase their chance of survival. Over time, certain traits develop in animals that enable them to thrive in these environments. Those animals with more of these traits, or better versions of these traits, gain an (7) advantage over others of their species. Therefore, the animal's chances to mate are increased and these useful (8) genes are passed into their offspring. With dog breeding, humans select traits that are desired and encourage more of these desired traits in other dogs by breeding dogs that already have them.

The reason for different breeds of dogs is that there were specific needs that humans wanted to fill with their animals. For example, sent hounds are known for their extraordinary ability to track game through scent. These breeds are also known for their endurance in seeking deer and other prey. Therefore, early hunters took dogs that displayed these abilities and bred them to encourage these traits. Later, these generations took on characteristics that aided these desired traits. (9) For example, Bloodhounds have broad snouts and droopy ears that fall to the ground when they smell. These physical qualities not only define the look of the Bloodhound, but also contribute to their amazing tracking ability. The broad snout is able to define and hold onto scents longer than many other breeds. The long floppy hears serve to collect and hold the scents the earth holds so that the smells are clearer and able to be distinguished.

1. Which of the following would be the best choice for this sentence (reproduced below)?

    While all dogs (1) descend through gray wolves, it's easy to notice that dog breeds come in a variety of shapes and sizes.

    a. NO CHANGE
    b. descend by gray wolves
    c. descend from gray wolves
    d. descended through gray wolves

2. Which of the following would be the best choice for this sentence (reproduced below)?

    With such a (2) drastic range of traits, appearances and body types, dogs are one of the most variable and adaptable species on the planet.

    a. NO CHANGE
    b. drastic range of traits, appearances, and body types,
    c. drastic range of traits and appearances and body types,
    d. drastic range of traits, appearances, as well as body types,

3. Which of the following would be the best choice for this sentence (reproduced below)?

(3) <u>But why so many differences.</u>

a. NO CHANGE
b. But are there so many differences?
c. But why so many differences are there.
d. But why so many differences?

4. Which of the following would be the best choice for this sentence (reproduced below)?

(4) <u>This was done through a process called selective breeding.</u>

a. NO CHANGE
b. This was done, through a process called selective breeding.
c. This was done, through a process, called selective breeding.
d. This was done through selective breeding, a process.

5. Which of the following would be the best choice for this sentence (reproduced below)?

(5) <u>Selective breeding which is also called artificial selection is the processes</u> in which animals with desired traits are bred in order to produce offspring that share the same traits.

a. NO CHANGE
b. Selective breeding, which is also called artificial selection is the processes
c. Selective breeding which is also called, artificial selection, is the processes
d. Selective breeding, which is also called artificial selection, is the processes

6. Which of the following would be the best choice for this sentence (reproduced below)?

In natural selection, (6) <u>animals must adapt to their environments increase their chance of survival.</u>

a. NO CHANGE
b. animals must adapt to their environments to increase their chance of survival.
c. animals must adapt to their environments, increase their chance of survival.
d. animals must adapt to their environments, increasing their chance of survival.

7. Which of the following would be the best choice for this sentence (reproduced below)?

Those animals with more of these traits, or better versions of these traits, gain an (7) <u>advantage over others of their species.</u>

a. NO CHANGE
b. advantage over others, of their species.
c. advantages over others of their species.
d. advantage over others.

8. Which of the following would be the best choice for this sentence (reproduced below)?

Therefore, the animal's chances to mate are increased and these useful (8) genes are passed into their offspring.

    a. NO CHANGE
    b. genes are passed onto their offspring.
    c. genes are passed on to their offspring.
    d. genes are passed within their offspring.

9. Which of the following would be the best choice for this sentence (reproduced below)?

(9) For example, Bloodhounds have broad snouts and droopy ears that fall to the ground when they smell.

    a. NO CHANGE
    b. For example, Bloodhounds,
    c. For example Bloodhounds
    d. For example, bloodhounds

Questions 10–18 are based on the following passage:

I'm not alone when I say that it's hard to pay attention sometimes. I can't count how many times I've sat in a classroom, lecture, speech, or workshop and (10) been bored to tears or rather sleep. (11) Usually I turn to doodling in order to keep awake. This never really helps; I'm not much of an artist. Therefore, after giving up on drawing a masterpiece, I would just concentrate on keeping my eyes open and trying to be attentive. This didn't always work because I wasn't engaged in what was going on.

(12) Sometimes in particularly dull seminars, I'd imagine comical things going on in the room or with the people trapped in the room with me. Why? (13) Because I wasn't invested in what was going on I wasn't motivated to listen. I'm not going to write about how I conquered the difficult task of actually paying attention in a difficult or unappealing class—it can be done, sure. I have sat through the very epitome of boredom (in my view at least) several times and come away learning something. (14) Everyone probably has had to at one time do this. What I want to talk about is that profound moment when curiosity is sparked (15) in another person drawing them to pay attention to what is before them and expand their knowledge.

What really makes people pay attention? (16) Easy it's interest. This doesn't necessarily mean (17) embellishing subject matter drawing people's attention. This won't always work. However, an individual can present material in a way that is clear to understand and actually engages the audience. Asking questions to the audience or class will make them a part of the topic at hand. Discussions that make people think about the content and (18) how it applies to there lives world and future is key. If math is being discussed, an instructor can explain the purpose behind the equations or perhaps use real-world applications to show how relevant the topic is. When discussing history, a lecturer can prompt students to imagine themselves in the place of key figures and ask how they might respond. The bottom line is to explore the ideas rather than just lecture. Give people the chance to explore material from multiple angles, and they'll be hungry to keep paying attention for more information.

10. Which of the following would be the best choice for this sentence (reproduced below)?

I can't count how many times I've sat in a classroom, lecture, speech, or workshop and (10) <u>been bored to tears or rather sleep.</u>

    a. NO CHANGE
    b. been bored to, tears, or rather sleep.
    c. been bored, to tears or rather sleep.
    d. been bored to tears or, rather, sleep.

11. Which of the following would be the best choice for this sentence (reproduced below)?

(11) <u>Usually I turn to doodling in order to keep awake.</u>

    a. NO CHANGE
    b. Usually, I turn to doodling in order to keep awake.
    c. Usually I turn to doodling, in order, to keep awake.
    d. Usually I turned to doodling in order to keep awake.

12. Which of the following would be the best choice for this sentence (reproduced below)?

(12) <u>Sometimes in particularly dull seminars,</u> I'd imagine comical things going on in the room or with the people trapped in the room with me.

    a. NO CHANGE
    b. Sometimes, in particularly, dull seminars,
    c. Sometimes in particularly dull seminars
    d. Sometimes in particularly, dull seminars,

13. Which of the following would be the best choice for this sentence (reproduced below)?

(13) <u>Because I wasn't invested in what was going on I wasn't motivated to listen.</u>

    a. NO CHANGE
    b. Because I wasn't invested, in what was going on, I wasn't motivated to listen.
    c. Because I wasn't invested in what was going on. I wasn't motivated to listen.
    d. I wasn't motivated to listen because I wasn't invested in what was going on.

14. Which of the following would be the best choice for this sentence (reproduced below)?

(14) <u>Everyone probably has had to at one time do this.</u>

    a. NO CHANGE
    b. Everyone probably has had to, at one time. Do this.
    c. Everyone's probably had to do this at some time.
    d. At one time everyone probably has had to do this.

15. Which of the following would be the best choice for this sentence (reproduced below)?

What I want to talk about is that profound moment when curiosity is sparked (15) <u>in another person drawing them to pay attention</u> to what is before them and expand their knowledge.

a. NO CHANGE
b. in another person, drawing them to pay attention
c. in another person; drawing them to pay attention to what is before them.
d. in another person, drawing them to pay attention to what is before them.

16. Which of the following would be the best choice for this sentence (reproduced below)?

(16) <u>Easy it's interest.</u>

a. NO CHANGE
b. Easy it is interest.
c. Easy. It's interest.
d. Easy—it's interest.

17. Which of the following would be the best choice for this sentence (reproduced below)?

This doesn't necessarily mean (17) <u>embellishing subject matter drawing people's attention.</u>

a. NO CHANGE
b. embellishing subject matter which draws people's attention.
c. embellishing subject matter to draw people's attention.
d. embellishing subject matter for the purpose of drawing people's attention.

18. Which of the following would be the best choice for this sentence (reproduced below)?

Discussions that make people think about the content and (18) <u>how it applies to there lives world and future is key.</u>

a. NO CHANGE
b. how it applies to their lives, world, and future is key.
c. how it applied to there lives world and future is key.
d. how it applies to their lives, world and future is key.

Questions 19–27 are based on the following passage:

Since the first discovery of dinosaur bones, (19) <u>scientists has made strides in technological development and methodologies used to investigate</u> these extinct animals. We know more about dinosaurs than ever before and are still learning fascinating new things about how they looked and lived. However, one has to ask, (20) <u>how if earlier perceptions of dinosaurs</u> continue to influence people's understanding of these creatures? Can these perceptions inhibit progress towards further understanding of dinosaurs?

(21) <u>The biggest problem with studying dinosaurs is simply that there are no living dinosaurs to observe.</u> All discoveries associated with these animals are based on physical remains. To gauge behavioral characteristics, scientists cross-examine these (22) <u>finds with living animals that seem</u>

similar in order to gain understanding. While this method is effective, these are still deductions. Some ideas about dinosaurs can't be tested and confirmed simply because humans can't replicate a living dinosaur. For example, a Spinosaurus has a large sail, or a finlike structure that grows from its back. Paleontologists know this sail exists and have ideas for the function of (23) the sail however they are uncertain of which idea is the true function. Some scientists believe (24) the sail serves to regulate the Spinosaurus' body temperature and yet others believe its used to attract mates. Still, other scientists think the sail is used to intimidate other predatory dinosaurs for self-defense. These are all viable explanations, but they are also influenced by what scientists know about modern animals. (25) Yet, it's quite possible that the sail could hold a completely unique function.

While it's (26) plausible, even likely that dinosaurs share many traits with modern animals, there is the danger of overattributing these qualities to a unique, extinct species. For much of the early nineteenth century, when people first started studying dinosaur bones, the assumption was that they were simply giant lizards. (27) For the longest time this image was the prevailing view on dinosaurs, until evidence indicated that they were more likely warm blooded. Scientists have also discovered that many dinosaurs had feathers and actually share many traits with modern birds.

19. Which of the following would be the best choice for this sentence (reproduced below)?

Since the first discovery of dinosaur bones, (19) scientists has made strides in technological development and methodologies used to investigate these extinct animals.

a. NO CHANGE
b. scientists has made strides in technological development, and methodologies, used to investigate
c. scientists have made strides in technological development and methodologies used to investigate
d. scientists, have made strides in technological development and methodologies used, to investigate

20. Which of the following would be the best choice for this sentence (reproduced below)?

However, one has to ask, (20) how if earlier perceptions of dinosaurs continue to influence people's understanding of these creatures?

a. NO CHANGE
b. how perceptions of dinosaurs
c. how, if, earlier perceptions of dinosaurs
d. whether earlier perceptions of dinosaurs

21. Which of the following would be the best choice for this sentence (reproduced below)?

(21) <u>The biggest problem with studying dinosaurs is simply that there are no living dinosaurs to observe.</u>

a. NO CHANGE
b. The biggest problem with studying dinosaurs is simple, that there are no living dinosaurs to observe.
c. The biggest problem with studying dinosaurs is simple. There are no living dinosaurs to observe.
d. The biggest problem with studying dinosaurs, is simply that there are no living dinosaurs to observe.

22. Which of the following would be the best choice for this sentence (reproduced below)?

To gauge behavioral characteristics, scientists cross-examine these (22) <u>finds with living animals that seem similar in order to gain understanding.</u>

a. NO CHANGE
b. finds with living animals to explore potential similarities.
c. finds with living animals to gain understanding of similarities.
d. finds with living animals that seem similar, in order, to gain understanding.

23. Which of the following would be the best choice for this sentence (reproduced below)?

Paleontologists know this sail exists and have ideas for the function of (23) <u>the sail however they are uncertain of which idea is the true function.</u>

a. NO CHANGE
b. the sail however, they are uncertain of which idea is the true function.
c. the sail however they are, uncertain, of which idea is the true function.
d. the sail; however, they are uncertain of which idea is the true function.

24. Which of the following would be the best choice for this sentence (reproduced below)?

Some scientists believe (24) <u>the sail serves to regulate the Spinosaurus' body temperature and yet others believe its used to attract mates.</u>

a. NO CHANGE
b. the sail serves to regulate the Spinosaurus' body temperature, yet others believe it's used to attract mates.
c. the sail serves to regulate the Spinosaurus' body temperature and yet others believe it's used to attract mates.
d. the sail serves to regulate the Spinosaurus' body temperature however others believe it's used to attract mates.

25. Which of the following would be the best choice for this sentence (reproduced below)?

(25) Yet, it's quite possible that the sail could hold a completely unique function.

    a. NO CHANGE
    b. Yet, it's quite possible,
    c. It's quite possible,
    d. Its quite possible

26. Which of the following would be the best choice for this sentence (reproduced below)?

While it's (26) plausible, even likely that dinosaurs share many traits with modern animals, there is the danger of over attributing these qualities to a unique, extinct species.

    a. NO CHANGE
    b. plausible, even likely that, dinosaurs share many
    c. plausible, even likely, that dinosaurs share many
    d. plausible even likely that dinosaurs share many

27. Which of the following would be the best choice for this sentence (reproduced below)?

(27) For the longest time this image was the prevailing view on dinosaurs, until evidence indicated that they were more likely warm blooded.

    a. NO CHANGE
    b. For the longest time this was the prevailing view on dinosaurs
    c. For the longest time, this image, was the prevailing view on dinosaurs
    d. For the longest time this was the prevailing image of dinosaurs

Questions 28–36 are based on the following passage:

Everyone has heard the (28) idea of the end justifying the means; that would be Weston's philosophy. Weston is willing to cross any line, commit any act no matter how heinous, to achieve success in his goal. (29) Ransom is reviled by this fact, seeing total evil in Weston's plan. To do an evil act in order (30) to gain a result that's supposedly good would ultimately warp the final act. (31) This opposing viewpoints immediately distinguishes Ransom as the hero. In the conflict with Un-man, Ransom remains true to his moral principles, someone who refuses to be compromised by power. Instead, Ransom makes it clear that by allowing such processes as murder and lying dictate how one attains a positive outcome, (32) the righteous goal becomes corrupted. The good end would not be truly good, but a twisted end that conceals corrupt deeds.

(33) This idea of allowing necessary evils to happen, is very tempting, it is what Weston fell prey to. (34) The temptation of the evil spirit Un-man ultimately takes over Weston and he is possessed. However, Ransom does not give into temptation. He remains faithful to the truth of what is right and incorrect. This leads him to directly face Un-man for the fate of Perelandra and its inhabitants.

Just as Weston was corrupted by the Un-man, (35) Un-man after this seeks to tempt the Queen of Perelandra to darkness. Ransom must literally (36) show her the right path, to accomplish this, he does this based on the same principle as the "means to an end" argument—that good follows good, and evil follows evil. Later in the plot, Weston/Un-man seeks to use deceptive reasoning to turn the queen to sin, pushing the queen to essentially ignore Melildil's rule to satisfy her own curiosity. In this sense, Un-man takes on the role of a false prophet, a tempter. Ransom must shed light on the truth, but this is difficult; his adversary is very clever and uses brilliant language. Ransom's lack of refinement heightens the weight of Un-man's corrupted logic, and so the Queen herself is intrigued by his logic.

Based on an excerpt from *Perelandra* by C.S. Lewis

28. Which of the following would be the best choice for this sentence (reproduced below)?

Everyone has heard the (28) idea of the end justifying the means; that would be Weston's philosophy.

a. NO CHANGE
b. idea of the end justifying the means; this is Weston's philosophy.
c. idea of the end justifying the means, this is the philosophy of Weston
d. idea of the end justifying the means. That would be Weston's philosophy.

29. Which of the following would be the best choice for this sentence (reproduced below)?

(29) Ransom is reviled by this fact, seeing total evil in Weston's plan.

a. NO CHANGE
b. Ransom is reviled by this fact; seeing total evil in Weston's plan.
c. Ransom, is reviled by this fact, seeing total evil in Weston's plan.
d. Ransom reviled by this, sees total evil in Weston's plan.

30. Which of the following would be the best choice for this sentence (reproduced below)?

To do an evil act in order (30) to gain a result that's supposedly good would ultimately warp the final act.

a. NO CHANGE
b. for an outcome that's for a greater good would ultimately warp the final act.
c. to gain a final act would warp its goodness.
d. to achieve a positive outcome would ultimately warp the goodness of the final act.

31. Which of the following would be the best choice for this sentence (reproduced below)?

(31) This opposing viewpoints immediately distinguishes Ransom as the hero.

a. NO CHANGE
b. This opposing viewpoints immediately distinguishes Ransom, as the hero.
c. This opposing viewpoint immediately distinguishes Ransom as the hero.
d. Those opposing viewpoints immediately distinguishes Ransom as the hero.

32. Which of the following would be the best choice for this sentence (reproduced below)?

Instead, Ransom makes it clear that by allowing such processes as murder and lying dictate how one attains a positive outcome, (32) the righteous goal becomes corrupted.

a. NO CHANGE
b. the goal becomes corrupted and no longer righteous.
c. the righteous goal becomes, corrupted.
d. the goal becomes corrupted, when once it was righteous.

33. Which of the following would be the best choice for this sentence (reproduced below)?

(33) This idea of allowing necessary evils to happen, is very tempting, it is what Weston fell prey to.

a. NO CHANGE
b. This idea of allowing necessary evils to happen, is very tempting. This is what Weston fell prey to.
c. This idea, allowing necessary evils to happen, is very tempting, it is what Weston fell prey to.
d. This tempting idea of allowing necessary evils to happen is what Weston fell prey to.

34. Which of the following would be the best choice for this sentence (reproduced below)?

(34) The temptation of the evil spirit Un-man ultimately takes over Weston and he is possessed.

a. NO CHANGE
b. The temptation of the evil spirit Un-man ultimately takes over and possesses Weston.
c. Weston is possessed as a result of the temptation of the evil spirit Un-man ultimately, who takes over.
d. The temptation of the evil spirit Un-man takes over Weston and he is possessed ultimately.

35. Which of the following would be the best choice for this sentence (reproduced below)?

Just as Weston was corrupted by the Un-man, (35) Un-man after this seeks to tempt the Queen of Perelandra to darkness.

a. NO CHANGE
b. Un-man, after this, would tempt the Queen of Perelandra
c. Un-man, after this, seeks to tempt the Queen of Perelandra
d. Un-man then seeks to tempt the Queen of Perelandra

36. Which of the following would be the best choice for this sentence (reproduced below)?

Ransom must literally (36) <u>show her the right path, to accomplish this, he does this based on the same principle as the "means to an end" argument</u>—that good follows good, and evil follows evil.

a. NO CHANGE
b. show her the right path. To accomplish this, he uses the same principle as the "means to an end" argument
c. show her the right path; to accomplish this he uses the same principle as the "means to an end" argument
d. show her the right path, to accomplish this, the same principle as the "means to an end" argument is applied

Questions 37–45 are based on the following passage:

(37) <u>What's clear about the news is today is that the broader the media</u> the more ways there are to tell a story. Even if different news groups cover the same story, individual newsrooms can interpret or depict the story differently than other counterparts. Stories can also change depending on the type of (38) <u>media in question incorporating different styles and unique</u> ways to approach the news. (39) <u>It is because of these respective media types that ethical and news-related subject matter can sometimes seem different or altered.</u> But how does this affect the narrative of the new story?

I began by investing a written newspaper article from the Baltimore Sun. Instantly striking are the bolded Headlines. (40) <u>These are clearly meant for direct the viewer</u> to the most exciting and important stories the paper has to offer. What was particularly noteworthy about this edition was that the first page dealt with two major ethical issues. (41) <u>On a national level there was a story</u> on the evolving Petraeus scandal involving his supposed affair. The other article was focused locally in Baltimore, a piece questioning the city's Ethic's Board and their current director. Just as a television newscaster communicates the story through camera and dialogue, the printed article applies intentional and targeted written narrative style. More so than any of the mediums, news article seems to be focused specifically on a given story without need to jump to another. Finer details are usually expanded on (42) <u>in written articles, usually people who</u> read newspapers or go online for web articles want more than a quick blurb. The diction of the story is also more precise and can be either straightforward or suggestive (43) <u>depending in earnest on the goal of the writer.</u> However, there's still plenty of room for opinions to be inserted into the text.

Usually, all news (44) <u>outlets have some sort of bias, it's just a question of how much</u> bias clouds the reporting. As long as this bias doesn't withhold information from the reader, it can be considered credible. (45) <u>However an over use of bias</u>, opinion, and suggestive language can rob readers of the chance to interpret the news events for themselves.

37. Which of the following would be the best choice for this sentence (reproduced below)?

(37) What's clear about the news today is that the broader the media the more ways there are to tell a story.

a. NO CHANGE
b. What's clear, about the news today, is that the broader the media
c. What's clear about today's news is that the broader the media
d. The news today is broader than earlier media

38. Which of the following would be the best choice for this sentence (reproduced below)?

Stories can also change depending on the type of (38) media in question incorporating different styles and unique ways to approach the news.

a. NO CHANGE
b. media in question; each incorporates unique styles and unique
c. media in question. To incorporate different styles and unique
d. media in question, incorporating different styles and unique

39. Which of the following would be the best choice for this sentence (reproduced below)?

(39) It is because of these respective media types that ethical and news-related subject matter can sometimes seem different or altered.

a. NO CHANGE
b. It is because of these respective media types, that ethical and news-related subject matter, can sometimes seem different or altered.
c. It is because of these respective media types, that ethical and news-related subject matter can sometimes seem different or altered.
d. It is because of these respective media types that ethical and news-related subject matter can sometimes seem different. Or altered.

40. Which of the following would be the best choice for this sentence (reproduced below)?

(40) These are clearly meant for direct the viewer to the most exciting and important stories the paper has to offer.

a. NO CHANGE
b. These are clearly meant for the purpose of giving direction to the viewer
c. These are clearly meant to direct the viewer
d. These are clearly meant for the viewer to be directed

41. Which of the following would be the best choice for this sentence (reproduced below)?

(41) <u>On a national level there was a story</u> on the evolving Petraeus scandal involving his supposed affair.

  a. NO CHANGE
  b. On a national level a story was there
  c. On a national level; there was a story
  d. On a national level, there was a story

42. Which of the following would be the best choice for this sentence (reproduced below)?

Finer details are usually expanded on (42) <u>in written articles, usually people who</u> read newspapers or go online for web articles want more than a quick blurb.

  a. NO CHANGE
  b. in written articles. People who usually
  c. in written articles, usually, people who
  d. in written articles usually people who

43. Which of the following would be the best choice for this sentence (reproduced below)?

The diction of the story is also more precise and can be either straightforward or suggestive (43) <u>depending in earnest on the goal of the writer.</u>

  a. NO CHANGE
  b. depending; in earnest on the goal of the writer.
  c. depending, in earnest, on the goal of the writer.
  d. the goal of the writer, in earnest, depends on the goal of the writer.

44. Which of the following would be the best choice for this sentence (reproduced below)?

Usually, all news (44) <u>outlets have some sort of bias, it's just a question of how much</u> bias clouds the reporting.

  a. NO CHANGE
  b. outlets have some sort of bias. Just a question of how much
  c. outlets have some sort of bias it can just be a question of how much
  d. outlets have some sort of bias, its just a question of how much

45. Which of the following would be the best choice for this sentence (reproduced below)?

(45) <u>However an over use of bias,</u> opinion, and suggestive language can rob readers of the chance to interpret the news events for themselves.

  a. NO CHANGE
  b. However, an over use of bias,
  c. However, with too much bias,
  d. However, an overuse of bias,

Math Test

1. Which of the following inequalities is equivalent to $3 - \frac{1}{2}x \geq 2$?

    a. $x \geq 2$
    b. $x \leq 2$
    c. $x \geq 1$
    d. $x \leq 1$

2. If $g(x) = x^3 - 3x^2 - 2x + 6$ and $f(x) = 2$, then what is $g(f(x))$?

    a. -26
    b. 6
    c. $2x^3 - 6x^2 - 4x + 12$
    d. -2

3. What is the definition of a factor of the number 36?

    a. A number that can be divided by 36 and have no remainder
    b. A number that 36 can be divided by and have no remainder
    c. A prime number that is multiplied times 36
    d. An even number that is multiplied times 36

4. What are the coordinates of the focus of the parabola $y = -9x^2$?

    a. $(-3, 0)$
    b. $\left(-\frac{1}{36}, 0\right)$
    c. $(0, -3)$
    d. $\left(0, -\frac{1}{36}\right)$

5. What is the volume of a cube with the side equal to 3 inches?

    a. 6 in³
    b. 27 in³
    c. 9 in³
    d. 3 in³

6. What is the cone prism with the height of 3 centimeters, a width of 5 centimeters, and a depth of 11 centimeters?

    a. 19 cm³
    b. 165 cm³
    c. 225 cm³
    d. 150 cm³

7. What is the volume of a cylinder, in terms of π, with a radius of 5 inches and a height of 10 inches?

    a. 250 π in³
    b. 50 π in³
    c. 100 π in³
    d. 200 π in³

8. What is the solution to the following system of equations?
$$x^2 - 2x + y = 8$$
$$x - y = -2$$
   a. $(-2, 3)$
   b. There is no solution.
   c. $(-2, 0)$ $(1, 3)$
   d. $(-2, 0)$ $(3, 5)$

9. An equation for the line passing through the origin and the point $(2, 1)$ is
   a. $y = 2x$
   b. $y = \frac{1}{2}x$
   c. $y = x - 2$
   d. $2y = x + 1$
   e. $y = x - 2$

10. A rectangle was formed out of pipe cleaner. Its length was $\frac{1}{2}$ feet and its width was $\frac{11}{2}$ inches. What is its area in square inches?
   a. $\frac{11}{4}$ inch^2
   b. $\frac{11}{2}$ inch^2
   c. 22 inch^2
   d. 33 inch^2

11. What type of function is modeled by the values in the following table?

X	f(x)
1	2
2	4
3	8
4	16
5	32

   a. Linear
   b. Exponential
   c. Quadratic
   d. Cubic

12. Two cards are drawn from a shuffled deck of 52 cards. What's the probability that both cards are Kings if the first card isn't replaced after it's drawn and is a King?
   a. $\frac{1}{169}$
   b. $\frac{1}{221}$
   c. $\frac{1}{13}$
   d. $\frac{4}{13}$

14. Write the expression for three times the sum of twice a number and one minus 6.

   a. $2x + 1 - 6$
   b. $3x + 1 - 6$
   c. $3(x + 1) - 6$
   d. $3(2x + 1) - 6$

16. $(2x - 4y)^2 =$

   a. $4x^2 - 16xy + 16y^2$
   b. $4x^2 - 8xy + 16y^2$
   c. $4x^2 - 16xy - 16y^2$
   d. $2x^2 - 8xy + 8y^2$

17. What are the zeros of $f(x) = x^2 + 4$?

   a. $x = -4$
   b. $x = \pm 2i$
   c. $x = \pm 2$
   d. $x = \pm 4i$

18. Which of the following shows the correct result of simplifying the following expression:
$$(7n + 3n^3 + 3) + (8n + 5n^3 + 2n^4)$$

   a. $9n^4 + 15n - 2$
   b. $2n^4 + 5n^3 + 15n - 2$
   c. $9n^4 + 8n^3 + 15n$
   d. $2n^4 + 8n^3 + 15n + 3$

19. Multiply and reduce $\frac{15}{23} \times \frac{54}{127}$.

   a. $\dfrac{810}{2,921}$

   b. $\dfrac{81}{292}$

   c. $\dfrac{69}{150}$

   d. $\dfrac{810}{2929}$

20. What is the product of the following expression?
$$(4x - 8)(5x^2 + x + 6)$$

   a. $20x^3 - 36x^2 + 16x - 48$
   b. $6x^3 - 41x^2 + 12x + 15$
   c. $204 + 11x^2 - 37x - 12$
   d. $2x^3 - 11x^2 - 32x + 20$

21. What is the solution for the following equation?
$$\frac{x^2 + x - 30}{x - 5} = 11$$

   a. $x = -6$
   b. There is no solution.
   c. $x = 16$
   d. $x = 5$

22. If x is not zero, then $\dfrac{3}{x} + \dfrac{5u}{2x} - \dfrac{u}{4} =$

   a. $\dfrac{12+10u-ux}{4x}$

   b. $\dfrac{3+5u-ux}{x}$

   c. $\dfrac{12x+10u+ux}{4x}$

   d. $\dfrac{12+10u-u}{4x}$

23. What are the zeros of the function: $f(x) = x^3 + 4x^2 + 4x$?
   a. -2
   b. 0, -2
   c. 2
   d. 0, 2

24. Is the following function even, odd, neither, or both?
$$y = \frac{1}{2}x^4 + 2x^2 - 6$$

   a. Even
   b. Odd
   c. Neither
   d. Both

25. Which of the following formulas would correctly calculate the perimeter of a legal-sized piece of paper that is 14 inches long and $8\frac{1}{2}$ inches wide?

   a. $P = 14 + 8\frac{1}{2}$

   b. $P = 14 + 8\frac{1}{2} + 14 + 8\frac{1}{2}$

   c. $P = 14 \times 8\frac{1}{2}$

   d. $P = 14 \times \frac{17}{2}$

26. A grocery store is selling individual bottles of water, and each bottle contains 750 milliliters of water. If 12 bottles are purchased, what conversion will correctly determine how many liters that customer will take home?
   a. 100 milliliters equals 1 liter
   b. 1,000 milliliters equals 1 liter
   c. 1,000 liters equals 1 milliliter
   d. 10 liters equals 1 milliliter

27. Given the following triangle, what's the length of the missing side? Round the answer to the nearest tenth.

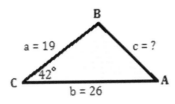

a. 17.0
b. 17.4
c. 18.0
d. 18.4

28. For the following similar triangles, what are the values of x and y (rounded to one decimal place)?

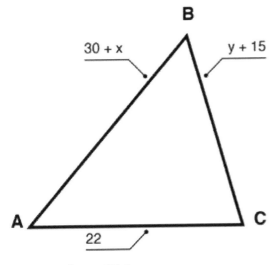
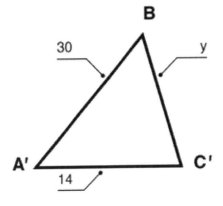

a. $x = 16.5, y = 25.1$
b. $x = 19.5, y = 24.1$
c. $x = 17.1, y = 26.3$
d. $x = 26.3, y = 17.1$

29. What are the center and radius of a circle with equation $4x^2 + 4y^2 - 16x - 24y + 51 = 0$?
    a. Center (3, 2) and radius ½
    b. Center (2, 3) and radius ½
    c. Center (3, 2) and radius ¼
    d. Center (2, 3) and radius ¼

30. What is the solution to $(2 \times 20) \div (7 + 1) + (6 \times 0.01) + (4 \times 0.001)$?
    a. 5.064
    b. 5.64
    c. 5.0064
    d. 48.064

31. A piggy bank contains 12 dollars' worth of nickels. A nickel weighs 5 grams, and the empty piggy bank weighs 1050 grams. What is the total weight of the full piggy bank?
    a. 1,110 grams
    b. 1,200 grams
    c. 2,250 grams
    d. 2,200 grams

32. Last year, the New York City area received approximately $27\frac{3}{4}$ inches of snow. The Denver area received approximately 3 times as much snow as New York City. How much snow fell in Denver?
    a. 60 inches
    b. $27\frac{1}{4}$ inches
    c. $9\frac{1}{4}$ inches
    d. $83\frac{1}{4}$ inches

33. If $-3(x + 4) \geq x + 8$, what is the value of x?
    a. $x = 4$
    b. $x \geq 2$
    c. $x \geq -5$
    d. $x \leq -5$

34. Karen gets paid a weekly salary and a commission for every sale that she makes. The table below shows the number of sales and her pay for different weeks.

Sales	2	7	4	8
Pay	$380	$580	$460	$620

Which of the following equations represents Karen's weekly pay?
    a. $y = 90x + 200$
    b. $y = 90x - 200$
    c. $y = 40x + 300$
    d. $y = 40x - 300$

35. The square and circle have the same center. The circle has a radius of r. What is the area of the shaded region?

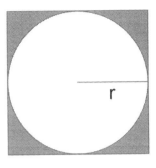

a. $r^2 - \pi r^2$
b. $4r^2 - 2\pi r$
c. $(4 - \pi)r^2$
d. $(\pi - 1)r^2$

36. The graph shows the position of a car over a 10-second time interval. Which of the following is the correct interpretation of the graph for the interval 1 to 3 seconds?

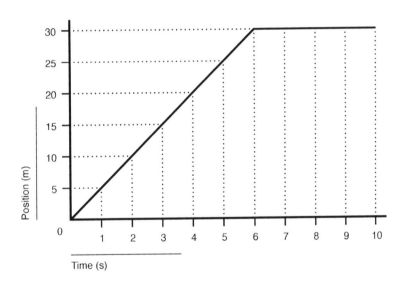

a. The car remains in the same position.
b. The car is traveling at a speed of 5m/s.
c. The car is traveling up a hill.
d. The car is traveling at 5mph.

37. Which of the ordered pairs below is a solution to the following system of inequalities?
$$y > 2x - 3$$
$$y < -4x + 8$$

    a. $(4, 5)$
    b. $(-3, -2)$
    c. $(3, -1)$
    d. $(5, 2)$

38. Which equation best represents the scatterplot below?

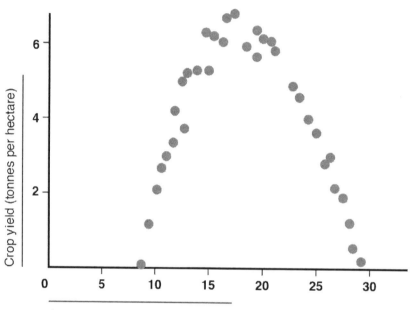

    a. $y = 3x - 4$
    b. $y = 2x^2 + 7x - 9$
    c. $y = (3)(4^x)$
    d. $y = -\frac{1}{14}x^2 + 2x - 8$

39. What is the solution to $9 \times 9 \div 9 + 9 - 9 \div 9$?
    a. 0
    b. 17
    c. 81
    d. 9

41. The hospital has a nurse to patient ratio of 1:25. If there are a maximum of 325 patients admitted at a time, how many nurses are there?
    a. 13 nurses
    b. 25 nurses
    c. 325 nurses
    d. 12 nurses

42. A hospital has a bed to room ratio of 2: 1. If there are 145 rooms, how many beds are there?
   a. 145 beds
   b. 2 beds
   c. 90 beds
   d. 290 beds

43. Solve for X: $\frac{2x}{5} - 1 = 59$.
   a. 60
   b. 145
   c. 150
   d. 115

44. A National Hockey League store in the state of Michigan advertises 50% off all items. Sales tax in Michigan is 6%. How much would a hat originally priced at $32.99 and a jersey originally priced at $64.99 cost during this sale? Round to the nearest penny.
   a. $97.98
   b. $103.86
   c. $51.93
   d. $48.99

45. Store brand coffee beans cost $1.23 per pound. A local coffee bean roaster charges $1.98 per 1 ½ pounds. How much more would 5 pounds from the local roaster cost than 5 pounds of the store brand?
   a. $0.55
   b. $1.55
   c. $1.45
   d. $0.45

46. Paint Inc. charges $2000 for painting the first 1,800 feet of trim on a house and $1.00 per foot for each foot after. How much would it cost to paint a house with 3125 feet of trim?
   a. $3125
   b. $2000
   c. $5125
   d. $3325

No Calculator Questions

47. A bucket can hold 11.4 liters of water. A kiddie pool needs 35 gallons of water to be full. How many times will the bucket need to be filled to fill the kiddie pool?
   a. 12
   b. 35
   c. 11
   d. 45

48. In Jim's school, there are 3 girls for every 2 boys. There are 650 students in total. Using this information, how many students are girls?
   a. 260
   b. 130
   c. 65
   d. 390

49. What is the volume of a pyramid, with a square base whose side is 6 inches, and the height is 9 inches?

     a. 324 in³

     b. 72 in³

     c. 108 in³

     d. 18 in³

50. Convert $\frac{2}{9}$ to a percentage.

     a. 22%

     b. 4.5%

     c. 450%

     d. 0.22%

51. What is the volume of a cone, in terms of π, with a radius of 10 centimeters and height of 12 centimeters?

     a. 400 cm³

     b. 200 cm³

     c. 120 cm³

     d. 140 cm³

52. What is 3 out of 8 expressed as a percent?

     a. 37.5%

     b. 37%

     c. 26.7%

     d. 2.67%

53. The area of a given rectangle is 24 centimeters. If the measure of each side is multiplied by 3, what is the area of the new figure?

     a. 48cm

     b. 72cm

     c. 216cm

     d. 13,824cm

54. If $4x - 3 = 5$, then $x =$

55. What is the solution to $4 \times 7 + (25 - 21)^2 \div 2$?

56. Solve the following:

$$\left(\sqrt{36} \times \sqrt{16}\right) - 3^2$$

57. What is the overall median of Dwayne's current test scores: 78, 92, 83, 97?

58. The total perimeter of a rectangle is 36 cm. If the length of each side is 12 cm, what is the width?

Answer Explanations #1

Reading Test

1. A: Choice *D* can be eliminated because the Salem witch trials aren't even mentioned. While sympathetic to the plight of the accused, the author doesn't demand or urge the reader to demand reparations to the descendants; therefore, Choice *B* can also be ruled out. It's clear that the author's main goal is to educate the reader and shed light on the facts and hidden details behind the case. However, his focus isn't on the occult, but the specific Lancashire case itself. He goes into detail about suspects' histories and ties to Catholicism, revealing how the fears of the English people at the time sealed the fate of the accused witches. Choice *A* is correct.

2. B: It's important to note that these terms may not be an exact analog for *enduring*. However, through knowledge of the definition of *enduring*, as well as the context in which it's used, an appropriate synonym can be found. Plugging "circumstantial" into the passage in place of "enduring" doesn't make sense. Nor does "un-original," this particular case of witchcraft, stand out in history. "Wicked" is very descriptive, but this is an attribute applied to people, not events; therefore, this is an inappropriate choice as well. *Enduring* literally means long lasting, referring to the continued interest in this particular case of witchcraft. Therefore, it's a popular topic of 1600s witch trials, making "popular," Choice *B*, the best choice.

3. D: Choices A and B are irrelevant. The use of quotes lends credibility to the author. However, the presence of quotes alone doesn't necessarily mean that the author has a qualified perspective. What establishes the writer as a reliable voice is that the author's previous writing on the subject has been published before. This qualification greatly establishes the author's credentials as a historical writer, making Choice D the correct answer.

4. B: Choice *A* is incorrect, clearly taking the statement somewhat literally. The remaining three choices appear somewhat interconnected, and though they may be proven at some point later in the article, the focus must remain on the given excerpt. It's very possible that evidence was tampered with or even falsified, but this statement doesn't refer to this. While the author alludes that there may have been evidence tampering and potentially corruption, what the writer is directly saying is that the documentation of the court indicates an elaborate trial. It's clear that exaggerations may have taken place both during the case and in the written account. The reasoning behind this was to gain the attention of the people and even the crown. Choice *B* is the best answer because it not only aligns with the above statement, but ultimately encompasses the potentiality of Choices *C* and D as well.

5. C: Several of these answers could have contributed to the fear and political motivations around the Lancashire witch trials. What this answer's looking for is very specific: political motivations and issues that played a major role in the case. Choice C clearly outlines the public fears of the time. It also describes how the government can use this fear to weed out and eliminate traces of Catholicism (and witchcraft too). Catholicism and witchcraft were seen as dangerous and undermining to English Protestantism and governance. Choice D can be eliminated; while this information may have some truth and is certainly consistent with the general fear of witchcraft, the details about Lancashire's ancient history aren't mentioned in the text. Choice A is true but not necessarily political in nature. Choice B is very promising, though not outright mentioned.

6. D: The best evidence comes from Alizon herself. The text mentions that she confessed to bewitching John Law, thinking that she did him harm. From here she names her grandmother, who she believes corrupted her. Choice B can be ruled out; spectral evidence isn't mentioned. The case draws on knowledge of superstition of witchcraft, but this in itself can't be considered evidence, so Choice A is incorrect. Choice C isn't evidence in a modern sense; rumors have no weight in court and therefore are not evidence. While this is used as evidence to some degree, this still isn't the bestevidence against Alizon and the witches.

7. D: Choice *D* is correct because the selection is told from first person but also addresses the reader as "you." *A* is incorrect because while the perspective is told from an "I" perspective, it also addresses the reader by the use of the word "you." *B* is incorrect because just like A, the selection addresses the reader, but also is told from a first person perspective. *C* is incorrect because there are no third-person pronouns in this selection.

8. A: Not only does the article provide examples to disprove a myth, the title also suggests that the article is trying to disprove a myth. Further, the sentence, "But the 'fact' that the majority of your body heat is lost through your head is a lie," and then the subsequent "let me explain," demonstrates the author's intention in disproving a myth. *B* is incorrect because although the selection does compare elephants and anteaters, it does so in order to prove a point, and is not the primary reason that the selection was written. *C* is incorrect because even though the article mentions somebody wearing clothes in the winter, and that doing so could save your life, wearing clothes in the winter is not the primary reason this article was written. *D* is incorrect because the article only mentions that people are gullible once, and makes no further comment on the matter, so this cannot be the primary purpose.

9. B: If the myth is that most of one's body heat is lost through their head, then the fact that heat loss is proportional to surface area exposed is the best evidence that disproves it, since one's head is a great deal less surface area than the rest of the body, making *B* the correct choice. "It is better to wear a shirt than a hat" does not provide evidence that disproves the fact that the head loses more heat than the rest of the body. Thus, *A* is incorrect. *C* is incorrect because gullibility is mentioned only once in this passage and the rest of the article ignores this statement, so clearly it is not the main idea. Finally, *D* is incorrect because though the article mentions that the human chest probably loses the most heat, it is to provide an example of the evidence that heat loss is proportional to surface area exposed, so this is not the main idea of the passage.

10. B: Choice *B* is correct because the author is trying to demonstrate the main idea, which is that heat loss is proportional to surface area, and so they compare two animals with different surface areas to clarify the main point. *A* is incorrect because the author uses elephants and anteaters to prove a point, that heat loss is proportional to surface area, not to express an opinion. *C* is incorrect because though the author does use them to show differences, they do so in order to give examples that prove the above points, so *C* is not the best answer. *D* is incorrect because there is no language to indicate favoritism between the two animals.

11. C: Since there is an opinion presented along with a fact, *C* is the correct answer. *A* is incorrect—"Not only would you look stupid," is an opinion because there is no way to prove that somebody would look stupid by not wearing a shirt in the cold, even if that may be a popular opinion. However, this opinion is sandwiched inside a factual statement. *B* is incorrect because again, this is a factual statement, but it has been editorialized by interjecting an opinion. Because of the presence of both a fact and an opinion, *D* is the opposite of the correct answer.

12. C: Because of the way that the author addresses the reader, and also the colloquial language that the author uses (i.e., "let me explain," "so," "well," didn't," "you would look stupid," etc.), *C* is the best answer because it has a much more casual tone than the usual informative article. Choice *A* may be a tempting choice because the author says the "fact" that most of one's heat is lost through their head is a "lie," and that someone who does not wear a shirt in the cold looks stupid, but it only happens twice within all the diction of the passage and it does not give an overall tone of harshness. *B* is incorrect because again, while not necessarily nice, the language does not carry an angry charge. The author is clearly not indifferent to the subject because of the passionate language that they use, so *D* is incorrect.

13. A: The author gives logical examples and reason in order to prove that most of one's heat is not lost through their head; therefore, *A* is correct. *B* is incorrect because there is not much emotionally charged language in this selection, and even the small amount present is greatly outnumbered by the facts and evidence. *C* is incorrect because there is no mention of ethics or morals in this selection. *D* is incorrect because the author never qualifies themself as someone who has the authority to be writing on this topic.

14. C: Choice *C* is correct because it contains factual evidence used to disprove a theory, and has no persuasive intent. *A* is incorrect because the selection does not follow a series of events or plot of any kind, nor does it have any elements of a narrative (plot, characters, setting, and theme). *B* is incorrect because the article does not attempt to persuade the reader that this is true; the author simply says that it is true, and is not asking the reader to take a stance on it. Finally, there are not any obvious descriptions within the passage, so *D* is incorrect.

15. B: Choice *B* is correct because since the primary purpose of the article is to provide evidence to disprove the myth that most of a person's heat is lost through their head, then each part of the body losing heat in proportion to its surface area is the best evidence to disprove the myth. *A* is incorrect because again, gullibility is not a main contributor to this article, but it may be common to see questions on the test that give the same wrong answer in order to try and trick the test taker. Choice *C* only suggests what you should do with this information; it is not the primary evidence itself. Choice *D*, while tempting, is actually not evidence. It does not give any reason for why it is a lie; it simply states that it is. Evidence is factual information that supports a claim.

16. D: To define and describe instances of spinoff technology. This is an example of a purpose question—*why* did the author write this? The article contains facts, definitions, and other objective information without telling a story or arguing an opinion. In this case, the purpose of the article is to inform the reader. The only answer choice that is related to giving information is answer Choice *D*: to define and describe.

17. A: A general definition followed by more specific examples. This organization question asks readers to analyze the structure of the essay. The topic of the essay is about spinoff technology; the first paragraph gives a general definition of the concept, while the following two paragraphs offer more detailed examples to help illustrate this idea.

18. C: They were looking for ways to add health benefits to food. This reading comprehension question can be answered based on the second paragraph—scientists were concerned about astronauts' nutrition and began researching useful nutritional supplements. A in particular is not true because it reverses the order of discovery (first NASA identified algae for astronaut use, and then it was further developed for use in baby food).

19. B: Related to the brain. This vocabulary question could be answered based on the reader's prior knowledge; but even for readers who have never encountered the word "neurological" before, the passage does provide context clues. The very next sentence talks about "this algae's potential to boost brain health," which is a paraphrase of "neurological benefits." From this context, readers should be able to infer that "neurological" is related to the brain.

20. D: To give an example of valuable space equipment. This purpose question requires readers to understand the relevance of the given detail. In this case, the author mentions "costly and crucial equipment" before mentioning space suit visors, which are given as an example of something that is very valuable. A is not correct because fashion is only related to sunglasses, not to NASA equipment. B can be eliminated because it is simply not mentioned in the passage. While C seems like it could be a true statement, it is also not relevant to what is being explained by the author.

21. C: It is difficult to make money from scientific research. The article gives several examples of how businesses have been able to capitalize on NASA research, so it is unlikely that the author would agree with this statement. Evidence for the other answer choices can be found in the article: A, the author mentions that "many consumers are unaware that products they are buying are based on NASA research"; B is a general definition of spinoff technology; and D is mentioned in the final paragraph.

22. D: The passage does not proceed in chronological order since it begins by pointing out Leif Erikson's explorations in America, so Choice A does not work. Although the author compares and contrasts Erikson with Christopher Columbus, this is not the main way in which the information is presented; therefore, Choice B does not work. Neither does Choice C because there is no mention of or reference to cause and effect in the passage. However, the passage does offer a conclusion (Leif Erikson deserves more credit) and premises (first European to set foot in the New World and first to contact the natives) to substantiate Erikson's historical importance. Thus, Choice D is correct.

23. C: Choice A is wrong because it describes facts: Leif Erikson was the son of Erik the Red and historians debate Leif's date of birth. These are not opinions. Choice B is wrong; that Erikson called the land "Vinland" is a verifiable fact, as is Choice D because he did contact the natives almost 500 years before Columbus. Choice C is the correct answer because it is the author's opinion that Erikson deserves more credit. That, in fact, is his conclusion in the piece, but another person could argue that Columbus or another explorer deserves more credit for opening up the New World to exploration. Rather than being an indisputable fact, it is a subjective value claim.

24. B: Choice A is wrong because the author aims to go beyond describing Erikson as a mere legendary Viking. Choice C is wrong because the author does not focus on Erikson's motivations, let alone name the spreading of Christianity as his primary objective. Choice D is wrong because it is a premise that Erikson contacted the natives 500 years before Columbus, which is simply a part of supporting the author's conclusion. Choice B is correct because, as stated in the previous answer, it accurately identifies the author's statement that Erikson deserves more credit than he has received for being the first European to explore the New World.

25. B: Choice A is wrong because the author is not in any way trying to entertain the reader. Choice D is wrong because he goes beyond a mere suggestion; "suggest" is too vague. Although the author is certainly trying to alert the readers (make them aware) of Leif Erikson's underappreciated and unheralded accomplishments, the nature of the writing does not indicate the author would be satisfied with the reader merely knowing of Erikson's exploration (Choice C). Rather, the author would want the reader to be informed about it, which is more substantial (Choice B).

26. D: Choice *A* is wrong because the author never addresses the Vikings' state of mind or emotions. Choice *B* is wrong because the author does not elaborate on Erikson's exile and whether he would have become an explorer if not for his banishment. Choice *C* is wrong because there is not enough information to support this premise. It is unclear whether Erikson informed the King of Norway of his finding. Although it is true that the King did not send a follow-up expedition, he could have simply chosen not to expend the resources after receiving Erikson's news. It is not possible to logically infer whether Erikson told him. Choice *D* is correct because there are two examples—Leif Erikson's date of birth and what happened during the encounter with the natives—of historians having trouble pinning down important dates in Viking history.

27. D: Although Washington is from a wealthy background, the passage does not say that his wealth led to his republican ideals, so Choice *A* is not supported. Choice *B* also does not follow from the passage. Washington's warning against meddling in foreign affairs does not mean that he would oppose wars of every kind, so Choice *B* is incorrect. Choice *C* is also unjustified since the author does not indicate that Alexander Hamilton's assistance was absolutely necessary. Choice *D* is correct because the farewell address clearly opposes political parties and partisanship. The author then notes that presidential elections often hit a fever pitch of partisanship. Thus, it is follows that George Washington would not approve of modern political parties and their involvement in presidential elections.

28. A: The author finishes the passage by applying Washington's farewell address to modern politics, so the purpose probably includes this application. Choice *B* is incorrect because George Washington is already a well-established historical figure; furthermore, the passage does not seek to introduce him. Choice *C* is incorrect because the author is not fighting a common perception that Washington was merely a military hero. Choice *D* is incorrect because the author is not convincing readers. Persuasion does not correspond to the passage. Choice *A* states the primary purpose.

29. A: The tone in this passage is informative. Choice *B*, excited, is incorrect, because there are not many word choices used that would indicate excitement from the author. Choice *C*, bitter, is incorrect. Although the author does make a suggestion in the last paragraph to Americans, the statement is not necessarily bitter, but based on the preceding information. Choice *D*, comic, is incorrect, as the author does not try to make the audience laugh, nor do they make light of the situation in any way.

30. C: Interfering. Meddling means to interfere in something. Choice *A* is incorrect. One helpful thing would be to use the word in the sentence: "Washington warned Americans against 'supporting' in foreign affairs" does not make that much sense, so we can mark it off. Choice *B*, speaking against, is incorrect. This phrase would make sense in the sentence, but it goes against the meaning that is intended. George Washington warned against interference in foreign affairs, not speaking *against* foreign affairs. Finally, gathering is also incorrect, because "gathering in foreign affairs" does not sound quite right. Interfering is the best choice for this question.

31. D: When Washington was offered a role as leader of the former colonies, he refused the offer. This is explained in the first sentence of the second paragraph. All of the other answer choices are incorrect and not mentioned in the passage.

32. C: The text mentions all of the listed properties of minerals except the instance of minerals being organically formed. Objects or substances must be naturally occurring, must be a homogeneous solid, and must have a definite chemical composition in order to be considered a mineral.

33. A: Choice *A* is the correct answer because geology is the study of earth related science. Choice *B* is incorrect because psychology is the study of the mind and behavior. Choice *C* is incorrect because biology is the study of life and living organisms. Choice *D* is incorrect because botany is the study of plants.

34. A: Choice *A* is the correct answer because the prefix "homo" means same. Choice *B* is incorrect because "differing in some areas" would be linked to the root word "hetero," meaning "different" or "other."

35: C: Choice *C* is the correct answer because *-logy* refers to the study of a particular subject matter.

36: C: Choice *C* is the correct answer because the counterargument is necessary to point to the fact that researchers don't always agree with findings. Choices *A* and *B* are incorrect because the counterargument isn't overcomplicated or expressing bias, but simply stating an objective dispute. Choice *D* is incorrect because the counterargument is not used to persuade readers to create a new subsection of minerals.

37. D: The author explains that Boethianism is a Medieval theological philosophy that attributes sin to temporary pleasure and righteousness with virtue and God's providence. Besides Choice *D*, the choices listed are all physical things. While these could still be divine rewards, Boethianism holds that the true reward for being virtuous is in God's favor. It is also stressed in the article that physical pleasures cannot be taken into the afterlife. Therefore, the best choice is *D*, God's favor.

38. C: *The Canterbury Tales* presents a manuscript written in the medieval period that can help illustrate Boethianism through stories and show how people of the time might have responded to the idea. Choices *A* and *B* are generalized statements, and we have no evidence to support Choice *B*. Choice *D* is very compelling, but it looks at Boethianism in a way that the author does not. The author does not mention "different levels of Boethianism" when discussing the tales, only that the concept appears differently in different tales. Boethianism also doesn't focus on enlightenment.

39. D: The author is referring to the principle that a desire for material goods leads to moral malfeasance punishable by a higher being. Choice *A* is incorrect; while the text does mention thieves ravaging others' possessions, it is only meant as an example and not as the principle itself. Choice *B* is incorrect for the same reason as *A*. Choice *C* is mentioned in the text and is part of the example that proves the principle, and also not the principle itself.

40. C: The word *avarice* most nearly means *parsimoniousness*, or an unwillingness to spend money. Choice *A* means *evil* or *mischief* and does not relate to the context of the sentence. Choice *B* is also incorrect, because *pithiness* means *shortness* or *conciseness*. Choice *D* is close because *precariousness* means dangerous or instability, which goes well with the context. However, we are told of the summoner's specific characteristic of greed, which makes Choice *C* the best answer.

41. D: Desire for pleasure can lead toward sin. Boethianism acknowledges desire as something that leads out of holiness, so Choice *A* is incorrect. Choice *B* is incorrect because in the passage, Boethianism is depicted as being wary of desire and anything that binds people to the physical world. Choice *C* can be eliminated because the author never says that desire indicates demonic.

attitude than Albert actually feels ("repugnance").

42. B: Narrative, Choice *A*, means a written account of connected events. Think of narrative writing as a story. Choice *C*, expository writing, generally seeks to explain or describe some phenomenon, whereas Choice *D*, technical writing, includes directions, instructions, and/or explanations. This passage is definitely persuasive writing, which hopes to change someone's beliefs based on an appeal to reason or emotion. The author is aiming to convince the reader that smoking is terrible. They use health, price, and beauty in their argument against smoking, so Choice *B*, persuasive, is the correct answer.

43. B: The author is clearly opposed to tobacco. He cites disease and deaths associated with smoking. He points to the monetary expense and aesthetic costs. Choice *A* is wrong because alternatives to smoking are not even addressed in the passage. Choice *C* is wrong because it does not summarize the passage; rather, it is just a premise. Choice *D* is wrong because, while these statistics do support the argument, they do not represent a summary of the piece. Choice *C* is the correct answer because it states the three critiques offered against tobacco and expresses the author's conclusion.

44. C: We are looking for something the author would agree with, so it will almost certainly be anti-smoking or an argument in favor of quitting smoking. Choice *A* is wrong because the author does not speak against means of cessation. Choice *B* is wrong because the author does not reference other substances, but does speak of how addictive nicotine—a drug in tobacco—is. Choice *D* is wrong because the author certainly would not encourage reducing taxes to encourage a reduction of smoking costs, thereby helping smokers to continue the habit. Choice *C* is correct because the author is definitely attempting to persuade smokers to quit smoking.

45. D: Here, we are looking for an opinion of the author's rather than a fact or statistic. Choice *A* is wrong because quoting statistics from the Centers of Disease Control and Prevention is stating facts, not opinions. Choice *B* is wrong because it expresses the fact that cigarettes sometimes cost more than a few gallons of gas. It would be an opinion if the author said that cigarettes were not affordable. Choice *C* is incorrect because yellow stains are a known possible adverse effect of smoking. Choice *D* is correct as an opinion because smell is subjective. Some people might like the smell of smoke, they might not have working olfactory senses, and/or some people might not find the smell of smoke akin to "pervasive nastiness," so this is the expression of an opinion. Thus, Choice *D* is the correct answer.

46. B: Strong dislike. This vocabulary question can be answered using context clues and common sense. Based on the rest of the conversation, the reader can gather that Albert isn't looking forward to his marriage. As the Count notes that "you don't appear to me to be very enthusiastic on the subject of this marriage," and also remarks on Albert's "objection to a young lady who is both rich and beautiful," readers can guess Albert's feelings. The answer choice that most closely matches "objection" and "not . . . very enthusiastic" is *B*, "strong dislike."

47. C: Their name is more respected than the Danglars'. This inference question can be answered by eliminating incorrect answers. Choice *A* is tempting, considering that Albert mentions money as a concern in his marriage. However, although he may not be as rich as his fiancée, his father still has a stable income of 50,000 francs a year. Choice *B* isn't mentioned at all in the passage, so it's impossible to make an inference. Finally, Choice *D* is clearly false because Albert's father arranged his marriage but his mother doesn't approve of it. Evidence for Choice *C* can be found in the Count's comparison of Albert and Eugénie: "she will enrich you, and you will ennoble her." In other words, the Danglars are wealthier but the Morcef family has a more noble background.

48. D: Apprehensive. As in question 7, there are many clues in the passage that indicate Albert's attitude towards his marriage—far from enthusiastic, he has many reservations. This question requires test takers to understand the vocabulary in the answer choices. "Pragmatic" is closest in meaning to "realistic," and "indifferent" means "uninterested." The only word related to feeling worried, uncertain, or unfavorable about the future is "apprehensive."

49. B: He is like a wise uncle, giving practical advice to Albert. Choice *A* is incorrect because the Count's tone is friendly and conversational. Choice *C* is also incorrect because the Count questions why Albert doesn't want to marry a young, beautiful, and rich girl. While the Count asks many questions, he isn't particularly "probing" or "suspicious"—instead, he's asking to find out more about Albert's situation and then give him advice about marriage.

50. A: She belongs to a noble family. Though Albert's mother doesn't appear in the scene, there's more than enough information to answer this question. More than once is his family's noble background mentioned (not to mention that Albert's mother is the Comtess de Morcef, a noble title). The other answer choices can be eliminated—she is obviously deeply concerned about her son's future; money isn't her highest priority because otherwise she would favor a marriage with the wealthy Danglars; and Albert describes her "clear and penetrating judgment," meaning she makes good decisions.

51. C: The richest people in society were also the most respected. The Danglars family is wealthier but the Morcef family has a more aristocratic name, which gives them a higher social standing. Evidence for the other answer choices can be found throughout the passage: Albert mentioned receiving money from his father's fortune after his marriage; Albert's father has arranged this marriage for him; and the Count speculates that Albert's mother disapproves of this marriage because Eugénie isn't from a noble background like the Morcef family, implying that she would prefer a match with a girl from aristocratic society.

52. A: He seems reluctant to marry Eugénie, despite her wealth and beauty. This is a reading comprehension question, and the answer can be found in the following lines: "'I confess,' observed Monte Cristo, 'that I have some difficulty in comprehending your objection to a young lady who is both rich and beautiful.'" Choice *B* is the opposite (Albert's father is the one who insists on the marriage), Choice *C* incorrectly represents Albert's eagerness to marry, and Choice *D* describes a more positive attitude than Albert actually feels ("repugnance").

Writing and Language Test

1. C: Choice *C* correctly uses *from* to describe the fact that dogs are related to wolves. The word *through* is incorrectly used here, so Choice *A* is incorrect. Choice *B* makes no sense. Choice *D* unnecessarily changes the verb tense in addition to incorrectly using *through*.

2. B: Choice *B* is correct because the Oxford comma is applied, clearly separating the specific terms. Choice *A* lacks this clarity. Choice *C* is correct but too wordy since commas can be easily applied. Choice *D* doesn't flow with the sentence's structure.

3. D: Choice *D* correctly uses the question mark, fixing the sentence's main issue. Thus, Choice *A* is incorrect because questions do not end with periods. Choice *B*, although correctly written, changes the meaning of the original sentence. Choice *C* is incorrect because it completely changes the direction of the sentence, disrupts the flow of the paragraph, and lacks the crucial question mark.

4. A: Choice *A* is correct since there are no errors in the sentence. Choices *B* and *C* both have extraneous commas, disrupting the flow of the sentence. Choice *D* unnecessarily rearranges the sentence.

5. D: Choice *D* is correct because the commas serve to distinguish that *artificial selection* is just another term for *selective breeding* before the sentence continues. The structure is preserved, and the sentence can flow with more clarity. Choice *A* is incorrect because the sentence needs commas to avoid being a run-on. Choice *B* is close but still lacks the required comma after *selection*, so this is incorrect. Choice *C* is incorrect because the comma to set off the aside should be placed after *breeding* instead of *called*.

6. B: Choice *B* is correct because the sentence is talking about a continuing process. Therefore, the best modification is to add the word *to* in front of *increase*. Choice *A* is incorrect because this modifier is missing. Choice *C* is incorrect because with the additional comma, the present tense of *increase* is inappropriate. Choice *D* makes more sense, but the tense is still not the best to use.

7. A: The sentence has no errors, so Choice *A* is correct. Choice *B* is incorrect because it adds an unnecessary comma. Choice *C* is incorrect because *advantage* should not be plural in this sentence without the removal of the singular *an*. Choice *D* is very tempting. While this would make the sentence more concise, this would ultimately alter the context of the sentence, which would be incorrect.

8. C: Choice *C* correctly uses *on to*, describing the way genes are passed generationally. The use of *into* is inappropriate for this context, which makes Choice *A* incorrect. Choice *B* is close, but *onto* refers to something being placed on a surface. Choice *D* doesn't make logical sense.

9. D: Choice *D* is correct, since only proper names should be capitalized. Because the name of a dog breed is not a proper name, Choice *A* is incorrect. In terms of punctuation, only one comma after *example* is needed, so Choices *B* and *C* are incorrect.

10. D: Choice *D* is the correct answer because "rather" acts as an interrupting word here and thus should be separated by commas. Choices *A, B,* and *C* all use commas unwisely, breaking the flow of the sentence.

11. B: Since the sentence can stand on its own without *Usually*, separating it from the rest of the sentence with a comma is correct. Choice *A* needs the comma after *Usually*, while Choice *C* uses commas incorrectly. Choice *D* is tempting but changing *turn* to past tense goes against the rest of the paragraph.

12. A: In Choice *A*, the dependent clause *Sometimes in particularly dull seminars* is seamlessly attached with a single comma after *seminars*. Choice *B* contain too many commas. Choice *C* does not correctly combine the dependent clause with the independent clause. Choice *D* introduces too many unnecessary commas.

13. D: Choice *D* rearranges the sentence to be more direct and straightforward, so it is correct. Choice *A* needs a comma after *on*. Choice *B* introduces unnecessary commas. Choice *C* creates an incomplete sentence, since *Because I wasn't invested in what was going on* is a dependent clause.

14. C: Choice *C* is fluid and direct, making it the best revision. Choice *A* is incorrect because the construction is awkward and lacks parallel structure. Choice *B* is clearly incorrect because of the unnecessary comma and period. Choice *D* is close, but its sequence is still awkward and overly complicated.

15. B: Choice *B* correctly adds a comma after *person* and cuts out the extraneous writing, making the sentence more streamlined. Choice *A* is poorly constructed, lacking proper grammar to connect the sections of the sentence correctly. Choice *C* inserts an unnecessary semicolon and doesn't enable this section to flow well with the rest of the sentence. Choice *D* is better but still unnecessarily long.

16. D: This sentence, though short, is a complete sentence. The only thing the sentence needs is an em-dash after "Easy." In this sentence the em-dash works to add emphasis to the word "Easy" and also acts in place of a colon, but in a less formal way. Therefore, Choice *D* is correct. Choices *A* and *B* lack the crucial comma, while Choice *C* unnecessarily breaks the sentence apart.

17. C: Choice *C* successfully fixes the construction of the sentence, changing *drawing* into *to draw*. Keeping the original sentence disrupts the flow, so Choice *A* is incorrect. Choice *B*'s use of *which* offsets the whole sentence. Choice *D* is incorrect because it unnecessarily expands the sentence content and makes it more confusing.

18. B: Choice *B* fixes the homophone issue. Because the author is talking about people, *their* must be used instead of *there*. This revision also appropriately uses the Oxford comma, separating and distinguishing *lives, world, and future*. Choice *A* uses the wrong homophone and is missing commas. Choice *C* neglects to fix these problems and unnecessarily changes the tense of *applies*. Choice *D* fixes the homophone but fails to properly separate *world* and *future*.

19. C: Choice *C* is correct because it fixes the core issue with this sentence: the singular *has* should not describe the plural *scientists*. Thus, Choice *A* is incorrect. Choices *B* and *D* add unnecessary commas.

20. D: Choice *D* correctly conveys the writer's intention of asking if, or *whether*, early perceptions of dinosaurs are still influencing people. Choice *A* makes no sense as worded. Choice *B* is better, but *how* doesn't coincide with the context. Choice *C* adds unnecessary commas.

21. A: Choice *A* is correct, as the sentence does not require modification. Choices *B* and *C* implement extra punctuation unnecessarily, disrupting the flow of the sentence. Choice *D* incorrectly adds a comma in an awkward location.

22. B: Choice *B* is the strongest revision, as adding *to explore* is very effective in both shortening the sentence and maintaining, even enhancing, the point of the writer. To explore is to seek understanding in order to gain knowledge and insight, which coincides with the focus of the overall sentence. Choice *A* is not technically incorrect, but it is overcomplicated. Choice *C* is a decent revision, but the sentence could still be more condensed and sharpened. Choice *D* fails to make the sentence more concise and inserts unnecessary commas.

23. D: Choice *D* correctly applies a semicolon to introduce a new line of thought while remaining in a single sentence. The comma after *however* is also appropriately placed. Choice *A* is a run-on sentence. Choice *B* is also incorrect because the single comma is not enough to fix the sentence. Choice *C* adds commas around *uncertain* which are unnecessary.

24. B: Choice *B* not only fixes the homophone issue from *its*, which is possessive, to *it's*, which is a contraction of *it is*, but also streamlines the sentence by adding a comma and eliminating *and*. Choice *A* is incorrect because of these errors. Choices *C* and *D* only fix the homophone issue.

25. A: Choice *A* is correct, as the sentence is fine the way it is. Choices *B* and *C* add unnecessary commas, while Choice *D* uses the possessive *its* instead of the contraction *it's*.

26. C: Choice *C* is correct because the phrase *even likely* is flanked by commas, creating a kind of aside, which allows the reader to see this separate thought while acknowledging it as part of the overall sentence and subject at hand. Choice *A* is incorrect because it seems to ramble after *even* due to a missing comma after *likely*. Choice *B* is better but inserting a comma after *that* warps the flow of the writing. Choice *D* is incorrect because there must be a comma after *plausible*.

27. D: Choice *D* strengthens the overall sentence structure while condensing the words. This makes the subject of the sentence, and the emphasis of the writer, much clearer to the reader. Thus, while Choice *A* is technically correct, the language is choppy and over-complicated. Choice *B* is better but lacks the reference to a specific image of dinosaurs. Choice *C* introduces unnecessary commas.

28. B: Choice *B* correctly joins the two independent clauses. Choice *A* is decent, but *that would be* is too verbose for the sentence. Choice *C* incorrectly changes the semicolon to a comma. Choice *D* splits the clauses effectively but is not concise enough.

29. A: Choice *A* is correct, as the original sentence has no error. Choices *B* and *C* employ unnecessary semicolons and commas. Choice *D* would be an ideal revision, but it lacks the comma after *Ransom* that would enable the sentence structure to flow.

30. D: By reorganizing the sentence, the context becomes clearer with Choice *D*. Choice *A* has an awkward sentence structure. Choice *B* offers a revision that doesn't correspond well with the original sentence's intent. Choice *C* cuts out too much of the original content, losing the full meaning.

31. C: Choice *C* fixes the disagreement between the singular *this* and the plural *viewpoints*. Choice *A*, therefore, is incorrect. Choice *B* introduces an unnecessary comma. In Choice *D*, *those* agrees with *viewpoints*, but neither agrees with *distinguishes*.

32. A: Choice *A* is direct and clear, without any punctuation errors. Choice *B* is well-written but too wordy. Choice *C* adds an unnecessary comma. Choice *D* is also well-written but much less concise than Choice *A*.

33. D: Choice *D* rearranges the sentence to improve clarity and impact, with *tempting* directly describing *idea*. On its own, Choice *A* is a run-on. Choice *B* is better because it separates the clauses, but it keeps an unnecessary comma. Choice *C* is also an improvement but still a run-on.

34. B: Choice *B* is the best answer simply because the sentence makes it clear that Un-man takes over and possesses Weston. In Choice *A*, these events sounded like two different things, instead of an action and result. Choices *C* and *D* make this relationship clearer, but the revisions don't flow very well grammatically.

35. D: Changing the phrase *after this* to *then* makes the sentence less complicated and captures the writer's intent, making Choice *D* correct. Choice *A* is awkwardly constructed. Choices *B* and *C* misuse their commas and do not adequately improve the clarity.

36. B: By starting a new sentence, the run-on issue is eliminated, and a new line of reasoning can be seamlessly introduced, making Choice *B* correct. Choice *A* is thus incorrect. While Choice *C* fixes the run-on via a semicolon, a comma is still needed after *this*. Choice *D* contains a comma splice. The independent clauses must be separated by more than just a comma, even with the rearrangement of the second half of the sentence.

37. C: Choice *C* condenses the original sentence while being more active in communicating the emphasis on changing times/media that the author is going for, so it is correct. Choice *A* is clunky because it lacks a comma after *today* to successfully transition into the second half of the sentence. Choice *B* inserts unnecessary commas. Choice *D* is a good revision of the underlined section, but not only does it not fully capture the original meaning, it also does not flow into the rest of the sentence.

38. B: Choice B clearly illustrates the author's point, with a well-placed semicolon that breaks the sentence into clearer, more readable sections. Choice A lacks punctuation. Choice C is incorrect because the period inserted after *question* forms an incomplete sentence. Choice D is a very good revision but does not make the author's point clearer than the original.

39. A: Choice A is correct: while the sentence seems long, it actually doesn't require any commas. The conjunction *that* successfully combines the two parts of the sentence without the need for additional punctuation. Choices B and C insert commas unnecessarily, incorrectly breaking up the flow of the sentence. Choice D alters the meaning of the original text by creating a new sentence, which is only a fragment.

40. C: Choice C correctly replaces *for* with *to*, the correct preposition for the selected area. Choice A is not the answer because of this incorrect preposition. Choice B is unnecessarily long and disrupts the original sentence structure. Choice D is also too wordy and lacks parallel structure.

41. D: Choice D is the answer because it inserts the correct punctuation to fix the sentence, linking the dependent and independent clauses. Choice A is therefore incorrect. Choice B is also incorrect since this revision only adds content to the sentence while lacking grammatical precision. Choice C overdoes the punctuation; only a comma is needed, not a semicolon.

42. B: Choice B correctly separates the section into two sentences and changes the word order to make the second part clearer. Choice A is incorrect because it is a run-on. Choice C adds an extraneous comma, while Choice D makes the run-on worse and does not coincide with the overall structure of the sentence.

43. C: Choice C is the best answer because of how the commas are used to flank *in earnest*. This distinguishes the side thought (*in earnest*) from the rest of the sentence. Choice A needs punctuation. Choice B inserts a semicolon in a spot that doesn't make sense, resulting in a fragmented sentence and lost meaning. Choice D is unnecessarily elaborate and leads to a run-on.

44. A: Choice A is correct because the sentence contains no errors. The comma after *bias* successfully links the two halves of the sentence, and the use of *it's* is correct as a contraction of *it is*. Choice B creates a sentence fragment, while Choice C creates a run-on. Choice D incorrectly changes *it's* to *its*.

45. D: Choice D correctly inserts a comma after *However* and fixes *over use* to *overuse*—in this usage, it is one word. Choice A is therefore incorrect, as is Choice B. Choice C is a good revision but does not fit well with the rest of the sentence.

Math Test

1. B: To simplify this inequality, subtract 3 from both sides to get $-\frac{1}{2}x \geq -1$. Then, multiply both sides by -2 (remembering this flips the direction of the inequality) to get $x \leq 2$.

2. D: This problem involves a composition function, where one function is plugged into the other function. In this case, the $f(x)$ function is plugged into the $g(x)$ function for each x-value. The composition equation becomes $g(f(x)) = 2^3 - 3(2^2) - 2(2) + 6$. Simplifying the equation gives the answer $g(f(x)) = 8 - 3(4) - 2(2) + 6 = 8 - 12 - 4 + 6 = -2$.

3. B: A factor of 36 is any number that can be divided into 36 and have no remainder. $36 = 36 \times 1, 18 \times 2, 9 \times 4,$ and 6×6. Therefore, it has 7 unique factors: 36, 18, 9, 6, 4, 2, and 1.

4. D: A parabola of the form $y = \frac{1}{4f}x^2$ has a focus $(0, f)$. Because $y = -9x^2$, set $-9 = \frac{1}{4f}$. Solving this equation for f results in $f = -\frac{1}{36}$. Therefore, the coordinates of the focus are $\left(0, -\frac{1}{36}\right)$.

5. B: The volume of a cube is the length of the side cubed, and 3 inches cubed is 27 in³. Choice A is not the correct answer because that is 2×3 inches. Choice C is not the correct answer because that is 3×3 inches, and Choice D is not the correct answer because there was no operation performed.

6. B: The volume of a rectangular prism is the $length \times width \times height$, and $3cm \times 5cm \times 11cm$ is 165 cm³. Choice A is not the correct answer because that is $3cm + 5cm + 11cm$. Choice C is not the correct answer because that is 15^2. Choice D is not the correct answer because that is $3cm \times 5cm \times 10cm$.

7. A: The volume of a cylinder is $\pi r^2 h$, and $\pi \times 5^2 \times 10$ is $250 \, \pi \, in^3$. Choice B is not the correct answer because that is $5^2 \times 2\pi$. Choice C is not the correct answer since that is $5in \times 10\pi$. Choice D is not the correct answer because that is $10^2 \times 2in$.

8. D: This system of equations involves one quadratic function and one linear function, as seen from the degree of each equation. One way to solve this is through substitution. Solving for y in the second equation yields $y = x + 2$. Plugging this equation in for the y of the quadratic equation yields $x^2 - 2x + x + 2 = 8$. Simplifying the equation, it becomes $x^2 - x + 2 = 8$. Setting this equal to zero and factoring, it becomes $x^2 - x - 6 = 0 = (x - 3)(x + 2)$. Solving these two factors for x gives the zeros $x = 3, -2$. To find the y-value for the point, each number can be plugged in to either original equation. Solving each one for y yields the points $(3, 5)$ and $(-2, 0)$.

9. B: The slope will be given by $\frac{1-0}{2-0} = \frac{1}{2}$. The y-intercept will be 0, since it passes through the origin. Using slope-intercept form, the equation for this line is $y = \frac{1}{2}x$.

10. D: Area = length x width. The answer must be in square inches, so all values must be converted to inches. $\frac{1}{2}$ ft is equal to 6 inches. Therefore, the area of the rectangle is equal to $6 \times \frac{11}{2} = \frac{66}{2} = 33$ square inches.

11. B: The table shows values that are increasing exponentially. The differences between the inputs are the same, while the differences in the outputs are changing by a factor of 2. The values in the table can be modeled by the equation $f(x) = 2^x$.

12. B: For the first card drawn, the probability of a King being pulled is $\frac{4}{52}$. Since this card isn't replaced, if a King is drawn first, the probability of a King being drawn second is $\frac{3}{51}$. The probability of a King being drawn in both the first and second draw is the product of the two probabilities: $\frac{4}{52} \times \frac{3}{51} = \frac{12}{2,652}$ which, divided by 12, equals $\frac{1}{221}$.

14. D: The expression is three times the sum of twice a number and 1, which is $3(2x + 1)$. Then, 6 is subtracted from this expression.

16. A: To expand a squared binomial, it's necessary use the *First, Inner, Outer, Last Method*

$$2x - 4y)^2$$

$$2x \times 2x + 2x(-4y) + (-4y)(2x) + (-4y)(-4y)$$

$$4x^2 - 8xy - 8xy + 16y^2$$

$$4x^2 - 16xy + 16y^2$$

17. B: The zeros of this function can be found by using the quadratic formula:

$$x = \frac{-b \pm \sqrt{b^2 - 4ac}}{2a}$$

Identifying a, b, and c can be done from the equation as well because it is in standard form. The formula becomes:

$$x = \frac{0 \pm \sqrt{0^2 - 4(1)(4)}}{2(1)} = \frac{\sqrt{-16}}{2}$$

Since there is a negative underneath the radical, the answer is a complex number.

18. D: The expression is simplified by collecting like terms. Terms with the same variable and exponent are like terms, and their coefficients can be added.

19. A: $\frac{810}{2921}$

Line up the fractions.

$$\frac{15}{23} \times \frac{54}{127}$$

Multiply across the top and across the bottom.

$$\frac{15 \times 54}{23 \times 127} = \frac{810}{2921}$$

20. A: Finding the product means distributing one polynomial to the other so that each term in the first is multiplied by each term in the second. Then, like terms can be collected. Multiplying the factors yields the expression $20x^3 + 4x^2 + 24x - 40x^2 - 8x - 48$. Collecting like terms means adding the x^2 terms and adding the x terms. The final answer after simplifying the expression is $20x^3 - 36x^2 + 16x - 48$.

21. B: The equation can be solved by factoring the numerator into $(x + 6)(x - 5)$. Since that same factor $(x - 5)$ exists on top and bottom, that factor cancels. This leaves the equation $x + 6 = 11$. Solving the equation gives the answer $x = 5$. When this value is plugged into the equation, it yields a zero in the denominator of the fraction. Since this is undefined, there is no solution.

22. C: The common denominator here will be $4x$. Rewrite these fractions as

$$\frac{3}{x} + \frac{5u}{2x} - \frac{u}{4} = \frac{12}{4x} + \frac{10u}{4x} - \frac{ux}{4x} = \frac{12x + 10u + ux}{4x}$$

23. B: There are two zeros for the given function. They are $x = 0, -2$. The zeros can be found a number of ways, but this particular equation can be factored into $f(x) = x(x^2 + 4x + 4) = x(x + 2)(x + 2)$. By setting each factor equal to zero and solving for x, there are two solutions. On a graph, these zeros can be seen where the line crosses the x-axis.

24. A: The equation is *even* because $f(-x) = f(x)$. Plugging in a negative value will result in the same answer as when plugging in the positive of that same value. The function:

$$f(-2) = \frac{1}{2}(-2)^4 + 2(-2)^2 - 6 = 8 + 8 - 6 = 10$$

yields the same value as:

$$f(2) = \frac{1}{2}(2)^4 + 2(2)^2 - 6 = 8 + 8 - 6 = 10$$

25. B: The perimeter of a rectangle is the sum of all four sides. Therefore, the answer is $P = 14 + 8\frac{1}{2} + 14 + 8\frac{1}{2} = 14 + 14 + 8 + \frac{1}{2} + 8 + \frac{1}{2} = 45$ square inches.

26. B: $12 \times 750 = 9,000$. Therefore, there are 9,000 milliliters of water, which must be converted to liters. 1,000 milliliters equals 1 liter; therefore, 9 liters of water are purchased.

27. B: Because this isn't a right triangle, SOHCAHTOA can't be used. However, the law of cosines can be used. Therefore:

$$c^2 = a^2 + b^2 - 2ab \cos C = 19^2 + 26^2 - 2 \cdot 19 \cdot 26 \cdot \cos 42° = 302.773$$

Taking the square root and rounding to the nearest tenth results in $c = 17.4$.

28. C: Because the triangles are similar, the lengths of the corresponding sides are proportional. Therefore:

$$\frac{30 + x}{30} = \frac{22}{14} = \frac{y + 15}{y}$$

This results in the equation $14(30 + x) = 22 \cdot 30$ which, when solved, gives $x = 17.1$. The proportion also results in the equation $14(y + 15) = 22y$ which, when solved, gives $y = 26.3$.

29. B: The technique of completing the square must be used to change $4x^2 + 4y^2 - 16x - 24y + 51 = 0$ into the standard equation of a circle. First, the constant must be moved to the right-hand side of the equals sign, and each term must be divided by the coefficient of the x^2 term (which is 4).

The x and y terms must be grouped together to obtain:

$$x^2 - 4x + y^2 - 6y = -\frac{51}{4}$$

Then, the process of completing the square must be completed for each variable. This gives:

$$(x^2 - 4x + 4) + (y^2 - 6y + 9) = -\frac{51}{4} + 4 + 9$$

The equation can be written as:

$$(x - 2)^2 + (y - 3)^2 = \frac{1}{4}$$

Therefore, the center of the circle is (2, 3) and the radius is:

$$\sqrt{\frac{1}{4}} = \frac{1}{2}$$

30. A: Operations within the parentheses must be completed first. Then, division is completed. Finally, addition is the last operation to complete. When adding decimals, digits within each place value are added together. Therefore, the expression is evaluated as $(2 \times 20) \div (7 + 1) + (6 \times 0.01) + (4 \times 0.001) = 40 \div 8 + 0.06 + 0.004 = 5 + 0.06 + 0.004 = 5.064$.

31. C: A dollar contains 20 nickels. Therefore, if there are 12 dollars' worth of nickels, there are $12 \times 20 = 240$ nickels. Each nickel weighs 5 grams. Therefore, the weight of the nickels is $240 \times 5 = 1,200$ grams. Adding in the weight of the empty piggy bank, the filled bank weighs 2,250 grams.

32. D: 3 must be multiplied times $27\frac{3}{4}$. In order to easily do this, the mixed number should be converted into an improper fraction. $27\frac{3}{4} = \frac{27*4+3}{4} = \frac{111}{4}$. Therefore, Denver had approximately $\frac{3x111}{4} = \frac{333}{4}$ inches of snow. The improper fraction can be converted back into a mixed number through division. $\frac{333}{4} = 83\frac{1}{4}$ inches.

33. D: $x \leq -5$. When solving a linear equation or inequality:

Distribution is performed if necessary: $-3(x + 4) \rightarrow -3x - 12 \geq x + 8$. This means that any like terms on the same side of the equation/inequality are combined.

The equation/inequality is manipulated to get the variable on one side. In this case, subtracting x from both sides produces $-4x - 12 \geq 8$.

The variable is isolated using inverse operations to undo addition/subtraction. Adding 12 to both sides produces $-4x \geq 20$.

The variable is isolated using inverse operations to undo multiplication/division. Remember if dividing by a negative number, the relationship of the inequality reverses, so the sign is flipped. In this case, dividing by -4 on both sides produces $x \leq -5$.

34. C: $y = 40x + 300$. In this scenario, the variables are the number of sales and Karen's weekly pay. The weekly pay depends on the number of sales. Therefore, weekly pay is the dependent variable (y) and the number of sales is the independent variable (x). Each pair of values from the table can be written as an ordered pair (x, y): (2,380), (7,580), (4,460), (8,620). The ordered pairs can be substituted into the equations to see which creates true statements (both sides equal) for each pair. Even if one ordered pair produces equal values for a given equation, the other three ordered pairs must be checked. The only equation which is true for all four ordered pairs is $y = 40x + 300$:

$$380 = 40(2) + 300 \rightarrow 380 = 380$$

$$580 = 40(7) + 300 \rightarrow 580 = 580$$

$$460 = 40(4) + 300 \rightarrow 460 = 460$$

$$620 = 40(8) + 300 \rightarrow 620 = 620$$

35. C: The area of the shaded region is the area of the square, minus the area of the circle. The area of the circle will be πr^2. The side of the square will be $2r$, so the area of the square will be $4r^2$. Therefore, the difference is $4r^2 - \pi r^2 = (4 - \pi)r^2$.

36. B: The car is traveling at a speed of five meters per second. On the interval from one to three seconds, the position changes by fifteen meters. By making this change in position over time into a rate, the speed becomes ten meters in two seconds or five meters in one second.

37. B: For an ordered pair to be a solution to a system of inequalities, it must make a true statement for BOTH inequalities when substituting its values for x and y. Substituting $(-3, -2)$ into the inequalities produces $(-2) > 2(-3) - 3 \rightarrow -2 > -9$ and $(-2) < -4(-3) + 8 \rightarrow -2 < 20$. Both are true statements.

38. D: The shape of the scatterplot is a parabola (U-shaped). This eliminates Choices A (a linear equation that produces a straight line) and C (an exponential equation that produces a smooth curve upward or downward). The value of a for a quadratic function in standard form ($y = ax^2 + bx + c$) indicates whether the parabola opens up (U-shaped) or opens down (upside-down U). A negative value for a produces a parabola that opens down; therefore, Choice B can also be eliminated.

39. B: According to the order of operations, multiplication and division must be completed first from left to right. Then, addition and subtraction are completed from left to right. Therefore:

$$9 \times 9 \div 9 + 9 - 9 \div 9$$

$$81 \div 9 + 9 - 9 \div 9$$

$$9 + 9 - 9 \div 9$$

$$9 + 9 - 1$$

$$18 - 1$$

$$17$$

40. B: When giving an answer to a math problem that is in fraction form, it always should be simplified. Both 3 and 15 have a common factor of 3 that can be divided out, so the correct answer is $\frac{3 \div 3}{15 \div 3} = \frac{1}{5}$.

41. A: 13 nurses

Using the given information of 1 nurse to 25 patients and 325 patients, set up an equation to solve for number of nurses (N):

$$\frac{N}{325} = \frac{1}{25}$$

Multiply both sides by 325 to get N by itself on one side.

$$\frac{N}{1} = \frac{325}{25} = 13 \; nurses$$

42. D: 290 beds

Using the given information of 2 beds to 1 room and 145 rooms, set up an equation to solve for number of beds (B):

$$\frac{B}{145} = \frac{2}{1}$$

Multiply both sides by 145 to get B by itself on one side.

$$\frac{B}{1} = \frac{290}{1} = 290 \; beds$$

43. C: X = 150

Set up the initial equation.

$$\frac{2X}{5} - 1 = 59$$

Add 1 to both sides.

$$\frac{2X}{5} - 1 + 1 = 59 + 1$$

Multiply both sides by 5/2.

$$\frac{2X}{5} \times \frac{5}{2} = 60 \times \frac{5}{2} = 150$$

$$X = 150$$

44. C: $51.93

List the givens.

$$Tax = 6.0\% = 0.06$$

$$Sale = 50\% = 0.5$$

$$Hat = \$32.99$$

$$Jersey = \$64.99$$

Calculate the sales prices.

$$Hat\ Sale\ =\ 0.5\ (32.99)\ =\ 16.495$$

$$Jersey\ Sale\ =\ 0.5\ (64.99)\ =\ 32.495$$

Total the sales prices.

$$Hat\ sale\ +\ jersey\ sale\ =\ 16.495\ +\ 32.495\ =\ 48.99$$

Calculate the tax and add it to the total sales prices.

$$Total\ after\ tax\ =\ 48.99\ +\ (48.99\ x\ 0.06)\ =\ \$51.93$$

45. D: $0.45

List the givens.

$$Store\ coffee\ =\ \$1.23/lbs$$

$$Local\ roaster\ coffee\ =\ \$1.98/1.5\ lbs$$

Calculate the cost for 5 lbs of store brand.

$$\frac{\$1.23}{1\ lbs}\ \times 5\ lbs\ =\ \$6.15$$

Calculate the cost for 5 lbs of the local roaster.

$$\frac{\$1.98}{1.5\ lbs}\ \times 5\ lbs\ =\ \$6.60$$

Subtract to find the difference in price for 5 lbs.

$$\begin{array}{r} \$6.60 \\ \underline{\$6.15} \\ \$0.45 \end{array}$$

46. D: $3,325

List the givens.

$$1,800\ ft.=\ \$2,000$$

$$Cost\ after\ 1,800\ ft.=\ \$1.00/ft.$$

Find how many feet left after the first 1,800 ft.

$$3,125 \text{ ft.}$$
$$- \underline{1,800 \text{ ft.}}$$
$$1,325 \text{ ft.}$$

Calculate the cost for the feet over 1,800 ft.

$$1,325 \, ft. \times \frac{\$1.00}{1 \, ft} = \$1,325$$

Total for entire cost.

$$\$2,000 + \$1,325 = \$3,325$$

47. A: 12

Calculate how many gallons the bucket holds.

$$11.4 \, L \times \frac{1 \, gal}{3.8 \, L} = 3 \, gal$$

Now how many buckets to fill the pool which needs 35 gallons.

$$35/3 = 11.67$$

Since the amount is more than 11 but less than 12, we must fill the bucket 12 times.

48. D: Three girls for every two boys can be expressed as a ratio: 3:2. This can be visualized as splitting the school into 5 groups: 3 girl groups and 2 boy groups. The number of students which are in each group can be found by dividing the total number of students by 5:

650 divided by 5 equals 1 part, or 130 students per group

To find the total number of girls, multiply the number of students per group (130) by how the number of girl groups in the school (3). This equals 390, answer *D*.

49. C: The volume of a pyramid is ($length \times width \times height$), divided by 3, and ($6 \times 6 \times 9$), divided by 3 is 108 in³. Choice *A* is incorrect because 324 in³ is ($length \times width \times height$) without dividing by 3. Choice *B* is incorrect because 6 is used for height instead of 9 (($6 \times 6 \times 6$) divided by 3) to get 72 in³. Choice *D* is incorrect because 18 in³ is (6×9), divided by 3 and leaving out a 6.

50. A: 22%

Converting from a fraction to a percentage generally involves two steps. First, the fraction needs to be converted to a decimal.

Divide 2 by 9 which results in $0.\overline{22}$. The top line indicates that the decimal actually goes on forever with an endless amount of 2's.

Second, the decimal needs to be moved two places to the right:

22%

51. A: The volume of a cone is $(\pi r^2 h)$, divided by 3, and $(\pi \times 10^2 \times 12)$, divided by 3 is 400 cm³. Choice B is $10^2 \times 2$. Choice C is incorrect because it is 10×12. Choice D is also incorrect because that is $10^2 + 40$.

52. A: 37.5%

Solve this by setting up the percent formula:

$$\frac{3}{8} = \frac{\%}{100}$$

Multiply 3 by 100 to get 300. Then divide 300 by 8:

$$300 \div 8 = 37.5\%$$

Note that with the percent formula, 37.5 is automatically a percentage and does not need to have any further conversions.

53. C: 216cm. Because area is a two-dimensional measurement, the dimensions are multiplied by a scale that is squared to determine the scale of the corresponding areas. The dimensions of the rectangle are multiplied by a scale of 3. Therefore, the area is multiplied by a scale of 3^2 (which is equal to 9): $24cm \times 9 = 216cm$.

54.

Add 3 to both sides to get $4x = 8$. Then divide both sides by 4 to get $x = 2$.

55.

To solve this correctly, keep in mind the order of operations with the mnemonic PEMDAS (Please Excuse My Dear Aunt Sally). This stands for Parentheses, Exponents, Multiplication, Division, Addition, Subtraction. Taking it step by step, solve the parentheses first:

$$4 \times 7 + (4)^2 \div 2$$

Then, apply the exponent:

$$4 \times 7 + 16 \div 2$$

Multiplication and division are both performed next:

$$28 + 8 = 36$$

56.

Follow the *order of operations* in order to solve this problem. Solve the parentheses first, and then follow the remainder as usual.

$$(6 \times 4) - 9$$

This equals $24 - 9$ or 15.

57.

For an even number of total values, the *median* is calculated by finding the *mean* or average of the two middle values once all values have been arranged in ascending order from least to greatest. In this case, $(92 + 83) \div 2$ would equal the median 87.5.

58.

6

The formula for the perimeter of a rectangle is P=2L+2W, where P is the perimeter, L is the length, and W is the width. The first step is to substitute all of the data into the formula:

$$36 = 2(12) + 2W$$

Simplify by multiplying 2x12:

$$36 = 24 + 2W$$

Simplifying this further by subtracting 24 on each side, which gives:

$$36-24 = 24-24+2W$$

$$12 = 2W$$

Divide by 2:

$$6 = W$$

The width is 6 cm. Remember to test this answer by substituting this value into the original formula:

$$36 = 2(12) + 2(6)$$

Practice Test #2

Reading Test

Passage #1

Questions 1–8 are based on the following passage:

People who argue that William Shakespeare is not responsible for the plays attributed to his name are known as anti-Stratfordians (from the name of Shakespeare's birthplace, Stratford-upon-Avon). The most common anti-Stratfordian claim is that William Shakespeare simply was not educated enough or from a high enough social class to have written plays overflowing with references to such a wide range of subjects like history, the classics, religion, and international culture. William Shakespeare was the son of a glove-maker, he only had a basic grade school education, and he never set foot outside of England—so how could he have produced plays of such sophistication and imagination? How could he have written in such detail about historical figures and events, or about different cultures and locations around Europe? According to anti-Stratfordians, the depth of knowledge contained in Shakespeare's plays suggests a well-traveled writer from a wealthy background with a university education, not a countryside writer like Shakespeare. But in fact, there is not much substance to such speculation, and most anti-Stratfordian arguments can be refuted with a little background about Shakespeare's time and upbringing.

First of all, those who doubt Shakespeare's authorship often point to his common birth and brief education as stumbling blocks to his writerly genius. Although it is true that Shakespeare did not come from a noble class, his father was a very *successful* glove-maker and his mother was from a very wealthy land owning family—so while Shakespeare may have had a country upbringing, he was certainly from a well-off family and would have been educated accordingly. Also, even though he did not attend university, grade school education in Shakespeare's time was actually quite rigorous and exposed students to classic drama through writers like Seneca and Ovid. It is not unreasonable to believe that Shakespeare received a very solid foundation in poetry and literature from his early schooling.

Next, anti-Stratfordians tend to question how Shakespeare could write so extensively about countries and cultures he had never visited before (for instance, several of his most famous works like *Romeo and Juliet* and *The Merchant of Venice* were set in Italy, on the opposite side of Europe!). But again, this criticism does not hold up under scrutiny. For one thing, Shakespeare was living in London, a bustling metropolis of international trade, the most populous city in England, and a political and cultural hub of Europe. In the daily crowds of people, Shakespeare would certainly have been able to meet travelers from other countries and hear firsthand accounts of life in their home country. And, in addition to the influx of information from world travelers, this was also the age of the printing press, a jump in technology that made it possible to print and circulate books much more easily than in the past. This also allowed for a freer flow of information across different countries, allowing people to read about life and ideas from throughout Europe. One needn't travel the continent in order to learn and write about its culture.

1. What is the main purpose of this article?
    a. To explain two sides of an argument and allow readers to choose which side they agree with
    b. To encourage readers to be skeptical about the authorship of famous poems and plays
    c. To give historical background about an important literary figure
    d. To criticize a theory by presenting counterevidence

2. Which sentence contains the author's thesis?
    a. People who argue that William Shakespeare is not responsible for the plays attributed to his name are known as anti-Stratfordians.
    b. But in fact, there is not much substance to such speculation, and most anti-Stratfordian arguments can be refuted with a little background about Shakespeare's time and upbringing.
    c. It is not unreasonable to believe that Shakespeare received a very solid foundation in poetry and literature from his early schooling.
    d. Next, anti-Stratfordians tend to question how Shakespeare could write so extensively about countries and cultures he had never visited before.

3. In the first paragraph, "How could he have written in such detail about historical figures and events, or about different cultures and locations around Europe?" is an example of which of the following?
    a. Hyperbole
    b. Onomatopoeia
    c. Rhetorical question
    d. Appeal to authority

4. How does the author respond to the claim that Shakespeare was not well-educated because he did not attend university?
    a. By insisting upon Shakespeare's natural genius
    b. By explaining grade school curriculum in Shakespeare's time
    c. By comparing Shakespeare with other uneducated writers of his time
    d. By pointing out that Shakespeare's wealthy parents probably paid for private tutors

5. What does the word "bustling" in the third paragraph most nearly mean?
    a. Busy
    b. Foreign
    c. Expensive
    d. Undeveloped

6. What can be inferred from the article?
    a. Shakespeare's peers were jealous of his success and wanted to attack his reputation.
    b. Until recently, classic drama was only taught in universities.
    c. International travel was extremely rare in Shakespeare's time.
    d. In Shakespeare's time, glove-makers were not part of the upper class.

7. Why does the author mention *Romeo and Juliet*?
    a. It is Shakespeare's most famous play.
    b. It was inspired by Shakespeare's trip to Italy.
    c. It is an example of a play set outside of England.
    d. It was unpopular when Shakespeare first wrote it.

8. Which statement would the author probably agree with?
   a. It is possible to learn things from reading rather than from firsthand experience.
   b. If you want to be truly cultured, you need to travel the world
   c. People never become successful without a university education.
   d. All of the world's great art comes from Italy.

Passage #2

Questions 9–14 are based on the following excerpt from "The Story of An Hour" by Kate Chopin:

Knowing that Mrs. Mallard was afflicted with heart trouble, great care was taken to break to her as gently as possible the news of her husband's death.

It was her sister Josephine who told her, in broken sentences; veiled hints that revealed in half concealing. Her husband's friend Richards was there, too, near her. It was he who had been in the newspaper office when intelligence of the railroad disaster was received, with Brently Mallard's name leading the list of "killed." He had only taken the time to assure himself of its truth by a second telegram, and had hastened to forestall any less careful, less tender friend in bearing the sad message.

She did not hear the story as many women have heard the same, with a paralyzed inability to accept its significance. She wept at once, with sudden, wild abandonment, in her sister's arms. When the storm of grief had spent itself she went away to her room alone. She would have no one follow her.

There stood, facing the open window, a comfortable, roomy armchair. Into this she sank, pressed down by a physical exhaustion that haunted her body and seemed to reach into her soul.

She could see in the open square before her house the tops of trees that were all aquiver with the new spring life. The delicious breath of rain was in the air. In the street below a peddler was crying his wares. The notes of a distant song which some one was singing reached her faintly, and countless sparrows were twittering in the eaves.

There were patches of blue sky showing here and there through the clouds that had met and piled one above the other in the west facing her window.

She sat with her head thrown back upon the cushion of the chair, quite motionless, except when a sob came up into her throat and shook her, as a child who has cried itself to sleep continues to sob in its dreams.

She was young, with a fair, calm face, whose lines bespoke repression and even a certain strength. But now here was a dull stare in her eyes, whose gaze was fixed away off yonder on one of those patches of blue sky. It was not a glance of reflection, but rather indicated a suspension of intelligent thought.

There was something coming to her and she was waiting for it, fearfully. What was it? She did not know; it was too subtle and elusive to name. But she felt it, creeping out of the sky, reaching toward her through the sounds, the scents, and color that filled the air.

Now her bosom rose and fell tumultuously. She was beginning to recognize this thing that was approaching to possess her, and she was striving to beat it back with her will—as powerless as her two white slender hands would have been. When she abandoned herself a little whispered word escaped her slightly parted lips. She said it over and over under her breath: "free, free, free!" The vacant stare and the look of terror that had followed it went from her eyes. They stayed keen and bright. Her pulses beat fast, and the coursing blood warmed and relaxed every inch of her body.

She did not stop to ask if it were or were not a monstrous joy that held her. A clear and exalted perception enabled her to dismiss the suggestion as trivial. She knew that she would weep again when she saw the kind, tender hands folded in death; the face that had never looked save with love upon her, fixed and gray and dead. But she saw beyond that bitter moment a long procession of years to come that would belong to her absolutely. And she opened and spread her arms out to them in welcome.

9. What point of view is the above passage told in?
   a. First person
   b. Second person
   c. Third person omniscient
   d. Third person limited

10. What kind of irony are we presented with in this story?
   a. The way Mrs. Mallard reacted to her husband's death.
   b. The way in which Mr. Mallard died.
   c. The way in which the news of her husband's death was presented to Mrs. Mallard.
   d. The way in which nature is compared with death in the story.

11. What is the meaning of the word "elusive" in paragraph 9?
   a. Horrible
   b. Indefinable
   c. Quiet
   d. Joyful

12. What is the best summary of the passage above?
   a. Mr. Mallard, a soldier during World War I, is killed by the enemy and leaves his wife widowed.
   b. Mrs. Mallard understands the value of friendship when her friends show up for her after her husband's death.
   c. Mrs. Mallard combats mental illness daily and will perhaps be sent to a mental institution soon.
   d. Mrs. Mallard, a newly widowed woman, finds unexpected relief in her husband's death.

13. What is the tone of this story?
   a. Confused
   b. Joyful
   c. Depressive
   d. All of the above

14. What is the meaning of the word "tumultuously" in paragraph 10?
    a. Orderly
    b. Unashamedly
    c. Violently
    d. Calmly

Passage #3

Questions 15–20 are based on the following excerpt from Civil Disobedience, *by Henry David Thoreau:*

I heartily accept the motto, "that government is best which governs least," and I should like to see it acted up to more rapidly and systematically. Carried out, it finally amounts to this, which also I believe—"that government is best which governs not at all," and when men are prepared for it, that will be the kind of government which they will have. Government is at best but an expedient; but most governments are usually, and all governments are sometimes, inexpedient. The objections which have been brought against a standing army, and they are many and weighty, and deserve to prevail, may also at last be brought against a standing government. The standing army is only an arm of the standing government. The government itself, which is only the mode which the people have chosen to execute their will, is equally liable to be abused and perverted before the people can act through it. Witness the present Mexican war, the work of comparatively a few individuals using the standing government as their tool; for, in the outset, the people would not have consented to this measure.

This American government—what is it but a tradition, though a recent one, endeavoring to transmit itself unimpaired to posterity, but each instant losing some of its integrity? It has not the vitality and force of a single living man; for a single man can bend it to his will. It is a sort of wooden gun to the people themselves. But it is not the less necessary for this; for the people must have some complicated machinery or other, and hear its din, to satisfy that idea of government which they have. Governments show thus how successfully men can be imposed on, even impose on themselves, for their own advantage. It is excellent, we must all allow. Yet this government never of itself furthered any enterprise, but by the alacrity with which it got out of its way. It does not keep the country free. It does not settle the West. It does not educate. The character inherent in the American people has done all that has been accomplished; and it would have done somewhat more, if the government had not sometimes got in its way. For government is an expedient by which men would fain succeed in letting one another alone; and, as has been said, when it is most expedient, the governed are most let alone by it. Trade and commerce, if they were not made of india-rubber, would never manage to bounce over the obstacles which legislators are continually putting in their way; and, if one were to judge these men wholly by the effects of their actions and not partly by their intentions, they would deserve to be classed and punished with those mischievous persons who put obstructions on the railroads.

But, to speak practically and as a citizen, unlike those who call themselves no-government men, I ask for, not at once no government, but at once a better government. Let every man make known what kind of government would command his respect, and that will be one step toward obtaining it.

15. Which phrase best encapsulates Thoreau's use of the term *expedient* in the first paragraph?
    a. A dead end
    b. A state of order
    c. A means to an end
    d. Rushed construction

16. Which best describes Thoreau's view on the Mexican War?
    a. Government is inherently corrupt because it must wage war.
    b. Government can easily be manipulated by a few individuals for their own agenda.
    c. Government is a tool for the people, but it can also act against their interest.
    d. The Mexican War was a necessary action, but not all the people believed this.

17. What is Thoreau's purpose for writing?
    a. His goal is to illustrate how government can function if ideals are maintained.
    b. He wants to prove that true democracy is the best government, but it can be corrupted easily.
    c. Thoreau reflects on the stages of government abuses.
    d. He is seeking to prove that government is easily corruptible and inherently restrictive of individual freedoms that can simultaneously affect the whole state.

18. Which example best supports Thoreau's argument?
    a. A vote carries in the Senate to create a new road tax.
    b. The president vetoes the new FARM bill.
    c. Prohibition is passed to outlaw alcohol.
    d. Trade is opened between the United States and Iceland.

19. Which best summarizes this section from the following passage?
    "This American government—what is it but a tradition, though a recent one, endeavoring to transmit itself unimpaired to posterity, but each instant losing some of its integrity? It has not the vitality and force of a single living man; for a single man can bend it to his will. It is a sort of wooden gun to the people themselves."

    a. The government may be instituted to ensure the protections of freedoms, but this is weakened by the fact that it is easily manipulated by individuals.
    b. Unlike an individual, government is uncaring.
    c. Unlike an individual, government has no will, making it more prone to be used as a weapon against the people.
    d. American government is modeled after other traditions but actually has greater potential to be used to control people.

20. According to Thoreau, what's the main reason why government eventually fails to achieve progress?
    a. There are too many rules.
    b. Legislation eventually becomes a hindrance to the lives and work of everyday people.
    c. Trade and wealth eventually become the driving factor of those in government.
    d. Government doesn't separate religion and state.

Passage #4

Questions 21–26 are based on the following passage, which is adapted from The Ideas of Physics, Third Edition by Douglas C. Giancoli:

The Electric Battery

The events that led to the discovery of the battery are interesting; for not only was this an important discovery, but it also gave rise to a famous scientific debate between Alessandro Volta and Luigi Galvani, eventually involving many others in the scientific world.

In the 1780's, Galvani, a professor at the University of Bologna (thought to be the world's oldest university still in existence), carried out a long series of experiments on the contraction of a frog's leg muscle through electricity produced by a static-electricity machine. In the course of these investigations, Galvani found, much to his surprise, that contraction of the muscle could be produced by other means as well: when a brass hook was pressed into the frog's spinal cord and then hung from an iron railing that also touched the frog, the leg muscles again would contract. Upon further investigation, Galvani found that this strange but important phenomenon occurred for other pairs of metals as well.fr

Galvani believed that the source of the electric charge was in the frog muscle or nerve itself and the wire merely transmitted the charge to the proper points. When he published his work in 1791, he termed it "animal electricity." Many wondered, including Galvani himself, if he had discovered the long-sought "life-force."

Volta, at the University of Pavia 125 miles away, was at first skeptical of Galvani's results, but at the urging of his colleagues, he soon confirmed and extended those experiments. Volta doubted Galvani's idea of "animal electricity." Instead he came to believe that the source of the electricity was not in the animal, but rather in the contact between the two metals.

During Volta's careful research, he soon realized that a moist conductor, such as a frog muscle or moisture at the contact point of the two dissimilar metals, was necessary if the effect was to occur. He also saw that the contracting frog muscle was a sensitive instrument for detecting electric potential or voltage, in fact more sensitive than the best available electroscopes that he and others had developed. Volta's research showed that certain combinations of metals produced a greater effect than others.

Volta then conceived his greatest contribution to science. Between a disc of zinc and one of silver he placed a piece of cloth or paper soaked in salt solution or dilute acid and piled a "battery" of such couplings, one on top of another; this "pile" or "battery" produced a much increased potential difference. Indeed, when strips of metal connected to the two ends of the pile were brought close, a spark was produced. Volta had designed and built the first battery.

21. Which statement best details the central idea in this passage?
    a. It details the story of how the battery was originally developed.
    b. It delves into the mechanics of battery operated machines.
    c. It defines the far-reaching effects of battery usage throughout the world.
    d. It invites readers to create innovations that make the world more efficient.

22. Which definition most closely relates to the usage of the word "battery" in the passage?
   a. A group of objects that work in tandem to create an unified effect
   b. A log of assessments
   c. A series
   d. A violent encounter

23. Which type of text structure is employed in this following text?

During Volta's careful research, he soon realized that a moist conductor, such as a frog muscle or moisture at the contact point of the two dissimilar metals, was necessary if the effect was to occur. He also saw that the contracting frog muscle was a sensitive instrument for detecting electric potential or voltage, in fact more sensitive than the best available electroscopes that he and others had developed. Volta's research showed that certain combinations of metals produced a greater effect than others.

Between a disc of zinc and one of silver he placed a piece of cloth or paper soaked in salt solution or dilute acid and piled a "battery" of such couplings, one on top of another; this "pile" or "battery" produced a much increased potential difference. Indeed, when strips of metal connected to the two ends of the pile were brought close, a spark was produced. Volta had designed and built the first battery."

   a. Problem and solution
   b. Sequence
   c. Description
   d. Cause and effect

24. Which researcher was ultimately credited with creating "the first battery"?
   a. Galvani
   b. Pavia
   c. Volta
   d. Bologna

25. Which of the statements reflect information that one could reasonably infer based on Volta's scientific contributions concerning batteries?
   a. The researcher died in a state of shame and obscurity.
   b. Other researchers doubted his ability to create the first battery.
   c. The term "voltage" was created to recognize him for his contribution in the production of batteries.
   d. Researchers now use plastic to further technological advances in the field of electrical current conduction.

26. According to the following passage, which statement best describes the contrast between Volta and Galvani's theory concerning "animal electricity"?

"Galvani believed that the source of the electric charge was in the frog muscle or nerve itself and the wire merely transmitted the charge to the proper points. When he published his work in 1791, he termed it "animal electricity." Many wondered, including Galvani himself, if he had discovered the long-sought "life-force."

Volta, at the University of Pavia 125 miles away, was at first skeptical of Galvani's results, but at the urging of his colleagues, he soon confirmed and extended those experiments. Volta doubted Galvani's idea of "animal electricity." Instead he came to believe that the source of the electricity was not in the animal, but rather in the contact between the two metals."

a. Galvani believed that only frogs were capable of serving as conductors for electricity.
b. Volta doubted that animals possessed the intellect necessary to properly direct electricity to the proper source.
c. Galvani believed that animals were carriers of the "life-force" necessary to conduct electricity while Volta felt that the meeting of metals was the catalyst for animal movement in the experiment.
d. Both researchers held fast to the belief that their theories were the foremost and premiere research in the field.

Passage #5

Questions 27–32 are based on the following passage, which is an excerpt adapted from The Immortal Cells of Henrietta Lacks by Rebecca Skloot:

Henrietta Lacks is an African American woman who died from an aggressive strain of cervical cancer. The word HeLa is used to refer to the cells grown from Henrietta Lacks's cervix. HeLa is known as the first immortal human cell line ever grown in culture.

The Cloning of HeLa

Today, when we hear the word clone, we imagine scientists creating entire living animals—like Dolly the famous cloned sheep—using DNA from one parent. But before the cloning of whole animals, there was the cloning of individual cells—Henrietta's cells.

To understand why cellular cloning was important, you need to know two things: First, HeLa didn't grow from one of Henrietta's cells. It grew from a sliver of her tumor, which was a cluster of cells. Second, cells often behave differently, even if they're all from the same sample, which means some grow faster than others, some produce more poliovirus, and some are resistant to certain antibiotics. Scientists wanted to grow cellular clones—lines of cells descended from individual cells—so they could harness those unique traits. With HeLa, a group of scientists in Colorado succeeded, and soon the world of science had not only HeLa but also its hundreds, then thousands, of clones.

The early cell culture and cloning technology developed using HeLa helped lead to many later advances that required the ability to grow single cells in culture, including isolating stem cells, cloning whole animals, and in vitro fertilization. Meanwhile, as the standard human cell in most labs, HeLa was also being used in research that would advance the new field of human genetics.

Researchers had long believed that human cells contained forty-eight chromosomes, the threads of DNA inside cells that contain all of our genetic information. But chromosomes clumped together, making it impossible to get an accurate count. Then, in 1953, a geneticist in Texas accidentally mixed the wrong liquid with HeLa and a few other cells, and it turned out to be a fortunate mistake. The chromosomes inside the cells swelled and spread out, and for the first time, scientists could see each of them clearly. That accidental discovery was the first of several developments that would allow two researchers from Spain and Sweden to discover that normal human cells have forty-six chromosomes.

Once scientists knew how many chromosomes people were supposed to have, they could tell when a person had too many or too few, which made it possible to diagnose genetic diseases. Researchers worldwide would soon begin identifying chromosomal disorders, discovering that patients with Down syndrome had an extra chromosome number 21, patients with Klinefelter syndrome had an extra sex chromosome, and those with Turner syndrome lacked all or part of one.

With all the new developments, demand for HeLa grew, and Tuskegee wasn't big enough to keep up. The owner of Microbiological Associates—a military man named Samuel Reader— knew nothing about science, but his business partner, Monroe Vincent, was a researcher who understood the potential market for cells. Many scientists needed cells, but few had the time or ability to grow them in large enough quantities. They just wanted to buy them. So together, Reader and Vincent used HeLa cells as the springboard to launch the first industrial-scale, for-profit cell distribution center.

27. The author's use of second person pronouns in the following text has all of the following effects except for? "To understand why cellular cloning was important, you need to know two things..."
   a. It personalizes the experience.
   b. It allows the reader to more easily understand the text.
   c. It encourages the reader to empathize with Henrietta Lack.
   d. It distances the reader from the text by overemphasizing the story.

28. The reference to "Dolly the famous cloned sheep" in the text points to which of the following facts?
   a. The HeLa cells research was not the only DNA-based research that has taken place.
   b. HeLa cells are the best evidence of cell mutation.
   c. HeLa cells provide no known evidence of the existence of immortal cells.
   d. Researchers doubt that HeLA cells exist.

29. What is the meaning of the word "harness" in the following text? "Scientists wanted to grow cellular clones—lines of cells descended from individual cells—so they could harness those unique traits."
   a. Tack
   b. Obtain
   c. Couple
   d. Duplicate

30. Where did HeLa cells initially originate?
   a. Within Henrietta Lack's heart
   b. Through Henrietta Lack's hair follicles
   c. Through DNA testing
   d. In a sliver of tumor from Henrietta Lack's cancerous cervical tissue

31. The discovery of HeLa cells has helped to further the scientific world through all of the following procedures except for?
   a. Isolating stem cells
   b. Cloning whole animals
   c. In vitro fertilization
   d. Separating Siamese twins

32. Normally developed humans have how many chromosomes?
   a. 48
   b. 47
   c. 46
   d. 41

Passage #6

Questions 33–38 are based on the following passage from The Curious Case of Benjamin Button *by F.S. Fitzgerald, 1922:*

As long ago as 1860 it was the proper thing to be born at home. At present, so I am told, the high gods of medicine have decreed that the first cries of the young shall be uttered upon the anesthetic air of a hospital, preferably a fashionable one. So young Mr. and Mrs. Roger Button were fifty years ahead of style when they decided, one day in the summer of 1860, that their first baby should be born in a hospital. Whether this anachronism had any bearing upon the astonishing history I am about to set down will never be known.

I shall tell you what occurred, and let you judge for yourself.

The Roger Buttons held an enviable position, both social and financial, in ante-bellum Baltimore. They were related to the This Family and the That Family, which, as every Southerner knew, entitled them to membership in that enormous peerage which largely populated the Confederacy. This was their first experience with the charming old custom of having babies— Mr. Button was naturally nervous. He hoped it would be a boy so that he could be sent to Yale College in Connecticut, at which institution Mr. Button himself had been known for four years by the somewhat obvious nickname of "Cuff."

On the September morning <u>consecrated</u> to the enormous event he arose nervously at six o'clock dressed himself, adjusted an impeccable stock, and hurried forth through the streets of Baltimore to the hospital, to determine whether the darkness of the night had borne in new life upon its bosom.

When he was approximately a hundred yards from the Maryland Private Hospital for Ladies and Gentlemen he saw Doctor Keene, the family physician, descending the front steps, rubbing his hands together with a washing movement—as all doctors are required to do by the unwritten ethics of their profession.

Mr. Roger Button, the president of Roger Button & Co., Wholesale Hardware, began to run toward Doctor Keene with much less dignity than was expected from a Southern gentleman of that picturesque period. "Doctor Keene!" he called. "Oh, Doctor Keene!"

The doctor heard him, faced around, and stood waiting, a curious expression settling on his harsh, medicinal face as Mr. Button drew near.

"What happened?" demanded Mr. Button, as he came up in a gasping rush. "What was it? How is she? A boy? Who is it? What—"

"Talk sense!" said Doctor Keene sharply. He appeared somewhat irritated.

"Is the child born?" begged Mr. Button.

Doctor Keene frowned. "Why, yes, I suppose so—after a fashion." Again he threw a curious glance at Mr. Button.

33. What major event is about to happen in this story?
    a. Mr. Button is about to go to a funeral.
    b. Mr. Button's wife is about to have a baby.
    c. Mr. Button is getting ready to go to the doctor's office.
    d. Mr. Button is about to go shopping for new clothes.

34. What kind of tone does the above passage have?
    a. Nervous and Excited
    b. Sad and Angry
    c. Shameful and Confused
    d. Grateful and Joyous

35. What is the meaning of the word "consecrated" in paragraph 4?
    a. Numbed
    b. Chained
    c. Dedicated
    d. Moved

36. What does the author mean to do by adding the following statement?

    "rubbing his hands together with a washing movement—as all doctors are required to do by the unwritten ethics of their profession."

    a. Suggesting that Mr. Button is tired of the doctor.
    b. Trying to explain the detail of the doctor's profession.
    c. Hinting to readers that the doctor is an unethical man.
    d. Giving readers a visual picture of what the doctor is doing.

37. Which of the following best describes the development of this passage?
    a. It starts in the middle of a narrative in order to transition smoothly to a conclusion.
    b. It is a chronological narrative from beginning to end.
    c. The sequence of events is backwards—we go from future events to past events.
    d. To introduce the setting of the story and its characters.

38. Which of the following is an example of an imperative sentence?
    a. "Oh, Doctor Keene!"
    b. "Talk sense!"
    c. "Is the child born?"
    d. "Why, yes, I suppose so—"

Passage #7

Questions 39–44 are based on the following excerpt from a novel:

When I got on the coach the driver had not taken his seat, and I saw him talking with the landlady. They were evidently talking of me, for every now and then they looked at me, and some of the people who were sitting on the bench outside the door came and listened, and then looked at me, most of them pityingly. I could hear a lot of words often repeated, queer words, for there were many nationalities in the crowd; so I quietly got my polyglot dictionary from my bag and looked them out. I must say they weren't cheering to me, for amongst them were "Ordog"—Satan, "pokol"—hell, "stregoica"—witch, "vrolok" and "vlkoslak"—both of which mean the same thing, one being Slovak and the other Servian for something that is either were-wolf or vampire.

When we started, the crowd round the inn door, which had by this time swelled to a considerable size, all made the sign of the cross and pointed two fingers towards me. With some difficulty I got a fellow-passenger to tell me what they meant; he wouldn't answer at first, but on learning that I was English, he explained that it was a charm or guard against the evil eye. This was not very pleasant for me, just starting for an unknown place to meet an unknown man; but everyone seemed so kind-hearted, and so sorrowful, and so sympathetic that I couldn't but be touched. I shall never forget the last glimpse which I had of the inn-yard and its crowd of picturesque figures, all crossing themselves, as they stood round the wide archway, with its background of rich foliage of oleander and orange trees in green tubs clustered in the centre of the yard. Then our driver cracked his big whip over his four small horses, which ran abreast, and we set off on our journey.

I soon lost sight and recollection of ghostly fears in the beauty of the scene as we drove along, although had I known the language, or rather languages, which my fellow-passengers were speaking, I might not have been able to throw them off so easily. Before us lay a green sloping land full of forests and woods, with here and there steep hills, crowned with clumps of trees or with farmhouses, the blank gable end to the road. There was everywhere a bewildering mass of fruit blossom—apple, plum, pear, cherry; and as we drove by I could see the green grass under the trees spangled with the fallen petals. In and out amongst these green hills of what they call here the "Mittel Land" ran the road, losing itself as it swept round the grassy curve, or was shut out by the straggling ends of pine woods, which here and there ran down the hillsides like tongues of flame. The road was rugged, but still we seemed to fly over it with a feverish haste. I couldn't understand then what the haste meant, but the driver was evidently bent on losing no time in reaching Borgo Prund.

39. What type of narrator is found in this passage?
    a. First person
    b. Second person
    c. Third-person limited
    d. Third-person omniscient

40. Which of the following is true of the traveler?
    a. He wishes the driver would go faster.
    b. He's returning to the country of his birth.
    c. He has some familiarity with the local customs.
    d. He doesn't understand all of the languages being used.

41. How does the traveler's mood change between the second and third paragraphs?
    a. From relaxed to rushed
    b. From fearful to charmed
    c. From confused to enlightened
    d. From comfortable to exhausted

42. Who is the traveler going to meet?
    a. A kind landlady
    b. A distant relative
    c. A friendly villager
    d. A complete stranger

43. Based on the details in this passage, what can readers probably expect to happen in the story?
    a. The traveler will become a farmer.
    b. The traveler will arrive late at his destination.
    c. The traveler will soon encounter danger or evil.
    d. The traveler will have a pleasant journey and make many new friends.

44. Which sentence from the passage provides a clue for question 39?
    a. "I must say they weren't cheering to me, for amongst them were "Ordog"—Satan, "pokol"—hell, "stregoica"—witch, "vrolok" and "vlkoslak"—both of which mean the same thing, one being Slovak and the other Servian for something that is either were-wolf or vampire."
    b. "When I got on the coach the driver had not taken his seat, and I saw him talking with the landlady."
    c. "Then our driver cracked his big whip over his four small horses, which ran abreast, and we set off on our journey."
    d. "There was everywhere a bewildering mass of fruit blossom—apple, plum, pear, cherry; and as we drove by I could see the green grass under the trees spangled with the fallen petals."

Passage #8

Questions 45–52 are based on the following passages:

Passage I

Lethal force, or deadly force, is defined as the physical means to cause death or serious harm to another individual. The law holds that lethal force is only accepted when you or another person are in immediate and unavoidable danger of death or severe bodily harm. For example, a person could be beating a weaker person in such a way that they are suffering severe enough trauma that could result in death or serious harm. This would be an instance where lethal force would be acceptable and possibly the only way to save that person from irrevocable damage.

Another example of when to use lethal force would be when someone enters your home with a deadly weapon. The intruder's presence and possession of the weapon indicate mal-intent and the ability to inflict death or severe injury to you and your loved ones. Again, lethal force can be used in this situation. Lethal force can also be applied to prevent the harm of another individual. If a woman is being brutally assaulted and is unable to fend off an attacker, lethal force can be used to defend her as a last-ditch effort. If she is in immediate jeopardy of rape, harm, and/or death, lethal force could be the only response that could effectively deter the assailant.

The key to understanding the concept of lethal force is the term *last resort*. Deadly force cannot be taken back; it should be used only to prevent severe harm or death. The law does distinguish whether the means of one's self-defense is fully warranted, or if the individual goes out of control in the process. If you continually attack the assailant after they are rendered incapacitated, this would be causing unnecessary harm, and the law can bring charges against you. Likewise, if you kill an attacker unnecessarily after defending yourself, you can be charged with murder. This would move lethal force beyond necessary defense, making it no longer a last resort but rather a use of excessive force.

Passage II

Assault is the unlawful attempt of one person to apply apprehension on another individual by an imminent threat or by initiating offensive contact. Assaults can vary, encompassing physical strikes, threatening body language, and even provocative language. In the case of the latter, even if a hand has not been laid, it is still considered an assault because of its threatening nature.

Let's look at an example: A homeowner is angered because his neighbor blows fallen leaves into his freshly mowed lawn. Irate, the homeowner gestures a fist to his fellow neighbor and threatens to bash his head in for littering on his lawn. The homeowner's physical motions and verbal threat heralds a physical threat against the other neighbor. These factors classify the homeowner's reaction as an assault. If the angry neighbor hits the threatening homeowner in retaliation, that would constitute an assault as well because he physically hit the homeowner.

Assault also centers on the involvement of weapons in a conflict. If someone fires a gun at another person, this could be interpreted as an assault unless the shooter acted in self-defense. If an individual drew a gun or a knife on someone with the intent to harm them, that would be considered assault. However, it's also considered an assault if someone simply aimed a weapon, loaded or not, at another person in a threatening manner.

45. What is the purpose of the second passage?
    a. To inform the reader about what assault is and how it is committed
    b. To inform the reader about how assault is a minor example of lethal force
    c. To disprove the previous passage concerning lethal force
    d. The author is recounting an incident in which they were assaulted

46. Which of the following situations, according to the passages, would not constitute an illegal use of lethal force?
    a. A disgruntled cashier yells obscenities at a customer.
    b. A thief is seen running away with stolen cash.
    c. A man is attacked in an alley by another man with a knife.
    d. A woman punches another woman in a bar.

47. Given the information in the passages, which of the following must be true about assault?
    a. Assault charges are more severe than unnecessary use of force charges.
    b. There are various forms of assault.
    c. Smaller, weaker people cannot commit assaults.
    d. Assault is justified only as a last resort.

48. Which of the following, if true, would most seriously undermine the explanation proposed by the author in Passage I in the third paragraph?

    a. An instance of lethal force in self-defense is not absolutely absolved from blame. The law considers the necessary use of force at the time it is committed.

    b. An individual who uses lethal force under necessary defense is in direct compliance of the law under most circumstances.

    c. Lethal force in self-defense should be forgiven in all cases for the peace of mind of the primary victim.

    d. The use of lethal force is not evaluated on the intent of the user, but rather the severity of the primary attack that warranted self-defense.

49. Based on the passages, what can be inferred about the relationship between assault and lethal force?

    a. An act of lethal force always leads to a type of assault.

    b. An assault will result in someone using lethal force.

    c. An assault with deadly intent can lead to an individual using lethal force to preserve their well-being.

    d. If someone uses self-defense in a conflict, it is called deadly force; if actions or threats are intended, it is called assault.

50. Which of the following best describes the way the passages are structured?

    a. Both passages open by defining a legal concept and then continue to describe situations that further explain the concept.

    b. Both passages begin with situations, introduce accepted definitions, and then cite legal ramifications.

    c. Passage I presents a long definition while the Passage II begins by showing an example of assault.

    d. Both cite specific legal doctrines, then proceed to explain the rulings.

51. What can be inferred about the role of intent in lethal force and assault?

    a. Intent is irrelevant. The law does not take intent into account.

    b. Intent is vital for determining the lawfulness of using lethal force.

    c. Intent is very important for determining both lethal force and assault; intent is examined in both parties and helps determine the severity of the issue.

    d. The intent of the assailant is the main focus for determining legal ramifications; it is used to determine if the defender was justified in using force to respond.

52. The author uses the example in the second paragraph of Passage II in order to do what?

    a. To demonstrate two different types of assault by showing how each specifically relates to the other

    b. To demonstrate a single example of two different types of assault, then adding in the third type of assault in the example's conclusion

    c. To prove that the definition of lethal force is altered when the victim in question is a homeowner and his property is threatened

    d. To suggest that verbal assault can be an exaggerated crime by the law and does not necessarily lead to physical violence

Writing and Language Test

Read the essay entitled "Education is Essential to Civilization" and answer Questions 1–15.

Early in my career, (1) a master's teacher shared this thought with me "Education is the last bastion of civility." While I did not completely understand the scope of those words at the time, I have since come to realize the depth, breadth, truth, and significance of what he said. (2) Education provides society with a vehicle for (3) raising it's children to be civil, decent, human beings with something valuable to contribute to the world. It is really what makes us human and what (4) distinguishes us as civilised creatures.

Being "civilized" humans means being "whole" humans. Education must address the mind, body, and soul of students. (5) It would be detrimental to society, only meeting the needs of the mind, if our schools were myopic in their focus. As humans, we are multi-dimensional, multi-faceted beings who need more than head knowledge to survive. (6) The human heart and psyche have to be fed in order for the mind to develop properly, and the body must be maintained and exercised to help fuel the working of the brain. Education is a basic human right, and it allows us to sustain a democratic society in which participation is fundamental to its success. It should inspire students to seek better solutions to world problems and to dream of a more equitable society. Education should never discriminate on any basis, and it should create individuals who are self-sufficient, patriotic, and tolerant of (7) others' ideas.

(8) All children can learn. Although not all children learn in the same manner. All children learn best, however, when their basic physical needs are met and they feel safe, secure, and loved. Students are much more responsive to a teacher who values them and shows them respect as individual people. Teachers must model at all times the way they expect students to treat them and their peers. If teachers set high expectations for (9) there students, the students will rise to that high level. Teachers must make the well-being of students their primary focus and must not be afraid to let students learn from their own mistakes.

In the modern age of technology, a teacher's focus is no longer the "what" of the content, (10) but more importantly, the 'why.' Students are bombarded with information and have access to ANY information they need right at their fingertips. Teachers have to work harder than ever before to help students identify salient information (11) so to think critically about the information they encounter. Students have to (12) read between the lines, identify bias, and determine who they can trust in the milieu of ads, data, and texts presented to them.

Schools must work in consort with families in this important mission. While children spend most of their time in school, they are dramatically and indelibly shaped (13) with the influences of their family and culture. Teachers must not only respect this fact, (14) but must strive to include parents in the education of their children and must work to keep parents informed of progress and problems. Communication between classroom and home is essential for a child's success.

Humans have always aspired to be more, do more, and to better ourselves and our communities. This is where education lies, right at the heart of humanity's desire to be all that we can be. Education helps us strive for higher goals and better treatment of ourselves and others. I shudder to think what would become of us if education ceased to be the "last bastion of civility." (15) We must be unapologetic about expecting excellence from our students? Our very existence depends upon it.

1. What edit is needed to correct sentence 1?
   a. NO CHANGE
   b. a master's teacher shared this thought with me: "Education is the last bastion of civility."
   c. a master's teacher shared this thought with me: "Education is the last bastion of civility".
   d. a master's teacher shared this thought with me. "Education is the last bastion of civility."

2. What edit is needed to correct sentence 2?
   a. NO CHANGE
   b. Education provide
   c. Education will provide
   d. Education providing

3. What edit is needed to correct sentence 3?
   a. NO CHANGE
   b. raises its children to be
   c. raising its' children to be
   d. raising its children to be

4. Which of these, if any, is misspelled?
   a. None of these are misspelled.
   b. distinguishes
   c. civilised
   d. creatures

5. What edit is needed to correct sentence 5?
   a. NO CHANGE
   b. It would be detrimental to society if our schools were myopic in their focus, only meeting the needs of the mind.
   c. Only meeting the needs of our mind, our schools were myopic in their focus, detrimental to society.
   d. Myopic is the focus of our schools, being detrimental to society for only meeting the needs of the mind.

6. Which of these sentences, if any, should begin a new paragraph?
   a. There should be no new paragraph.
   b. The human heart and psyche have to be fed in order for the mind to develop properly, and the body must be maintained and exercised to help fuel the working of the brain.
   c. Education is a basic human right, and it allows us to sustain a democratic society in which participation is fundamental to its success.
   d. It should inspire students to seek better solutions to world problems and to dream of a more equitable society.

7. What edit is needed to correct sentence 7?
   a. NO CHANGE
   b. other's ideas
   c. others ideas
   d. others's ideas

8. What edit is needed to correct sentence 8?
   a. NO CHANGE
   b. All children can learn although not all children learn in the same manner.
   c. All children can learn although, not all children learn in the same manner.
   d. All children can learn, although not all children learn in the same manner.

9. What edit is needed to correct sentence 9?
   a. NO CHANGE
   b. they're students
   c. their students
   d. thare students

10. What edit is needed to correct sentence 10?
    a. NO CHANGE
    b. but more importantly, the "why."
    c. but more importantly, the 'why'.
    d. but more importantly, the "why".

11. What edit is needed to correct sentence 11?
    a. NO CHANGE
    b. and to think critically
    c. but to think critically
    d. nor to think critically

12. What edit is needed to correct sentence 12?
    a. NO CHANGE
    b. read between the lines, identify bias, and determining
    c. read between the lines, identifying bias, and determining
    d. reads between the lines, identifies bias, and determines

13. What edit is needed to correct sentence 13?
    a. NO CHANGE
    b. for the influences
    c. to the influences
    d. by the influences

14. What edit is needed to correct sentence 14?
    a. NO CHANGE
    b. but to strive
    c. but striving
    d. but strived

15. What edit is needed to correct sentence 15?
    a. NO CHANGE
    b. We must be unapologetic about expecting excellence from our students, our very existence depends upon it.
    c. We must be unapologetic about expecting excellence from our students—our very existence depends upon it.
    d. We must be unapologetic about expecting excellence from our students our very existence depends upon it.

Questions 16–24 are based on the following passage:

(16) <u>One of the icon's of romantic and science fiction literature</u> remains Mary Shelley's classic, *Frankenstein, or The Modern Prometheus.* Schools throughout the world still teach the book in literature and philosophy courses. Scientific communities also engage in discussion on the novel. But why? Besides the novel's engaging (17) <u>writing style the story's central theme</u> remains highly relevant in a world of constant discovery and moral dilemmas. Central to the core narrative is the (18) <u>struggle between enlightenment and the cost of overusing power</u>.

The subtitle, *The Modern Prometheus*, encapsulates the inner theme of the story more than the main title of *Frankenstein*. As with many romantic writers, Shelley invokes the classical myths and (19) <u>symbolism of Ancient Greece and Rome to high light core ideas</u>. Looking deeper into the myth of Prometheus sheds light not only on the character of Frankenstein (20) <u>but also poses a psychological dilemma to the audience.</u> Prometheus is the titan who gave fire to mankind. (21) <u>However, more than just fire he gave people knowledge and power.</u> The power of fire advanced civilization. Yet, for giving fire to man, Prometheus is (22) <u>punished by the gods bound to a rock and tormented for his act</u>. This is clearly a parallel to Frankenstein—he is the modern Prometheus.

Frankenstein's quest for knowledge becomes an obsession. It leads him to literally create new life, breaking the bounds of conceivable science to illustrate that man can create life out of nothing. (523) <u>Yet he ultimately faltered as a creator,</u> abandoning his progeny in horror of what he created. Frankenstein then suffers his creature's wrath, (24) <u>the result of his pride, obsession for power and lack of responsibility.</u>

Shelley isn't condemning scientific achievement. Rather, her writing reflects that science and discovery are good things, but, like all power, it must be used wisely. The text alludes to the message that one must have reverence for nature and be mindful of the potential consequences. Frankenstein did not take responsibility or even consider how his actions would affect others. His scientific brilliance ultimately led to suffering.

Based on an excerpt from *Frankenstein* by Mary Shelley

16. Which of the following would be the best choice for this sentence (reproduced below)?

(16) <u>One of the icon's of romantic and science fiction literature</u> remains Mary Shelley's classic, Frankenstein, or The Modern Prometheus.

a. NO CHANGE
b. One of the icons of romantic and science fiction literature
c. One of the icon's of romantic, and science fiction literature,
d. The icon of romantic and science fiction literature

17. Which of the following would be the best choice for this sentence (reproduced below)?

Besides the novel's engaging (17) <u>writing style the story's central theme</u> remains highly relevant in a world of constant discovery and moral dilemmas.

a. NO CHANGE
b. writing style the central theme of the story
c. writing style, the story's central theme
d. the story's central theme's writing style

18. Which of the following would be the best choice for this sentence (reproduced below)?

Central to the core narrative is the (18) <u>struggle between enlightenment and the cost of overusing</u> <u>power.</u>

a. NO CHANGE
b. struggle between enlighten and the cost of overusing power.
c. struggle between enlightenment's cost of overusing power.
d. struggle between enlightening and the cost of overusing power.

19. Which of the following would be the best choice for this sentence (reproduced below)?

As with many romantic writers, Shelley invokes the classical myths and (19) <u>symbolism of Ancient</u> <u>Greece and Rome to high light core ideas.</u>

a. NO CHANGE
b. symbolism of Ancient Greece and Rome to highlight core ideas.
c. symbolism of ancient Greece and Rome to highlight core ideas.
d. symbolism of Ancient Greece and Rome highlighting core ideas.

20. Which of the following would be the best choice for this sentence (reproduced below)?

Looking deeper into the myth of Prometheus sheds light not only on the character of Frankenstein (20) <u>but also poses a psychological dilemma to the audience.</u>

a. NO CHANGE
b. but also poses a psychological dilemma with the audience.
c. but also poses a psychological dilemma for the audience.
d. but also poses a psychological dilemma there before the audience.

21. Which of the following would be the best choice for this sentence (reproduced below)?

(21) <u>However, more than just fire he gave people knowledge and power.</u>

a. NO CHANGE
b. However, more than just fire he gave people, knowledge, and power.
c. However, more than just fire, he gave people knowledge and power.
d. Besides actual fire, Prometheus gave people knowledge and power.

22. Which of the following would be the best choice for this sentence (reproduced below)?

Yet, for giving fire to man, Prometheus is (22) punished by the gods bound to a rock and tormented for his act.

   a. NO CHANGE
   b. punished by the gods, bound to a rock and tormented for his act.
   c. bound to a rock and tormented as punishment by the gods.
   d. punished for his act by being bound to a rock and tormented as punishment from the gods.

23. Which of the following would be the best choice for this sentence (reproduced below)?

(23) Yet he ultimately faltered as a creator, abandoning his progeny in horror of what he created.

   a. NO CHANGE
   b. Yet, he ultimately falters as a creator by
   c. Yet, he ultimately faltered as a creator,
   d. Yet he ultimately falters as a creator by

24. Which of the following would be the best choice for this sentence (reproduced below)?

Frankenstein then suffers his creature's wrath, (24) the result of his pride, obsession for power and lack of responsibility.

   a. NO CHANGE
   b. the result of his pride, obsession for power and lacking of responsibility.
   c. the result of his pride, obsession for power, and lack of responsibility.
   d. the result of his pride and also his obsession for power and lack of responsibility.

Questions 25–33 are based on the following passage:

The power of legends continues to enthrall our imagination, provoking us both to wonder and explore. (25) Who doesnt love a good legend? Some say legends never (26) die and this is certainly the case for the most legendary creature of all, Bigfoot. To this day, people still claim sightings of the illusive cryptid. Many think of Bigfoot as America's monster, yet many nations have legends of a similar creature. In my own research I have found that Australia has the Yowie, China has the Yerin, and Russia has the Almas. (27) Their all over the world, the bigfoots and the legends tied to them. Does this mean they could exist?

There are many things to consider when addressing (28) this question but the chief factor is whether there is credible evidence. (29) For science to formally recognize that such a species exists, there needs to be physical proof. While people have found supposed footprints and even (30) captured photos and film of the creature, this validity of such evidence is up for debate. There is room for uncertainty. Most visual evidence is out of focus, thus (31) there is often skepticism whether such images are real. Some researchers have even claimed to have hair and blood samples, but still there is doubt in the scientific community. The reason is simple: there needs to be a body or living specimen found and actively studied in order to prove the Bigfoots' existence.

Yet, one cannot ignore the fact that (32) <u>hundreds of witnesses continuing to describe a creature</u> with uniform features all over the world. These bigfoot sightings aren't a modern occurrence either. Ancient civilizations have reported (33) <u>seeing Bigfoot as well including Native Americans</u>. It is from Native Americans that we gained the popular term Sasquatch, which is the primary name for the North American bigfoot. How does their testimony factor in? If indigenous people saw these animals, could they not have existed at some point? After all, when Europeans first arrived in Africa, they disbelieved the native accounts of the gorilla. But sure enough, Europeans eventually found gorillas and collected a body.

25. Which of the following would be the best choice for this sentence (reproduced below)?

   (25) <u>Who doesnt love a good legend?</u>

   a. NO CHANGE
   b. Who does not love a good legend?
   c. A good legend, who doesn't love one?
   d. Who doesn't love a good legend?

26. Which of the following would be the best choice for this sentence (reproduced below)?

   Some say legends never (26) <u>die and this is certainly the case</u> for the most legendary creature of all, Bigfoot.

   a. NO CHANGE
   b. die, and this is certainly the case
   c. die; this is certainly the case
   d. die. This is certainly the case

27. Which of the following would be the best choice for this sentence (reproduced below)?

   (27) <u>Their all over the world, the</u> bigfoots and the legends tied to them.

   a. NO CHANGE
   b. There all over the world, the
   c. They're all over the world, the
   d. All over the world they are, the

28. Which of the following would be the best choice for this sentence (reproduced below)?

   There are many things to consider when addressing (28) <u>this question but the chief factor</u> is whether there is credible evidence.

   a. NO CHANGE
   b. this question, but the chief factor
   c. this question however the chief factor
   d. this question; but the chief factor

29. Which of the following would be the best choice for this sentence (reproduced below)?

(29) For science to formally recognize that such a species exists, there needs to be physical proof.

a. NO CHANGE
b. Physical proof are needed in order for science to formally recognize that such a species exists.
c. For science to formally recognize that such a species exists there needs to be physical proof.
d. For science, to formally recognize that such a species exists, there needs to be physical proof.

30. Which of the following would be the best choice for this sentence (reproduced below)?

While people have found supposed footprints and even (30) captured photos and film of the creature, this validity of such evidence is up for debate.

a. NO CHANGE
b. captured photos and film of the creature. This validity of such evidence is up for debate.
c. captured photos and film of the creature, the validities of such evidence is up for debate.
d. captured photos and film of the creature, the validity of such evidence is up for debate.

31. Which of the following would be the best choice for this sentence (reproduced below)?

Most visual evidence is out of focus, thus there is (31) often skepticism whether such images are real.

a. NO CHANGE
b. often skepticism whether such images are real.
c. there is often skepticism, whether such images are real.
d. there is often skepticism weather such images are real.

32. Which of the following would be the best choice for this sentence (reproduced below)?

Yet, one cannot ignore the fact that (32) hundreds of witnesses continuing to describe a creature with uniform features all over the world.

a. NO CHANGE
b. hundreds of witnesses continuing to describing a creature
c. hundreds of witnesses continue to describe a creature
d. hundreds of the witnesses continue to described a creature

33. Which of the following would be the best choice for this sentence (reproduced below)?

Ancient civilizations have reported (33) seeing Bigfoot as well including Native Americans.

a. NO CHANGE
b. seeing Bigfoot, Native Americans as well.
c. seeing Bigfoot also the Native Americans.
d. seeing Bigfoot, including Native Americans.

Questions 34–40 are based on the following passage:

I have to admit that when my father bought a recreational vehicle (RV), I thought he was making a huge mistake. I didn't really know anything about RVs, but I knew that my dad was as big a "city slicker" as there was. (34) <u>In fact, I even thought he might have gone a little bit crazy.</u> On trips to the beach, he preferred to swim at the pool, and whenever he went hiking, he avoided touching any plants for fear that they might be poison ivy. Why would this man, with an almost irrational fear of the outdoors, want a 40-foot camping behemoth?

(35) <u>The RV</u> was a great purchase for our family and brought us all closer together. Every morning (36) <u>we would wake up, eat breakfast, and broke camp.</u> We laughed at our own comical attempts to back The Beast into spaces that seemed impossibly small. (37) <u>We rejoiced as "hackers."</u> When things inevitably went wrong and we couldn't solve the problems on our own, we discovered the incredible helpfulness and friendliness of the RV community. (38) <u>We even made some new friends in the process.</u>

(39) <u>Above all, it allowed us to share adventures. While travelling across America,</u> which we could not have experienced in cars and hotels. Enjoying a campfire on a chilly summer evening with the mountains of Glacier National Park in the background or waking up early in the morning to see the sun rising over the distant spires of Arches National Park are memories that will always stay with me and our entire family. (40) <u>Those are also memories that my siblings and me</u> have now shared with our own children.

34. Which of the following would be the best choice for this sentence (reproduced below)?

(34) <u>In fact, I even thought he might have gone a little bit crazy.</u>

a. NO CHANGE
b. Move the sentence so that it comes before the preceding sentence.
c. Move the sentence to the end of the first paragraph.
d. Omit the sentence.

35. In context, which is the best version of the underlined Frankenstein then suffers his creature's wrath portion of this sentence (reproduced below)?

(35) <u>The RV</u> was a great purchase for our family and brought us all closer together.

a. NO CHANGE
b. Not surprisingly, the RV
c. Furthermore, the RV
d. As it turns out, the RV

36. Which is the best version of the underlined portion of this sentence (reproduced below)?

Every morning (36) <u>we would wake up, eat breakfast, and broke camp.</u>

a. NO CHANGE
b. we would wake up, eat breakfast, and break camp.
c. would we wake up, eat breakfast, and break camp?
d. we are waking up, eating breakfast, and breaking camp.

98

37. Which is the best version of the underlined portion of this sentence (reproduced below)?

(37) <u>We rejoiced as "hackers."</u>

a. NO CHANGE
b. To a nagging problem of technology, we rejoiced as "hackers."
c. We rejoiced when we figured out how to "hack" a solution to a nagging technological problem.
d. To "hack" our way to a solution, we had to rejoice.

38. Which is the best version of the underlined portion of this sentence (reproduced below)?

(38) <u>We even made some new friends in the process.</u>

a. NO CHANGE
b. In the process was the friends we were making.
c. We are even making some new friends in the process.
d. We will make new friends in the process.

39. Which is the best version of the underlined portion of this sentence (reproduced below)?

(39) <u>Above all, it allowed us to share adventures. While travelling across America</u>, which we could not have experienced in cars and hotels.

a. NO CHANGE
b. Above all, it allowed us to share adventures while traveling across America
c. Above all, it allowed us to share adventures; while traveling across America
d. Above all, it allowed us to share adventures—while traveling across America

40. Which is the best version of the underlined portion of this sentence (reproduced below)?

(40) <u>Those are also memories that my siblings and me</u> have now shared with our own children.

a. NO CHANGE
b. Those are also memories that me and my siblings
c. Those are also memories that my siblings and I
d. Those are also memories that I and my siblings

Questions 41–45 are based on the following passage:

We live in a savage world; that's just a simple fact. It is a time of violence, when the need for self-defense is imperative. (41) <u>Martial arts, like Ju-jitsu, still play a vital role in ones survival.</u> (42) <u>Ju-jitsu, however doesn't justify kicking people around</u>, even when being harassed or attacked. Today, laws prohibit the (43) <u>use of unnecessary force in self-defense; these serve to eliminate</u> beating someone to a pulp once they have been neutralized. Such laws are needed. Apart from being unnecessary to continually strike a person when (44) <u>their down, its immoral</u>. Such over-aggressive retaliation turns the innocent into the aggressor. Ju-jitsu provides a way for defending oneself while maintaining the philosophy of restraint and self-discipline. (45) <u>Ingratiated into its core philosophy</u>, Ju-jitsu tempers the potential to do great physical harm with respect for that power and for life.

41. Which of the following would be the best choice for this sentence (reproduced below)?

(41) <u>Martial arts, like Ju-jitsu, still play a vital role in ones survival.</u>

a. NO CHANGE
b. Martial arts, like Ju-jitsu, still play a vital role in one's survival.
c. Martial arts, like Ju-jitsu still play a vital role in ones survival.
d. Martial arts, like Ju-jitsu, still plays a vital role in one's survival.

42. Which of the following would be the best choice for this sentence (reproduced below)?

(42) <u>Ju-jitsu, however doesn't justify kicking people around,</u> even when being harassed or attacked.

a. NO CHANGE
b. Ju-jitsu, however, isn't justified by kicking people around,
c. However, Ju-jitsu doesn't justify kicking people around,
d. Ju-jitsu however doesn't justify kicking people around,

43. Which of the following would be the best choice for this sentence (reproduced below)?

Today, laws prohibit the (43) <u>use of unnecessary force in self-defense; these serve to eliminate</u> beating someone to a pulp once they have been neutralized.

a. NO CHANGE
b. use of unnecessary force in self-defense serving to eliminate
c. use of unnecessary force, in self-defense, these serve to eliminate
d. use of unnecessary force. In self-defense, these serve to eliminate

44. Which of the following would be the best choice for this sentence (reproduced below)?

Apart from being unnecessary to continually strike a person when (44) <u>their down, its immoral.</u>

a. NO CHANGE
b. their down, it's immoral.
c. they're down, its immoral.
d. they're down, it's immoral.

45. Which of the following would be the best choice for this sentence (reproduced below)?

(45) <u>Ingratiated into its core philosophy,</u> Ju-jitsu tempers the potential to do great physical harm with respect for that power, and for life.

a. NO CHANGE
b. Ingratiated into its core philosophy,
c. Ingratiated into it's core philosophy,
d. Ingratiated into its' core philosophy,

Math Test

1. If a car can travel 300 miles in 4 hours, how far can it go in an hour and a half?
    a. 100 miles
    b. 112.5 miles
    c. 135.5 miles
    d. 150 miles

2. At the store, Jan spends $90 on apples and oranges. Apples cost $1 each and oranges cost $2 each. If Jan buys the same number of apples as oranges, how many oranges did she buy?
    a. 20
    b. 25
    c. 30
    d. 35

3. What is the volume of a box with rectangular sides 5 feet long, 6 feet wide, and 3 feet high?
    a. 60 cubic feet
    b. 75 cubic feet
    c. 90 cubic feet
    d. 14 cubic feet

4. A train traveling 50 miles per hour takes a trip lasting 3 hours. If a map has a scale of 1 inch per 10 miles, how many inches apart are the train's starting point and ending point on the map?
    a. 14
    b. 12
    c. 13
    d. 15

5. A traveler takes an hour to drive to a museum, spends 3 hours and 30 minutes there, and takes half an hour to drive home. What percentage of his or her time was spent driving?
    a. 15%
    b. 30%
    c. 40%
    d. 60%

6. A truck is carrying three cylindrical barrels. Their bases have a diameter of 2 feet and they have a height of 3 feet. What is the total volume of the three barrels in cubic feet?
    a. 3π
    b. 9π
    c. 12π
    d. 15π

7. Greg buys a $10 lunch with 5% sales tax. He leaves a $2 tip after his bill. How much money does he spend?
    a. $12.50
    b. $12
    c. $13
    d. $13.25

8. Marty wishes to save $150 over a 4-day period. How much must Marty save each day on average?
   a. $37.50
   b. $35
   c. $45.50
   d. $41

9. Bernard can make $80 per day. If he needs to make $300 and only works full days, how many days will this take?
   a. 6
   b. 3
   c. 5
   d. 4

10. A couple buys a house for $150,000. They sell it for $165,000. By what percentage did the house's value increase?
   a. 10%
   b. 13%
   c. 15%
   d. 17%

11. A school has 15 teachers and 20 teaching assistants. They have 200 students. What is the ratio of faculty to students?
   a. 3:20
   b. 4:17
   c. 5:54
   d. 7:40

12. A map has a scale of 1 inch per 5 miles. A car can travel 60 miles per hour. If the distance from the start to the destination is 3 inches on the map, how long will it take the car to make the trip?
   a. 12 minutes
   b. 15 minutes
   c. 17 minutes
   d. 20 minutes

13. Taylor works two jobs. The first pays $20,000 per year. The second pays $10,000 per year. She donates 15% of her income to charity. How much does she donate each year?
   a. $4500
   b. $5000
   c. $5500
   d. $6000

14. A box with rectangular sides is 24 inches wide, 18 inches deep, and 12 inches high. What is the volume of the box in cubic feet?
   a. 2
   b. 3
   c. 4
   d. 5

15. Kristen purchases $100 worth of CDs and DVDs. The CDs cost $10 each and the DVDs cost $15. If she bought four DVDs, how many CDs did she buy?

    a. 5

    b. 6

    c. 3

    d. 4

16. If Sarah reads at an average rate of 21 pages in four nights, how long will it take her to read 140 pages?

    a. 6 nights

    b. 26 nights

    c. 8 nights

    d. 27 nights

17. Mom's car drove 72 miles in 90 minutes. There are 5280 feet per mile. How fast did she drive in feet per second?

    a. 0.8 feet per second

    b. 48.9 feet per second

    c. 0.009 feet per second

    d. 70. 4 feet per second

18. This chart indicates how many sales of CDs, vinyl records, and MP3 downloads occurred over the last year. Approximately what percentage of the total sales was from CDs?

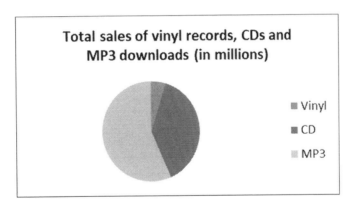

    a. 55%

    b. 25%

    c. 40%

    d. 5%

19. After a 20% sale discount, Frank purchased a new refrigerator for $850. How much did he save from the original price?

    a. $170

    b. $212.50

    c. $105.75

    d. $200

20. Which of the following is NOT a way to write 40 percent of N?

    a. $(0.4)N$

    b. $\frac{2}{5}N$

    c. $40N$

    d. $\frac{4N}{10}$

21. The graph of which function has an x-intercept of -2?

    a. $y = 2x - 3$

    b. $y = 4x + 2$

    c. $y = x^2 + 5x + 6$

    d. $y = -\frac{1}{2} \times 2^x$

22. The table below displays the number of three-year-olds at Kids First Daycare who are potty-trained and those who still wear diapers.

	Potty-trained	Wear diapers	
Boys	26	22	48
Girls	34	18	52
	60	40	

What is the probability that a three-year-old girl chosen at random from the school is potty-trained?

    a. 52 percent

    b. 34 percent

    c. 65 percent

    d. 57 percent

23. A clothing company with a target market of U.S. boys surveys 2000 twelve-year-old boys to find their height. The average height of the boys is 61 inches. For the above scenario, 61 inches represents which of the following?

    a. Sample statistic

    b. Population parameter

    c. Confidence interval

    d. Measurement error

24. A government agency is researching the average consumer cost of gasoline throughout the United States. Which data collection method would produce the most valid results?

    a. Randomly choosing one hundred gas stations in the state of New York

    b. Randomly choosing ten gas stations from each of the fifty states

    c. Randomly choosing five hundred gas stations from across all fifty states with the number chosen proportional to the population of the state

    d. Methods A, B, and C would each produce equally valid results.

25. Suppose an investor deposits $1200 into a bank account that accrues 1 percent interest per month. Assuming x represents the number of months since the deposit and y represents the money in the account, which of the following exponential functions models the scenario?

    a. $y = (0.01)(1200^x)$
    b. $y = (1200)(0.01^x)$
    c. $y = (1.01)(1200^x)$
    d. $y = (1200)(1.01^x)$

26. A student gets an 85% on a test with 20 questions. How many answers did the student solve correctly?

    a. 15
    b. 16
    c. 17
    d. 18

27. Four people split a bill. The first person pays for $\frac{1}{5}$, the second person pays for $\frac{1}{4}$, and the third person pays for $\frac{1}{3}$. What fraction of the bill does the fourth person pay?

    a. $\frac{13}{60}$

    b. $\frac{47}{60}$

    c. $\frac{1}{4}$

    d. $\frac{4}{15}$

32. Five of six numbers have a sum of 25. The average of all six numbers is 6. What is the sixth number?

    a. 8
    b. 10
    c. 11
    d. 12

33. Suppose the function $y = \frac{1}{8}x^3 + 2x - 21$ approximates the population of a given city between the years 1900 and 2000 with x representing the year (1900 = 0) and y representing the population (in 1000s). Which of the following domains are relevant for the scenario?

    a. $[\infty, \infty]$
    b. [1900, 2000]
    c. [0, 100]
    d. [0, 0]

34. What is the equation of a circle whose center is (0, 0) and whole radius is 5?

    a. $(x - 5)^2 + (y - 5)^2 = 25$
    b. $(x)^2 + (y)^2 = 5$
    c. $(x)^2 + (y)^2 = 25$
    d. $(x + 5)^2 + (y + 5)^2 = 25$

35. What is the equation of a circle whose center is (1, 5) and whole radius is 4?
    a. $(x - 1)^2 + (y - 25)^2 = 4$
    b. $(x - 1)^2 + (y - 25)^2 = 16$
    c. $(x + 1)^2 + (y + 5)^2 = 16$
    d. $(x - 1)^2 + (y - 5)^2 = 16$

36. Where does the point (-3, -4) lie on the circle with the equation $(x)^2 + (y)^2 = 25$?
    a. Inside of the circle.
    b. Outside of the circle.
    c. On the circle.
    d. There is not enough information to tell.

37. A drug needs to be stored at room temperature (68 °F). What is the equivalent temperature in degrees Celsius?
    a. 36 °C
    b. 72 °C
    c. 68 °C
    d. 20 °C

38. What is the slope of this line?

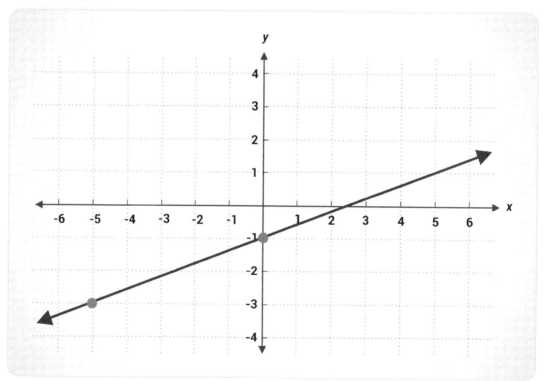

    a. 2

    b. $\frac{5}{2}$

    c. $\frac{1}{2}$

    d. $\frac{2}{5}$

39. What is the perimeter of the figure below? Note that the solid outer line is the perimeter.

9 ft

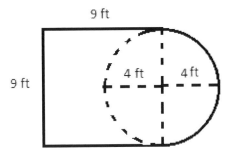

9 ft   4 ft   4 ft

a. 48.565 ft
b. 39.565 ft
c. 19.78 ft
d. 30.565 ft

40. Which of the following equations best represents the problem below?
The width of a rectangle is 2 centimeters less than the length. If the perimeter of the rectangle is 44 centimeters, then what are the dimensions of the rectangle?
a. $2l + 2(l - 2) = 44$
b. $l + 2) + (l + 2) + l = 48$
c. $l \times (l - 2) = 44$
d. $(l + 2) + (l + 2) + l = 44$

41. How will the following algebraic expression be simplified: $(5x^2 - 3x + 4) - (2x^2 - 7)$?
a. x^5
b. $3x^2 - 3x + 11$
c. $3x^2 - 3x - 3$
d. $x - 3$

42. What is 39% of 164?
a. 63.96%
b. 23.78%
c. 6,396%
d. 2.38%

43. Kimberley earns $10 an hour babysitting, and after 10 p.m., she earns $12 an hour, with the amount paid being rounded to the nearest hour accordingly. On her last job, she worked from 5:30 p.m. to 11 p.m. In total, how much did Kimberley earn for that job?
a. $45
b. $57
c. $62
d. $42

44. Keith's bakery had 252 customers go through its doors last week. This week, that number increased to 378. By what percentage did his customer volume increase?
a. 26%
b. 50%
c. 35%
d. 12%

No Calculator Questions

45. A family purchases a vehicle in 2005 for $20,000. In 2010, they decide to sell it for a newer model. They are able to sell the car for $8,000. By what percentage did the value of the family's car drop?
    a. 40%
    b. 68%
    c. 60%
    d. 33%

46. In May of 2010, a couple purchased a house for $100,000. In September of 2016, the couple sold the house for $93,000 so they could purchase a bigger one to start a family. How many months did they own the house?
    a. 76
    b. 54
    c. 85
    d. 93

47. At the beginning of the day, Xavier has 20 apples. At lunch, he meets his sister Emma and gives her half of his apples. After lunch, he stops by his neighbor Jim's house and gives him 6 of his apples. He then uses ¾ of his remaining apples to make an apple pie for dessert at dinner. At the end of the day, how many apples does Xavier have left?
    a. 4
    b. 6
    c. 2
    d. 1

48. If $\frac{5}{2} \div \frac{1}{3} = n$, then n is between:
    a. 5 and 7
    b. 7 and 9
    c. 9 and 11
    d. 3 and 5

49. A closet is filled with red, blue, and green shirts. If $\frac{1}{3}$ of the shirts are green and $\frac{2}{5}$ are red, what fraction of the shirts are blue?
    a. $\frac{4}{15}$

    b. $\frac{1}{5}$

    c. $\frac{7}{15}$

    d. $\frac{1}{2}$

50. Shawna buys $2\frac{1}{2}$ gallons of paint. If she uses $\frac{1}{3}$ of it on the first day, how much does she have left?

a. $1\frac{5}{6}$ gallons

b. $1\frac{1}{2}$ gallons

c. $1\frac{2}{3}$ gallons

d. 2 gallons

51. What is the volume of a cylinder, in terms of π, with a radius of 6 centimeters and a height of 2 centimeters?
- a. $36\,\pi$ cm³
- b. $24\,\pi$ cm³
- c. $72\,\pi$ cm³
- d. $48\,\pi$ cm³

52. What is the length of the hypotenuse of a right triangle with one leg equal to 3 centimeters and the other leg equal to 4 centimeters?
- a. 7 cm
- b. 5 cm
- c. 25 cm
- d. 12 cm

53. Twenty is 40% of what number?
- a. 50
- b. 8
- c. 200
- d. 5000

54. If Danny takes 48 minutes to walk 3 miles, how many minutes should it take him to walk 5 miles maintaining the same speed?

55. The perimeter of a 6-sided polygon is 56 cm. The length of three sides is 9 cm each. The length of two other sides is 8 cm each. What is the length of the missing side?

56. If sine of 30° = x, the cosine of what angle, in degrees, also equals x?

57. What is the value of $x^2 - 2xy + 2y^2$ when $x = 2, y = 3$?

58. If $4x - 3 = 5$, then $x =$

Answer Explanations #2

Reading Test

1. D: To criticize a theory by presenting counterevidence. The author mentions anti-Stratfordian arguments in the first paragraph, but then goes on to debunk these theories with more facts about Shakespeare's life in the second and third paragraphs. *A* is not correct because, while the author does present arguments from both sides, the author is far from unbiased; in fact, the author clearly disagrees with anti-Stratfordians. *B* is also not correct because it is more closely aligned to the beliefs of anti-Stratfordians, whom the author disagrees with. *C* can be eliminated because, while it is true that the author gives historical background, the main purpose of the article is using that information to disprove a theory.

2. B: But in fact, there is not much substance to such speculation, and most anti-Stratfordian arguments can be refuted with a little background about Shakespeare's time and upbringing. The thesis is a statement that contains the author's topic and main idea. As seen in question 27, the main purpose of this article is to use historical evidence to provide counterarguments to anti-Stratfordians. *A* is simply a definition; *C* is a supporting detail, not a main idea; and *D* represents an idea of anti-Stratfordians, not the author's opinion.

3. C: Rhetorical question. This requires readers to be familiar with different types of rhetorical devices. A rhetorical question is a question that is asked not to obtain an answer but to encourage readers to more deeply consider an issue.

4. B: By explaining grade school curriculum in Shakespeare's time. This question asks readers to refer to the organizational structure of the article and demonstrate understanding of how the author provides details to support their argument. This particular detail can be found in the second paragraph: "even though he did not attend university, grade school education in Shakespeare's time was actually quite rigorous."

5. A: Busy. This is a vocabulary question that can be answered using context clues. Other sentences in the paragraph describe London as "the most populous city in England" filled with "crowds of people," giving an image of a busy city full of people. *B* is not correct because London was in Shakespeare's home country, not a foreign one. *C* is not mentioned in the passage. *D* is not a good answer choice because the passage describes how London was a popular and important city, probably not an underdeveloped one.

6. D: In Shakespeare's time, glove-makers were not part of the upper class. Anti-Stratfordians doubt Shakespeare's ability because he was not from the upper class; his father was a glove-maker; therefore, in at least this instance, glove-makers were not included in the upper class (this is an example of inductive reasoning, or using two specific pieces of information to draw a more general conclusion).

7. C: It is an example of a play set outside of England. This detail comes from the third paragraph, where the author responds to skeptics who claim that Shakespeare wrote too much about places he never visited, so *Romeo and Juliet* is mentioned as a famous example of a play with a foreign setting. In order to answer this question, readers need to understand the author's main purpose in the third paragraph and how the author uses details to support this purpose. *A* and *D* are not mentioned in the passage, and *B* is clearly not true because the passage mentions more than once that Shakespeare never left England.

8. A: It is possible to learn things from reading rather than from firsthand experience. This inference can be made from the final paragraph, where the author refutes anti-Stratfordian skepticism by pointing out that books about life in Europe could easily circulate throughout London. From this statement, readers can conclude that the author believes it is possible that Shakespeare learned about European culture from books, rather than visiting the continent on his own. *B* is not true because the author believes that Shakespeare contributed to English literature without traveling extensively. Similarly, *C* is not a good answer because the author explains how Shakespeare got his education without university. *D* can also be eliminated because the author describes Shakespeare's genius and clearly Shakespeare is not from Italy.

9. C: The point of view is told in third person omniscient. We know this because the story starts out with us knowing something that the character does not know: that her husband has died. Mrs. Mallard eventually comes to know this, but we as readers know this information before it is broken to her. In third person limited, Choice *D*, we would only see and know what Mrs. Mallard herself knew, and we would find out the news of her husband's death when she found out the news, not before.

10. A: The way Mrs. Mallard reacted to her husband's death. The irony in this story is called situational irony, which means the situation that takes place is different than what the audience anticipated. At the beginning of the story, we see Mrs. Mallard react with a burst of grief to her husband's death. However, once she's alone, she begins to contemplate her future and says the word "free" over and over. This is quite a different reaction from Mrs. Mallard than what readers expected from the first of the story.

11. B: The word "elusive" most closely means "indefinable." Horrible, Choice *A*, doesn't quite fit with the tone of the word "subtle" that comes before it. Choice *C*, "quiet," is more closely related to the word "subtle." Choice *D*, "joyful," also doesn't quite fit the context here. "Indefinable" is the best option.

12. D: Mrs. Mallard, a newly widowed woman, finds unexpected relief in her husband's death. A summary is a brief explanation of the main point of a story. The story mostly focuses on Mrs. Mallard and her reaction to her husband's death, especially in the room when she's alone and contemplating the present and future. All of the other answer choices except Choice *C* are briefly mentioned in the story; however, they are not the main focus of the story.

13. D: The interesting thing about this story is that feelings that are confused, joyful, and depressive all play a unique and almost equal part of this story. There is no one right answer here, because the author seems to display all of these emotions through the character of Mrs. Mallard. She displays feelings of depressiveness by her grief at the beginning; then, when she receives feelings of joy, she feels moments of confusion. We as readers cannot help but go through these feelings with the character. Thus, the author creates a tone of depression, joy, and confusion, all in one story.

14. C: The word "tumultuously" most nearly means "violently." Even if you don't know the word "tumultuously," look at the surrounding context to figure it out. The next few sentences we see Mrs. Mallard striving to "beat back" the "thing that was approaching to possess her." We see a fearful and almost violent reaction to the emotion that she's having. Thus, her chest would rise and fall turbulently, or violently.

15. C: This is a tricky question, but it can be solved through careful context analysis and vocabulary knowledge. One can infer that the use of "expedient," while not necessarily very positive, isn't inherently bad in this context either. Note how in the next line, he says, "but most governments are usually, and all governments are sometimes, inexpedient." This use of "inexpedient" indicates that a government becomes a hindrance rather than a solution; it slows progress rather than helps facilitate progress. Thus, Choice *A* and Choice *D* can be ruled out because these are more of the result of government, not the intention or initial design. Choice *B* makes no logical sense. Therefore, Choice *C* is the best description of *expedient*. Essentially, Thoreau is saying that government is constructed as a way of developing order and people's rights, but the rigidness of government soon inhibits justice and human rights.

16. B: While Choice *D* is the only answer that mentions the Mexican War directly, Thoreau clearly thinks the war is unnecessary because the people generally didn't consent to the war. Choices *A*, *B*, and *C* are all correct to a degree, but the answer asks for the best description. Therefore, Choice *B* is the most accurate representation of Thoreau's views. Essentially, Thoreau brings to light the fact that the few people in power can twist government and policy for their own needs.

17. D: Choice *C* and Choice *B* are completely incorrect. Thoreau is not defending government in any way. His views are set against government. As mentioned in the text, he appreciates little government but favors having no government structure at all. The text is reflective by nature, but what makes Choice *D* a more appropriate answer is the presence of evidence in the text. Thoreau cites current events and uses them to illustrate the point he's trying to make.

18. C: One of Thoreau's biggest criticisms of government is its capacity to impose on the people's freedoms and liberties, enacting rules that the people don't want and removing power from the individual. None of the scenarios directly impose specific regulations or restrictions on the people, except Prohibition. Prohibition removed the choice to consume alcohol in favor of abstinence, which was favored by the religious conservatives of the time. Thus, Thoreau would point out that this is a clear violation of free choice and an example of government meddling.

19. A: Choice *B* is totally irrelevant. Choice *C* is also incorrect; Thoreau never personifies government. Also, this doesn't coincide with his wooden gun analogy. Choice *D* is compelling because of its language but doesn't define the statement. Choice *A* is the most accurate summary of the main point of Thoreau's statement.

20. B: Thoreau specifically cites that legislators "are continually putting in their way." This reflects his suspicion and concern of government intervention. Recall that Thoreau continually mentions that government, while meant as a way to establish freedom, is easily used to suppress freedom, piling on regulations and rules that inhibit progress. Choice *B* is the answer that most directly states how Thoreau sees government getting in the way of freedom.

21. A: The story is dedicated to telling about the origin of the battery. It doesn't explicitly explain the mechanics of battery operated machines or the far-reaching effects of battery usage, like Choices *B* and *C* suggest. Choice *D* also doesn't work because it does not explicitly encourage readers to take part in new innovations.

22. A: Choices *B* and *D* are incorrect because the text makes no mention of an assessment or a violent encounter. Choice *C* is a possibility; however, Choice *A* is the correct answer because Volta placed things in a particular order to achieve a given result.

23. A: Choice *A*, problem and solution, is the correct answer because the passage details the problem of trying to use electricity to induce muscle contraction and the solution of causing metals to touch instead of muscles, which later lead to the development of the battery.

24. C: The text states that Volta is credited with creating the first battery. Choice *A,* Galvani, had a part in the discovery of the battery because Volta built upon Galvani's previous research. Choice *B,* Pavia, is the university that Volta attended. Choice *D,* Bologna, is the name of the university that Galvani attended.

25. C: The text supports the idea that the term "voltage" has a direct correlation to the fact that Volta is the scientist credited with originally developing batteries. *A* is incorrect because the text does not explain how the researcher died, or that he had failed in any way. *B* is incorrect because information about the researcher's peers is not represented in the text. *D* is incorrect because the text does not divulge the advances of modern researchers.

26. C: The text corroborates the assertion concerning Galvani's belief about the role of animals' life-force in inducing muscle movements. Volta's initial doubt in Galvani's belief led Volta to further the research Galvani had started. *A* is incorrect because it leaves out any information concerning Volta. *B* is incorrect because Volta was not concerned with the intellect of the animals, but rather their ability to contain the "life-force" of electricity. *D* is incorrect because the text does not depict either researcher believing their own theories were the foremost research in the field.

27. D: The use of "you" could have all of the effects for the reader with the Choices *A, B,* and *C;* it could serve to personalize the text, make the passage easier to understand, and cause the reader to empathize with Henrietta Lack's story. However, it doesn't distance the reader from Lack's experiences, 15us eliminating Choice *D.*

28. A: Choices *C* and *D* are incorrect because they are disproven in the text. Choice *B* is incorrect because there is no mention of what the best evidence of cell mutation is. The author references Dolly to point the reader to another popular case of DNA research.

29. D: The word "harness" in the text means to duplicate because the scientists' desire is to develop more immortal cells. *A,* "tack," means to pinpoint in place with tacks, which is physically impossible in this context. *B,* "obtain," doesn't logically make sense, because the scientists couldn't obtain traits at this stage in their development. *C,* "couple," is also incorrect, as scientists in this context are more prone to duplicating unique traits than coupling them.

30. D: Choice *D* is correct because the text states that HeLa cells came from a sliver of one of the Henrietta Lack's tumor. Choice *A* and *B* are not mentioned in the text, and Choice *C* is incorrect, as the HeLa cells did not come through DNA testing.

31. D: The discovery of HeLa cells has helped to further the scientific world through *A,* isolating stem cells, *B,* cloning whole animals, and *D,* in vitro fertilization. Choice *D,* separating Siamese twins, is not mentioned in the text.

32. C: The text states that normally developed humans have 46 chromosomes. Originally scientists thought that human cells contained 48 chromosomes, but later a geneticist in Texas proved that incorrect.

33. B: Mr. Button's wife is about to have a baby. The passage begins by giving the reader information about traditional birthing situations. Then, we are told that Mr. and Mrs. Button decide to go against tradition to have their baby in a hospital. The next few passages are dedicated to letting the reader know how Mr. Button dresses and goes to the hospital to welcome his new baby. There is a doctor in this excerpt, as Choice *C* indicates, and Mr. Button does put on clothes, as Choice *D* indicates. However, Mr. Button is not going to the doctor's office nor is he about to go shopping for new clothes.

34. A: The tone of the above passage is nervous and excited. We are told in the fourth paragraph that Mr. Button "arose nervously." We also see him running without caution to the doctor to find out about his wife and baby—this indicates his excitement. We also see him stuttering in a nervous yet excited fashion as he asks the doctor if it's a boy or girl. Though the doctor may seem a bit abrupt at the end, indicating a bit of anger or shame, neither of these choices is the overwhelming tone of the entire passage.

35. C: Dedicated. Mr. Button is dedicated to the task before him. Choice *A*, numbed, Choice *B*, chained, and Choice *D*, moved, all could grammatically fit in the sentence. However, they are not synonyms with *consecrated* like Choice *C* is.

36. D: Giving readers a visual picture of what the doctor is doing. The author describes a visual image—the doctor rubbing his hands together—first and foremost. The author may be trying to make a comment about the profession; however, the author does not "explain the detail of the doctor's profession" as Choice *B* suggests.

37. D: To introduce the setting of the story and its characters. We know we are being introduced to the setting because we are given the year in the very first paragraph along with the season: "one day in the summer of 1860." This is a classic structure of an introduction of the setting. We are also getting a long explanation of Mr. Button, what his work is, who is related to him, and what his life is like in the third paragraph.

38. B: "Talk sense!" is an example of an imperative sentence. An imperative sentence gives a command. The doctor is commanding Mr. Button to talk sense. Choice *A* is an example of an exclamatory sentence, which expresses excitement. Choice *C* is an example of an interrogative sentence—these types of sentences ask questions. Choice *D* is an example of a declarative sentence. This means that the character is simply making a statement.

39. A: First person. This is a straightforward question that requires readers to know that a first-person narrator speaks from an "I" point of view.

40. D: He doesn't understand all of the languages being used. This can be inferred from the fact that the traveler must refer to his dictionary to understand those around him. Choice *A* isn't a good choice because the traveler seems to wonder why the driver needs to drive so fast. Choice *B* isn't mentioned in the passage and doesn't seem like a good answer choice because he seems wholly unfamiliar with his surroundings. This is why Choice *C* can also be eliminated.

41. B: From fearful to charmed. This can be found in the first sentence of the third paragraph, which states, "I soon lost sight and recollection of ghostly fears in the beauty of the scene as we drove along." Also, readers should get a sense of foreboding from the first two paragraphs, where superstitious villagers seem frightened on the traveler's behalf. However, the final paragraph changes to delighted descriptions of the landscape's natural beauty. Choices *A* and *D* can be eliminated because the traveler is anxious, not relaxed or comfortable at the beginning of the passage. Choice *C* can also be eliminated because the traveler doesn't gain any particular insights in the last paragraph, and in fact continues to lament that he cannot understand the speech of those around him.

42. D: A complete stranger. The answer to this reading comprehension question can be found in the second paragraph, when the traveler is "just starting for an unknown place to meet an unknown man"—in other words, a complete stranger.

43. C: The traveler will soon encounter danger or evil. Answering this prediction question requires readers to understand foreshadowing, or hints that the author gives about what will happen next. There are numerous hints scattered throughout this passage: the villager's sorrow and sympathy for the traveler and their superstitious actions; the spooky words that the traveler overhears; the driver's unexplained haste. All of these point to a danger that awaits the protagonist.

44. A: "I must say they weren't cheering to me, for amongst them were "Ordog"—Satan, "pokol"—hell, "stregoica"—witch, "vrolok" and "vlkoslak"—both of which mean the same thing, one being Slovak and the other Servian for something that is either were-wolf or vampire." As mentioned in question 39, this sentence is an example of how the author hints at evil to come for the traveler. The other answer choices aren't related to the passage's grim foreshadowing.

45. A: The purpose is to inform the reader about what assault is and how it is committed. Choice *B* is incorrect because the passage does not state that assault is a lesser form of lethal force, only that an assault can use lethal force, or alternatively, lethal force can be utilized to counter a dangerous assault. Choice *C* is incorrect because the passage is informative and does not have a set agenda. Finally, Choice *D* is incorrect because although the author uses an example in order to explain assault, it is not indicated that this is the author's personal account.

46. C: If the man being attacked in an alley by another man with a knife used self-defense by lethal force, it would not be considered illegal. The presence of a deadly weapon indicates mal-intent and because the individual is isolated in an alley, lethal force in self-defense may be the only way to preserve his life. Choices *A* and *B* can be ruled out because in these situations, no one is in danger of immediate death or bodily harm by someone else. Choice *D* is an assault and does exhibit intent to harm, but this situation isn't severe enough to merit lethal force; there is no intent to kill.

47. B: As discussed in the second passage, there are several forms of assault, like assault with a deadly weapon, verbal assault, or threatening posture or language. Choice *A* is incorrect because the author does mention what the charges are on assaults; therefore, we cannot assume that they are more or less than unnecessary use of force charges. Choice *C* is incorrect because anyone is capable of assault; the author does not state that one group of people cannot commit assault. Choice *D* is incorrect because assault is never justified. Self-defense resulting in lethal force can be justified.

48. D: The use of lethal force is not evaluated on the intent of the user, but rather on the severity of the primary attack that warranted self-defense. This statement most undermines the last part of the passage because it directly contradicts how the law evaluates the use of lethal force. Choices *A* and *B* are stated in the paragraph, so they do not undermine the explanation from the author. Choice *C* does not necessarily undermine the passage, but it does not support the passage either. It is more of an opinion that does not offer strength or weakness to the explanation.

49. C: An assault with deadly intent can lead to an individual using lethal force to preserve their well-being. Choice *C* is correct because it clearly establishes what both assault and lethal force are and gives the specific way in which the two concepts meet. Choice *A* is incorrect because lethal force doesn't necessarily result in assault. This is also why Choice *B* is incorrect. Not all assaults would necessarily be life-threatening to the point where lethal force is needed for self-defense. Choice *D* is compelling but ultimately too vague; the statement touches on aspects of the two ideas but fails to present the concrete way in which the two are connected to each other.

50. A: Both passages open by defining a legal concept and then continue to describe situations in order to further explain the concept. Choice *D* is incorrect because while the passages utilize examples to help explain the concepts discussed, the author doesn't indicate that they are specific court cases. It's also clear that the passages don't open with examples, but instead, they begin by defining the terms addressed in each passage. This eliminates Choice *B,* and ultimately reveals Choice *A* to be the correct answer. Choice *A* accurately outlines the way both passages are structured. Because the passages follow a nearly identical structure, the Choice *C* can easily be ruled out.

51. C: Intent is very important for determining both lethal force and assault; intent is examined in both parties and helps determine the severity of the issue. Choices *A* and *B* are incorrect because it is clear in both passages that intent is a prevailing theme in both lethal force and assault. Choice *D* is compelling, but if a person uses lethal force to defend himself or herself, the intent of the defender is also examined in order to help determine if there was excessive force used. Choice *C* is correct because it states that intent is important for determining both lethal force and assault, and that intent is used to gauge the severity of the issues. Remember, just as lethal force can escalate to excessive use of force, there are different kinds of assault. Intent dictates several different forms of assault.

52. B: The example is used to demonstrate a single example of two different types of assault, then adding in a third type of assault to the example's conclusion. The example mainly provides an instance of "threatening body language" and "provocative language" with the homeowner gesturing threats to his neighbor. It ends the example by adding a third type of assault: physical strikes. This example is used to show the variant nature of assaults. Choice *A* is incorrect because it doesn't mention the "physical strike" assault at the end and is not specific enough. Choice *C* is incorrect because the example does not say anything about the definition of lethal force or how it might be altered. Choice *D* is incorrect, as the example mentions nothing about cause and effect.

Writing and Language Test

1. B: Choice *B* is correct. Here, a colon is used to introduce an explanation. Colons either introduce explanations or lists. Additionally, the quote ends with the punctuation inside the quotes, unlike Choice *C.*

2. A: The verb tense in this passage is predominantly in the present tense, so Choice *A* is the correct answer. Choice *B* is incorrect because the subject and verb do not agree. It should be "Education provides," not "Education provide." Choice *C* is incorrect because the passage is in present tense, and "Education will provide" is future tense. Choice *D* doesn't make sense when placed in the sentence.

3. D: The possessive form of the word "it" is "its." The contraction "it's" denotes "it is." Thus, Choice *A* is wrong. The word "raises" in Choice *B* makes the sentence grammatically incorrect. Choice *C* adds an apostrophe at the end of "its." While adding an apostrophe to most words would indicate possession, adding *'s* to the word "it" indicates a contraction.

4. C: The word *civilised* should be spelled *civilized.* The words "distinguishes" and "creatures" are both spelled correctly.

5. B: Choice *B* is correct because it provides clarity by describing what "myopic" means right after the word itself. Choice *A* is incorrect because the explanation of "myopic" comes before the word; thus, the meaning is skewed. It's possible that Choice *C* makes sense within context. However, it's not the *best* way to say this. Choice *D* is confusingly worded. Using "myopic focus" is not detrimental to society; however, the way *D* is worded makes it seem so.

6. C: Again, we see where the second paragraph can be divided into two parts due to separate topics. The first section's main focus is education addressing the mind, body, and soul. The first section, then, could end with the concluding sentence, "The human heart and psyche . . ." The next sentence to start a new paragraph would be "Education is a basic human right." The rest of this paragraph talks about what education is and some of its characteristics.

7. A: Choice *A* is correct because the phrase "others' ideas" is both plural and indicates possession. Choice *B* is incorrect because "other's" indicates only one "other" that's in possession of "ideas," which is incorrect. Choice *C* is incorrect because no possession is indicated. Choice *D* is incorrect because the word "other" does not end in *s*. *Others's* is not a correct form of the word in any situation.

8. D: This sentence must have a comma before "although" because the word "although" is connecting two independent clauses. Thus, Choices *B* and *C* are incorrect. Choice *A* is incorrect because the second sentence in the underlined section is a fragment.

9. C: Choice *C* is the correct choice because the word "their" indicates possession, and the text is talking about "their students," or the students of someone. Choice *A*, "there," means at a certain place and is incorrect. Choice *B*, "they're," is a contraction and means "they are." Choice *D* is not a word.

10. B: Choice *B* uses all punctuation correctly in this sentence. In American English, single quotes should only be used if they are quotes within a quote, making choices *A* and *C* incorrect. Additionally, punctuation here should go inside the quotes, making Choice *D* incorrect.

11. B: Choice *B* is correct because the conjunction "and" is used to connect phrases that are to be used jointly, such as teachers working hard to help students "identify salient information" and to "think critically." The conjunctions *so*, *but*, and *nor* are incorrect in the context of this sentence.

12. A: Choice *A* has consistent parallel structure with the verbs "read," "identify," and "determine." Choices *B* and *C* have faulty parallel structure with the words "determining" and "identifying." Choice *D* has incorrect subject/verb agreement. The sentence should read, "Students have to read . . . identify . . . and determine."

13. D: The correct choice for this sentence is that "they are . . . shaped by the influences." The prepositions "for," "to," and "with" do not make sense in this context. People are *shaped by*, not *shaped for, shaped to,* or *shaped with*.

14. A: To see which answer is correct, it might help to place the subject, "Teachers," near the verb. Choice *A* is correct: "Teachers . . . must strive" makes grammatical sense here. Choice B is incorrect because "Teachers . . . to strive" does not make grammatical sense. Choice C is incorrect because "Teachers must not only respect . . . but striving" eschews parallel structure. Choice *D* is incorrect because it is in past tense, and this passage is in present tense.

15. C: Choice *C* is correct because it uses an em-dash. Em-dashes are versatile. They can separate phrases that would otherwise be in parenthesis, or they can stand in for a colon. In this case, a colon would be another decent choice for this punctuation mark because the second sentence expands upon the first sentence. Choice *A* is incorrect because the statement is not a question. Choice *B* is incorrect because adding a comma here would create a comma splice. Choice *D* is incorrect because this creates a run-on sentence since the two sentences are independent clauses.

16. B: Choice *B* is correct because it removes the apostrophe from *icon's*, since the noun *icon* is not possessing anything. This conveys the author's intent of setting *Frankenstein* apart from other icons of the romantic and science fiction genres. Choices *A* and *C* are therefore incorrect. Choice *D* is a good revision but alters the meaning of the sentence—*Frankenstein* is one of the icons, not the sole icon.

17 C: Choice *C* correctly adds a comma after *style*, successfully joining the dependent and the independent clause as a single sentence. Choice *A* is incorrect because the dependent and independent clauses remain unsuccessfully combined without the comma. Choices *B* and *D* do nothing to fix this.

18. A: Choice *A* is correct, as the sentence doesn't require changes. Choice *B* incorrectly changes the noun *enlightenment* into the verb *enlighten*. Choices *C* and *D* alter the original meaning of the sentence.

19. B: Choice *B* is correct, fixing the incorrect split of *highlight*. This is a polyseme, a word combined from two unrelated words to make a new word. On their own, *high* and *light* make no sense for the sentence, making Choice *A* incorrect. Choice *C* incorrectly decapitalizes *Ancient*—since it modifies *Greece* and works with the noun to describe a civilization, *Ancient Greece* functions as a proper noun, which should be capitalized. Choice *D* uses *highlighting*, a gerund, but the present tense of *highlight* is what works with the rest of the sentence; to make this change, a comma would be needed after *Rome*.

20. A: Choice *A* is correct, as *not only* and *but also* are correlative pairs. In this sentence, *but* successfully transitions the first part into the second half, making punctuation unnecessary. Additionally, the use of *to* indicates that an idea or challenge is being presented to the reader. Choice *B*'s *with*, *C*'s *for*, and *D*'s *there before* are not as active, meaning these revisions weaken the sentence.

21. D: Choice *D* is correct, adding finer details to help the reader understand exactly what Prometheus did and his impact: fire came with knowledge and power. Choice *A* lacks a comma after *fire*. Choice *B* inserts unnecessary commas since *people* is not part of the list *knowledge and power*. Choice *C* is a strong revision but could be confusing, hinting that the fire was knowledge and power itself, as opposed to being symbolized by the fire.

22. C: Choice *C* reverses the order of the section, making the sentence more direct. Choice *A* lacks a comma after *gods*, and although Choice *B* adds this, the structure is too different from the first half of the sentence to flow correctly. Choice *D* is overly complicated and repetitious in its structure even though it doesn't need any punctuation.

23. B: Choice *B* fixes the two problems of the sentence, changing *faltered* to present tense in agreement with the rest of the passage, and correctly linking the two dependent clauses. Choice *A* is therefore incorrect. Choice *C* does not correct the past tense of *faltered*. Choice *D* correctly adds the conjunction *by*, but it lacks a comma after the conjunction *Yet*.

24. C: Choice *C* successfully applies a comma after *power*, distinguishing the causes of Frankenstein's suffering and maintaining parallel structure. Choice *A* is thus incorrect. Choice *B* lacks the necessary punctuation and unnecessarily changes *lack* to a gerund. Choice *D* adds unnecessary wording, making the sentence more cumbersome.

25. D: Choice *D* correctly inserts an apostrophe into the contraction *doesn't*. Choice *A* is incorrect because of this omission. Choices *B* and *C* are better than the original but do not fit well with the informal tone of the passage.

26. B: Choice *B* is correct, successfully combining the two independent clauses of this compound sentence by adding a comma before "and" to create the effective pause and transition between clauses. Choice *A* does not join the independent clauses correctly. Choices *C* and *D* offer alternate ways of joining these clauses, but since "and" is already part of the sentence, adding the comma is the most logical choice. This also keeps the informal tone set by the rest of the passage.

27. C: Choice *C* correctly fixes the homophone issue of *their* and *they're*. *Their* implies ownership, which is not needed here. The author intends *they're*, a contraction of *they are*. Thus, Choice *A* is incorrect, as is Choice *B*, using the homophone *there*. Choice *D* eliminates the homophone issue altogether, but the sentence becomes more clunky because of that.

28. B: Choice *B* correctly joins the two independent clauses with a comma before *but*. Choice *A* is incorrect because, without the comma, it is a run-on sentence. Choice *C* also lacks punctuation and uses *however*, which should be reserved for starting a new sentence or perhaps after a semicolon. Choice *D* is incorrect because the semicolon throws off the sentence structure and is incorrectly used; the correct revision would have also removed *but*.

29. A: Choice *A* is correct because the sentence does not require modification. Choice *B* is incorrect because it uses the faulty subject/verb agreement, "Physical proof are." Choice *C* is incorrect because a comma would need to follow *exists*. Choice *D* is incorrect because the comma after *science* is unnecessary.

30. D: Choice *D* correctly changes *this* to *the* and retains *validity*, making it the right choice. Choices *A* and *B* keep *this*, which is not as specific as "the." Choice *C* incorrectly pluralizes *validity*.

31. A: Choice *A* is correct because the sentence is fine without revisions. Choice *B* is incorrect, since removing *there is* is unnecessary and confusing. Choice *C* is incorrect since it inserts an unnecessary comma. Choice *D* introduces a homophone issue: *weather* refers to climatic states and atmospheric events, while *whether* expresses doubt, which is the author's intent.

32. C: Choice *C* correctly changes *continuing* to the present tense. Choice *A* is incorrect because of this out-of-place gerund use. Choice *B* not only does not fix this issue but also incorrectly changes *describe* into a gerund. While Choice *D* correctly uses *continue*, *describe* is incorrectly put in the past tense.

33. D: Choice *D* is correct, since it eliminates the unnecessary *as well* and adds a comma to separate the given example, making the sentence more direct. Choice *A* seems repetitive with *as well*, since it has *including*, and at the least needs punctuation. Choice *B* is poorly constructed, taking out the clearer *including*. Choice *C* also makes little sense.

34. B: Move the sentence so that it comes before the preceding sentence. For this question, place the underlined sentence in each prospective choice's position. To keep as-is is incorrect because the father *going crazy* doesn't logically follow the fact that he was a *city slicker*. Choice *C* is incorrect because the sentence in question is not a concluding sentence and does not transition smoothly into the second paragraph. Choice *D* is incorrect because the sentence doesn't necessarily need to be omitted since it logically follows the very first sentence in the passage.

35. D: Choice *D* is correct because "As it turns out" indicates a contrast from the previous sentiment, that the RV was a great purchase. Choice *A* is incorrect because the sentence needs an effective transition from the paragraph before. Choice *B* is incorrect because the text indicates it *is* surprising that the RV was a great purchase because the author was skeptical beforehand. Choice *C* is incorrect because the transition "Furthermore" does not indicate a contrast.

36. B: This sentence calls for parallel structure. Choice *B* is correct because the verbs "wake," "eat," and "break" are consistent in tense and parts of speech. Choice *A* is incorrect because the words "wake" and "eat" are present tense while the word "broke" is in past tense. Choice *C* is incorrect because this turns the sentence into a question, which doesn't make sense within the context. Choice *D* is incorrect because it breaks tense with the rest of the passage. "Waking," "eating," and "breaking" are all present participles, and the context around the sentence is in past tense.

37. C: Choice *C* is correct because it is clear, concise, and fits within the context of the passage. Choice *A* is incorrect because "We rejoiced as 'hackers'" does not give reason *why* hacking was rejoiced. Choice *B* is incorrect because it does not mention a solution being found and is therefore not specific enough. Choice *D* is incorrect because the meaning is eschewed by the helping verb "had to rejoice," and the sentence does not give enough detail as to what the problem entails.

38. A: The original sentence is correct because the verb tense as well as the order of the sentence makes sense in the given context. Choice *B* is incorrect because the order of the words makes the sentence more confusing than it otherwise would be. Choice *C* is incorrect because "We are even making" is in present tense. Choice *D* is incorrect because "We will make" is future tense. The surrounding text of the sentence is in past tense.

39. B: Choice *B* is correct because there is no punctuation needed if a dependent clause ("while traveling across America") is located behind the independent clause ("it allowed us to share adventures"). Choice *A* is incorrect because there are two dependent clauses connected and no independent clause, and a complete sentence requires at least one independent clause. Choice *C* is incorrect because of the same reason as Choice *A*. Semicolons have the same function as periods: there must be an independent clause on either side of the semicolon. Choice *D* is incorrect because the dash simply interrupts the complete sentence.

40. C: The rules for "me" and "I" is that one should use "I" when it is the subject pronoun of a sentence, and "me" when it is the object pronoun of the sentence. Break the sentence up to see if "I" or "me" should be used. To say "Those are memories that I have now shared" makes more sense than to say "Those are memories that me have now shared." Choice *D* is incorrect because "my siblings" should come before "I."

41. B: Choice *B* is correct because it adds an apostrophe to *ones*, which indicates *one's* possession of *survival*. Choice *A* doesn't do this, so it is incorrect. This is the same for Choice *C*, but that option also takes out the crucial comma after *Ju-jitsu*. Choice *D* is incorrect because it changes *play* to *plays*. This disagrees with the plural *Martial arts*, exemplified by having an example of its many forms, *Ju-jitsu*. Therefore, *play* is required.

42. C: Choice *C* is the best answer because it most clearly defines the point that the author is trying to make. The original sentence would need a comma after *however* in order to continue the sentence fluidly—but this option isn't available. Choice *B* is close, but this option changes the meaning of the sentence. Therefore, the best alternative is to begin the sentence with *However* and have a comma follow right after it in order to introduce a new idea. The original context is still maintained, but the flow of the language is more streamlined. Thus, Choice *A* is incorrect. Choice *D* would need a comma before and after *however*, so it is also incorrect.

43. A: Choice *A* is the best answer for several reasons. To begin, the section is grammatically correct in using a semicolon to connect the two independent clauses. This allows the two ideas to be connected without separating them. In this context, the semicolon makes more sense for the overall sentence structure and passage as a whole. Choice *B* is incorrect because it forms a run-on. Choice *C* applies a comma in incorrect positions. Choice *D* separates the sentence in a place that does not make sense for the context.

44. D: Choice *D* is the correct answer because it fixes two key issues. First, *their* is incorrectly used. *Their* is a possessive indefinite pronoun and also an antecedent—neither of these fit the context of the sentence, so Choices *A* and *B* are incorrect. What should be used instead is *they're*, which is the contraction of *they are*, emphasizing action or the result of action in this case. Choice *D* also corrects another contraction-related issue with *its*. Again, *its* indicates possession, while *it's* is the contraction of *it is*. The latter is what's needed for the sentence to make sense and be grammatically correct. Thus, Choice *C* is also incorrect.

45. A: Choice *A* is correct because the section contains no errors and clearly communicates the writer's point. Choice *B* is incorrect because it lacks a comma after *philosophy*, needed to link the first clause with the second. Choice *C* also has this issue but additionally alters *its* to *it's*; since *it is* does not make sense in this sentence, this is incorrect. Choice *D* is incorrect because *its* is already plural possessive and does not need an apostrophe on the end.

Math Test

1. B: 300 miles in 4 hours is $\frac{300}{4}$ = 75 miles per hour. In 1.5 hours, the car will go 1.5×75 miles, or 112.5 miles.

2. C: One apple/orange pair costs $3 total. Therefore, Jan bought 90/3 = 30 total pairs, and hence, she bought 30 oranges.

3. C: The formula for the volume of a box with rectangular sides is the length times width times height, so $5 \times 6 \times 3 = 90$ cubic feet.

4. D: First, the train's journey in the real word is 3 x 50 = 150 miles. On the map, 1 inch corresponds to 10 miles, so there is 150/10 = 15 inches on the map.

5. B: The total trip time is 1 + 3.5 + 0.5 = 5 hours. The total time driving is 1 + 0.5 = 1.5 hours. So, the fraction of time spent driving is 1.5/5 or 3/10. To get the percentage, convert this to a fraction out of 100. The numerator and denominator are multiplied by 10, with a result of 30/100. The percentage is the numerator in a fraction out of 100, so 30%.

6. B: The formula for the volume of a cylinder is $\pi r^2 h$, where *r* is the radius and *h* is the height. The diameter is twice the radius, so these barrels have a radius of 1 foot. That means each barrel has a volume of $\pi \times 1^2 \times 3 = 3\pi$ cubic feet. Since there are three of them, the total is $3 \times 3\pi = 9\pi$ cubic feet.

7. A: The tip is not taxed, so he pays 5% tax only on the $10. 5% of $10 is $0.05 \times 10 = \$0.50$. Add up $10 + $2 + $0.50 to get $12.50.

8. A: The first step is to divide up $150 into four equal parts. 150/4 is 37.5, so she needs to save an average of $37.50 per day.

9. D: 300/80 =30/8 = 15/4 =3.75. But Bernard is only working full days, so he will need to work 4 days, since 3 days is not sufficient.

10. A: The value went up by $165,000 − $150,000 = $15,000. Out of $150,000, this is $\frac{15,000}{150,000} = \frac{1}{10}$. Convert this to having a denominator of 100, the result is $\frac{10}{100}$ or 10%.

11. D: The total faculty is 15 + 20 = 35. Therefore, the faculty to student ratio is 35:200. Then, to simplify this ratio, both the numerator and the denominator are divided by 5, since 5 is a common factor of both, which yields 7:40.

12. B: The journey will be $5 \times 3 = 15$ miles. A car travelling at 60 miles per hour is travelling at 1 mile per minute. So, it will take 15/1 = 15 minutes to take the journey.

13. A: Taylor's total income is $20,000 + $10,000 = $30,000. 15% of this is $\frac{15}{100} = \frac{3}{20}$. So $\frac{3}{20} \times \$30,000 = \frac{90,000}{20} = \frac{9000}{2} = \$4500$.

14. B: Since the answer will be in cubic feet rather than inches, the first step is to convert from inches to feet for the dimensions of the box. There are 12 inches per foot, so the box is 24/12 = 2 feet wide, 18/12 = 1.5 feet deep, and 12/12 = 1 foot high. The volume is the product of these three together: $2 \times 1.5 \times 1 = 3$ cubic feet.

15. D: Kristen bought four DVDs, which would cost a total of $4 \times 15 = \$60$. She spent a total of $100, so she spent $100 − $60 = $40 on CDs. Since they cost $10 each, she must have purchased 40/10 = four CDs.

16. D: This problem can be solved by setting up a proportion involving the given information and the unknown value. The proportion is $\frac{21\ pages}{4\ nights} = \frac{140\ pages}{x\ nights}$. Solving the proportion by cross-multiplying, the equation becomes $21x = 4 * 140$, where $x = 26.67$. Since it is not an exact number of nights, the answer is rounded up to 27 nights. Twenty-six nights would not give Sarah enough time.

17. D: This problem can be solved by using unit conversion. The initial units are miles per minute. The final units need to be feet per second. Converting miles to feet uses the equivalence statement 1 mile = 5,280 feet. Converting minutes to seconds uses the equivalence statement 1 minute = 60 seconds. Setting up the ratios to convert the units is shown in the following equation:

$$\frac{72\ miles}{90\ minutes} * \frac{1\ minute}{60\ seconds} * \frac{5280\ feet}{1\ mile} = 70.4\ feet\ per\ second$$

The initial units cancel out, and the new units are left.

18. C: The sum total percentage of a pie chart must equal 100%. Since the CD sales take up less than half of the chart and more than a quarter (25%), it can be determined to be 40% overall. This can also be measured with a protractor. The angle of a circle is 360°. Since 25% of 360 would be 90° and 50% would be 180°, the angle percentage of CD sales falls in between; therefore, it would be Choice *C*.

19. B: Since $850 is the price *after* a 20% discount, $850 represents 80% of the original price. To determine the original price, set up a proportion with the ratio of the sale price (850) to original price (unknown) equal to the ratio of sale percentage:

$$\frac{850}{x} = \frac{80}{100}$$

(where *x* represents the unknown original price)

To solve a proportion, cross multiply the numerators and denominators and set the products equal to each other: (850) x (100) = (80) x (x). Multiplying each side results in the equation 85,000 = 80x.

To solve for *x*, both sides get divided by 80: $\frac{85,000}{80} = \frac{80x}{80}$, resulting in x = 1062.5. Remember that *x* represents the original price. Subtracting the sale price from the original price ($1062.50 – $850) indicates that Frank saved $212.50.

20. C: 40*N* would be 4000% of *N*. It's possible to check that each of the others is actually 40% of *N*.

21. C: An *x*-intercept is the point where the graph crosses the *x*-axis. At this point, the value of *y* is 0. To determine if an equation has an *x*-intercept of −2, substitute −2 for *x*, and calculate the value of *y*. If the value of −2 for *x* corresponds with a *y*-value of 0, then the equation has an *x*-intercept of −2. The only answer choice that produces this result is Choice $C \rightarrow 0 = (-2)2 + 5(-2) + 6$.

22. C: The conditional frequency of a girl being potty-trained is calculated by dividing the number of potty-trained girls by the total number of girls: $34 \div 52 = 0.65$. To determine the conditional probability, multiply the conditional frequency by 100: $0.65 \times 100 = 65\%$.

23. A: A sample statistic indicates information about the data that was collected (in this case, the heights of those surveyed). A population parameter describes an aspect of the entire population (in this case, all twelve-year-old boys in the United States). A confidence interval would consist of a range of heights likely to include the actual population parameter. Measurement error relates to the validity of the data that was collected.

24. C: To ensure valid results, samples should be taken across the entire scope of the study. Since all states are not equally populated, representing each state proportionately would result in a more accurate statistic.

25. D: Exponential functions can be written in the form: $y = a \cdot b^x$. The equation for an exponential function can be written given the *y*-intercept (*a*) and the growth rate (*b*). The *y*-intercept is the output (*y*) when the input (*x*) equals zero. It can be thought of as an "original value," or starting point. The value of *b* is the rate at which the original value increases ($b > 1$) or decreases ($b < 1$). In this scenario, the *y*-intercept, *a*, would be $1200, and the growth rate, *b*, would be 1.01 (100% of the original value + 1% interest = 101% = 1.01).

26. C: 85% of a number means multiplying that number by 0.85. So, $0.85 \times 20 = \frac{85}{100} \times \frac{20}{1}$, which can be simplified to $\frac{17}{20} \times \frac{20}{1} = 17$.

27. A: To find the fraction of the bill that the first three people pay, the fractions need to be added, which means finding common denominator. The common denominator will be 60.

$$\frac{1}{5} + \frac{1}{4} + \frac{1}{3} = \frac{12}{60} + \frac{15}{60} + \frac{20}{60} = \frac{47}{60}$$

The remainder of the bill is $1 - \frac{47}{60} = \frac{60}{60} - \frac{47}{60} = \frac{13}{60}$.

28. D: $9\frac{3}{10}$

To convert a decimal to a fraction, remember that any number to the left of the decimal point will be a whole number. Then, sense 0.3 goes to the tenths place, it can be placed over 10.

29. A: These numbers to improper fractions: $\frac{11}{3} - \frac{9}{5}$. Take 15 as a common denominator:

$$\frac{11}{3} - \frac{9}{5} =: \frac{55}{15} - \frac{27}{15} = \frac{28}{15} = 1\frac{13}{15}$$

(when rewritten to get rid of the partial fraction).

30. B: Dividing by 98 can be approximated by dividing by 100, which would mean shifting the decimal point of the numerator to the left by 2. The result is 4.2 and rounds to 4.

31. B: $4\frac{1}{3} + 3\frac{3}{4} = 4 + 3 + \frac{1}{3} + \frac{3}{4} = 7 + \frac{1}{3} + \frac{3}{4}$

Adding the fractions gives:

$$\frac{1}{3} + \frac{3}{4} = \frac{4}{12} + \frac{9}{12} = \frac{13}{12} = 1 + \frac{1}{12}$$

Thus:

$$7 + \frac{1}{3} + \frac{3}{4} 7 + 1 + \frac{1}{12} = 8\frac{1}{12}$$

32. C: The average is calculated by adding all six numbers, then dividing by 6. The first five numbers have a sum of 25. If the total divided by 6 is equal to 6, then the total itself must be 36. The sixth number must be 36 – 25 = 11.

33. C: The domain consists of all possible inputs, or x-values. The scenario states that the function approximates the population between the years 1900 and 2000. It also states that $x = 0$ represents the year 1900. Therefore, the year 2000 would be represented by $x = 100$. Only inputs between 0 and 100 are relevant in this case.

34. C: Nothing is added to x and y since the center is 0 and 5^2 is 25. Choice A is not the correct answer because you do not subtract the radius from x and y. Choice B is not the correct answer because you must square the radius on the right side of the equation. Choice D is not the correct answer because you do not add the radius to x and y in the equation.

35. D: Subtract the center from the x and y values of the equation and square the radius on the right side of the equation. Choice A is not the correct answer because you need to square the radius of the equation. Choice *B* is not the correct answer because you do not square the centers of the equation. Choice *C* is not the correct answer because you need to subtract (not add) the centers of the equation.

36. C: Plug in the values for *x* and *y* to discover that the solution works, which is $(-3)^2 + (-4)^2 = 25$. Choices *A* and *B* are not the correct answers since the solution works. Choice *D* is not the correct answer because there is enough information to tell where the given point lies on the circle.

37. D: The correct answer of 20 °C can be found using the appropriate temperature conversion formula:

$$°C = (°F - 32) \times \frac{5}{9}$$

38. D: The slope is given by the change in *y* divided by the change in *x*. Specifically, it's:

$$slope = \frac{y_2 - y_1}{x_2 - x_1}$$

The first point is (-5,-3) and the second point is (0,-1). Work from left to right when identifying coordinates. Thus the point on the left is point 1 (-5,-3) and the point on the right is point 2 (0,-1).

Now we need to just plug those numbers into the equation:

$$slope = \frac{-1 - (-3)}{0 - (-5)}$$

It can be simplified to:

$$slope = \frac{-1 + 3}{0 + 5}$$

$$slope = \frac{2}{5}$$

39. B: The figure is composed of three sides of a square and a semicircle. The sides of the square are simply added: 9 + 9 + 9 = 27 feet. The circumference of a circle is found by the equation C = 2πr. The radius is 4, so the circumference of the circle is 25.13 ft. Only half of the circle makes up the outer border of the figure (part of the perimeter) so half of 25.13 feet is 12.565 ft. Therefore, the total perimeter is: 27 ft + 12.565 ft = 39.565 ft. The other answer choices use the incorrect formula or fail to include all of the necessary sides.

40. A: The first step is to determine the unknown, which is in terms of the length, *l*.

The second step is to translate the problem into the equation using the perimeter of a rectangle, $P = 2l + 2w$. The width is the length minus 2 centimeters. The resulting equation is $2l + 2(l - 2) = 44$. The equation can be solved as follows:

$2l + 2l - 4 = 44$	Apply the distributive property on the left side of the equation
$4l - 4 = 44$	Combine like terms on the left side of the equation
$4l = 48$	Add 4 to both sides of the equation
$l = 12$	Divide both sides of the equation by 4

The length of the rectangle is 12 centimeters. The width is the length minus 2 centimeters, which is 10 centimeters. Checking the answers for length and width forms the following equation:

$$44 = 2(12) + 2(10)$$

The equation can be solved using the order of operations to form a true statement: $44 = 44$.

41. B: $3x^2 - 3x + 11$. By distributing the implied one in front of the first set of parentheses and the -1 in front of the second set of parentheses, the parenthesis can be eliminated:

$$1(5x^2 - 3x + 4) - 1(2x^2 - 7) = 5x^2 - 3x + 4 - 2x^2 + 7$$

Next, like terms (same variables with same exponents) are combined by adding the coefficients and keeping the variables and their powers the same: $5x^2 - 3x + 4 - 2x^2 + 7 = 3x^2 - 3x + 11$.

42. A: 63.96%

This question involves the percent formula. Since, we're beginning with a percent, also known as a number over 100, we'll put 39 on the right side of the equation:

$$\frac{x}{164} = \frac{39}{100}$$

Now, multiple 164 and 39 to get 6,396, which then needs to be divided by 100.

$$6,396 \div 100 = 63.96$$

43. C: Kimberley worked 4.5 hours at the rate of \$10/h and 1 hour at the rate of \$12/h. The problem states that her pay is rounded to the nearest hour, so the 4.5 hours would round up to 5 hours at the rate of \$10/h. (5h) x (\$10/h) + (1h) x (\$12/h) = \$50 + \$12 = \$62.

44. B: The first step is to calculate the difference between the larger value and the smaller value.

$$378 - 252 = 126$$

To calculate this difference as a percentage of the original value, and thus calculate the percentage *increase*, 126 is divided by 252, then this result is multiplied by 100 to find the percentage = 50%, answer *B*.

45. C: In order to find the percentage by which the value of the car has been reduced, the current cash value should be subtracted from the initial value and then the difference divided by the initial value. The result should be multiplied by 100 to find the percentage decrease.

$$\frac{20,000 - 8,000}{20,000} = .6$$

$$(.60) \times 100 = 60\%$$

46. A: This problem can be solved by simple multiplication and addition. Since the sale date is over six years apart, 6 can be multiplied by 12 for the number of months in a year, and then the remaining 4 months can be added.

$$(6 \times 12) + 4 = ?$$

$$72 + 4 = 76$$

47. D: This problem can be solved using basic arithmetic. Xavier starts with 20 apples, then gives his sister half, so 20 divided by 2.

$$\frac{20}{2} = 10$$

He then gives his neighbor 6, so 6 is subtracted from 10.

$$10 - 6 = 4$$

Lastly, he uses ¾ of his apples to make an apple pie, so to find remaining apples, the first step is to subtract ¾ from one and then multiply the difference by 4.

$$\left(1 - \frac{3}{4}\right) \times 4 = ?$$

$$\left(\frac{4}{4} - \frac{3}{4}\right) \times 4 = ?$$

$$\left(\frac{1}{4}\right) \times 4 = 1$$

48. B: $\frac{5}{2} \div \frac{1}{3} = \frac{5}{2} \times \frac{3}{1} = \frac{15}{2} = 7.5$.

49. A: The total fraction taken up by green and red shirts will be $\frac{1}{3} + \frac{2}{5} = \frac{5}{15} + \frac{6}{15} = \frac{11}{15}$. The remaining fraction is $1 - \frac{11}{15} = \frac{15}{15} - \frac{11}{15} = \frac{4}{15}$.

50. C: If she has used 1/3 of the paint, she has 2/3 remaining. $2\frac{1}{2}$ gallons are the same as $\frac{5}{2}$ gallons. The calculation is $\frac{2}{3} \times \frac{5}{2} = \frac{5}{3} = 1\frac{2}{3}$ gallons.

51. C: The volume of a cylinder is $\pi r^2 h$, and $\pi \times 6^2 \times 2$ is $72\,\pi$ cm³. Choice A is not the correct answer because that is only $6^2 \times \pi$. Choice B is not the correct answer because that is $2^2 \times 6 \times \pi$. Choice D is not the correct answer because that is $2^3 \times 6 \times \pi$.

52. B: This answer is correct because $3^2 + 4^2$ is $9 + 16$, which is 25. Taking the square root of 25 is 5. Choice A is not the correct answer because that is $3 + 4$. Choice C is not the correct answer because that is stopping at $3^2 + 4^2$ is $9 + 16$, which is 25. Choice D is not the correct answer because that is 3×4.

53. A: Setting up a proportion is the easiest way to represent this situation. The proportion becomes $\frac{20}{x} = \frac{40}{100}$, where cross-multiplication can be used to solve for x. The answer can also be found by observing the two fractions as equivalent, knowing that twenty is half of forty, and fifty is half of one-hundred.

54.

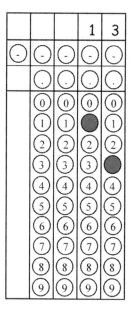

To solve the problem, a proportion is written consisting of ratios comparing distance and time. One way to set up the proportion is: $\frac{3}{48} = \frac{5}{x}\left(\frac{distance}{time} = \frac{distance}{time}\right)$ where x represents the unknown value of time. To solve a proportion, the ratios are cross-multiplied: $(3)(x) = (5)(48) \rightarrow 3x = 240$. The equation is solved by isolating the variable, or dividing by 3 on both sides, to produce $x = 80$.

55.

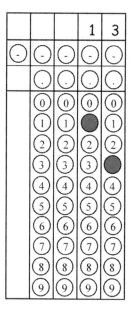

Perimeter is found by calculating the sum of all sides of the polygon. $9 + 9 + 9 + 8 + 8 + s = 56$, where s is the missing side length. Therefore, 43 plus the missing side length is equal to 56. The missing side length is 13 cm.

56.

			3	0
-	-	-	-	-
	.	.	.	.
0	0	0	●	
1	1	1	1	
2	2	2	2	
3	3	●	3	
4	4	4	4	
5	5	5	5	
6	6	6	6	
7	7	7	7	
8	8	8	8	
9	9	9	9	

Because x and y are complementary, the $\sin(x) = \cos(y)$. Therefore, the answer is 30 degrees.

57.

			1	0
-	-	-	-	-
	.	.	.	.
0	0	0	●	
1	1	●	1	
2	2	2	2	
3	3	3	3	
4	4	4	4	
5	5	5	5	
6	6	6	6	
7	7	7	7	
8	8	8	8	
9	9	9	9	

Each instance of x is replaced with a 2, and each instance of y is replaced with a 3 to get $2^2 - 2 \cdot 2 \cdot 3 + 2 \cdot 3^2 = 4 - 12 + 18 = 10$.

58.

Add 3 to both sides to get $4x = 8$. Then divide both sides by 4 to get $x = 2$.

Practice Test #3

Reading Test

Passage #1

Questions 1-6 are based upon the following passage:

This excerpt is an adaptation of Jonathan Swift's *Gulliver's Travels into Several Remote Nations of the World.*

My gentleness and good behaviour had gained so far on the emperor and his court, and indeed upon the army and people in general, that I began to conceive hopes of getting my liberty in a short time. I took all possible methods to cultivate this favourable disposition. The natives came, by degrees, to be less apprehensive of any danger from me. I would sometimes lie down, and let five or six of them dance on my hand; and at last the boys and girls would venture to come and play at hide-and-seek in my hair. I had now made a good progress in understanding and speaking the language. The emperor had a mind one day to entertain me with several of the country shows, wherein they exceed all nations I have known, both for dexterity and magnificence. I was diverted with none so much as that of the rope-dancers, performed upon a slender white thread, extended about two feet, and twelve inches from the ground. Upon which I shall desire liberty, with the reader's patience, to enlarge a little.

This diversion is only practised by those persons who are candidates for great employments, and high favour at court. They are trained in this art from their youth, and are not always of noble birth, or liberal education. When a great office is vacant, either by death or disgrace (which often happens,) five or six of those candidates petition the emperor to entertain his majesty and the court with a dance on the rope; and whoever jumps the highest, without falling, succeeds in the office. Very often the chief ministers themselves are commanded to show their skill, and to convince the emperor that they have not lost their faculty. Flimnap, the treasurer, is allowed to cut a caper on the straight rope, at least an inch higher than any other lord in the whole empire. I have seen him do the summerset several times together, upon a trencher fixed on a rope which is no thicker than a common packthread in England. My friend Reldresal, principal secretary for private affairs, is, in my opinion, if I am not partial, the second after the treasurer; the rest of the great officers are much upon a par.

1. Which of the following statements best summarize the central purpose of this text?
   a. Gulliver details his fondness for the archaic yet interesting practices of his captors.
   b. Gulliver conjectures about the intentions of the aristocratic sector of society.
   c. Gulliver becomes acquainted with the people and practices of his new surroundings.
   d. Gulliver's differences cause him to become penitent around new acquaintances.

2. What is the word *principal* referring to in the following text?

> My friend Reldresal, principal secretary for private affairs, is, in my opinion, if I am not partial, the second after the treasurer; the rest of the great officers are much upon a par.

    a. Primary or chief
    b. An acolyte
    c. An individual who provides nurturing
    d. One in a subordinate position

3. What can the reader infer from this passage?

> I would sometimes lie down, and let five or six of them dance on my hand; and at last the boys and girls would venture to come and play at hide-and-seek in my hair.

    a. The children tortured Gulliver.
    b. Gulliver traveled because he wanted to meet new people.
    c. Gulliver is considerably larger than the children who are playing around him.
    d. Gulliver has a genuine love and enthusiasm for people of all sizes.

4. What is the significance of the word *mind* in the following passage?

> The emperor had a mind one day to entertain me with several of the country shows, wherein they exceed all nations I have known, both for dexterity and magnificence.

    a. The ability to think
    b. A collective vote
    c. A definitive decision
    d. A mythological question

5. Which of the following assertions does not support the fact that games are a commonplace event in this culture?

    a. My gentlest and good behavior . . . short time.
    b. They are trained in this art from their youth . . . liberal education.
    c. Very often the chief ministers themselves are commanded to show their skill . . . not lost their faculty.
    d. Flimnap, the treasurer, is allowed to cut a caper on the straight rope . . . higher than any other lord in the whole empire.

6. How does Gulliver's description of Flimnap's, the treasurer's, ability to *cut a caper on the straight rope*, and Reldresal, principal secretary for private affairs, being the *second to the treasurer,* serve as evidence of the community's emphasis in regards to the correlation between physical strength and leadership abilities?

    a. Only children used Gulliver's hands as a playground.
    b. The two men who exhibited superior abilities held prominent positions in the community.
    c. Only common townspeople, not leaders, walk the straight rope.
    d. No one could jump higher than Gulliver.

Passage #2

Questions 7-12 are based upon the following passage:

This excerpt is adaptation of Robert Louis Stevenson's *The Strange Case of Dr. Jekyll and Mr. Hyde.*

"Did you ever come across a protégé of his—one Hyde?" He asked.

"Hyde?" repeated Lanyon. "No. Never heard of him. Since my time."

That was the amount of information that the lawyer carried back with him to the great, dark bed on which he tossed to and fro until the small hours of the morning began to grow large. It was a night of little ease to his toiling mind, toiling in mere darkness and besieged by questions.

Six o'clock struck on the bells of the church that was so conveniently near to Mr. Utterson's dwelling, and still he was digging at the problem. Hitherto it had touched him on the intellectual side alone; but; but now his imagination also was engaged, or rather enslaved; and as he lay and tossed in the gross darkness of the night in the curtained room, Mr. Enfield's tale went by before his mind in a scroll of lighted pictures. He would be aware of the great field of lamps in a nocturnal city; then of the figure of a man walking swiftly; then of a child running from the doctor's; and then these met, and that human Juggernaut trod the child down and passed on regardless of her screams. Or else he would see a room in a rich house, where his friend lay asleep, dreaming and smiling at his dreams; and then the door of that room would be opened, the curtains of the bed plucked apart, the sleeper recalled, and, lo! There would stand by his side a figure to whom power was given, and even at that dead hour he must rise and do its bidding. The figure in these two phrases haunted the lawyer all night; and if at anytime he dozed over, it was but to see it glide more stealthily through sleeping houses, or move the more swiftly, and still the more smoothly, even to dizziness, through wider labyrinths of lamplighted city, and at every street corner crush a child and leave her screaming. And still the figure had no face by which he might know it; even in his dreams it had no face, or one that baffled him and melted before his eyes; and thus there it was that there sprung up and grew apace in the lawyer's mind a singularly strong, almost an inordinate, curiosity to behold the features of the real Mr. Hyde. If he could but once set eyes on him, he thought the mystery would lighten and perhaps roll altogether away, as was the habit of mysterious things when well examined. He might see a reason for his friend's strange preference or bondage, and even for the startling clauses of the will. And at least it would be a face worth seeing: the face of a man who was without bowels of mercy: a face which had but to show itself to raise up, in the mind of the unimpressionable Enfield, a spirit of enduring hatred.

From that time forward, Mr. Utterson began to haunt the door in the by street of shops. In the morning before office hours, at noon when business was plenty of time scares, at night under the face of the full city moon, by all lights and at all hours of solitude or concourse, the lawyer was to be found on his chosen post.

"If he be Mr. Hyde," he had thought, "I should be Mr. Seek."

7. What is the purpose of the use of repetition in the following passage?

> It was a night of little ease to his toiling mind, toiling in mere darkness and besieged by questions.

a. It serves as a demonstration of the mental state of Mr. Lanyon.
b. It is reminiscent of the church bells that are mentioned in the story.
c. It mimics Mr. Utterson's ambivalence.
d. It emphasizes Mr. Utterson's anguish in failing to identify Hyde's whereabouts.

8. What is the setting of the story in this passage?

a. In the city
b. On the countryside
c. In a jail
d. In a mental health facility

9. What can one infer about the meaning of the word "Juggernaut" from the author's use of it in the passage?

a. It is an apparition that appears at daybreak.
b. It scares children.
c. It is associated with space travel.
d. Mr. Utterson finds it soothing.

10. What is the definition of the word *haunt* in the following passage?

> From that time forward, Mr. Utterson began to haunt the door in the by street of shops. In the morning before office hours, at noon when business was plenty of time scares, at night under the face of the full city moon, by all lights and at all hours of solitude or concourse, the lawyer was to be found on his chosen post.

a. To levitate
b. To constantly visit
c. To terrorize
d. To daunt

11. The phrase *labyrinths of lamplighted city* contains an example of what?

a. Hyperbole
b. Simile
c. Metaphor
d. Alliteration

12. What can one reasonably conclude from the final comment of this passage?

> "If he be Mr. Hyde," he had thought, "I should be Mr. Seek."

a. The speaker is considering a name change.
b. The speaker is experiencing an identity crisis.
c. The speaker has mistakenly been looking for the wrong person.
d. The speaker intends to continue to look for Hyde.

Passage #3

Questions 13-18 are based upon the following passage:

This excerpt is adaptation from "What to the Slave is the Fourth of July?" Rochester, New York July 5, 1852

Fellow citizens—Pardon me, and allow me to ask, why am I called upon to speak here today? What have I, or those I represent, to do with your national independence? Are the great principles of political freedom and of natural justice embodied in that Declaration of Independence, Independence extended to us? And am I therefore called upon to bring our humble offering to the national altar, and to confess the benefits, and express devout gratitude for the blessings, resulting from your independence to us?

Would to God, both for your sakes and ours, ours that an affirmative answer could be truthfully returned to these questions! Then would my task be light, and my burden easy and delightful. For who is there so cold that a nation's sympathy could not warm him? Who so obdurate and dead to the claims of gratitude, gratitude that that would not thankfully acknowledge such priceless benefits? Who so stolid and selfish, that would not give his voice to swell the hallelujahs of a nation's jubilee, when the chains of servitude had been torn from his limbs? I am not that man. In a case like that, the dumb may eloquently speak, and the lame man leap as an hart.

But, such is not the state of the case. I say it with a sad sense of the disparity between us. I am not included within the pale of this glorious anniversary. Oh pity! Your high independence only reveals the immeasurable distance between us. The blessings in which you this day rejoice, I do not enjoy in common. The rich inheritance of justice, liberty, prosperity, and independence, bequeathed by your fathers, is shared by *you*, not by *me*. This Fourth of July is *yours,* not *mine*. You may rejoice, *I* must mourn. To drag a man in fetters into the grand illuminated temple of liberty, and call upon him to join you in joyous anthems, were inhuman mockery and sacrilegious irony. Do you mean, citizens, to mock me, by asking me to speak today? If so there is a parallel to your conduct. And let me warn you that it is dangerous to copy the example of a nation whose crimes, towering up to heaven, were thrown down by the breath of the Almighty, burying that nation and irrecoverable ruin! I can today take up the plaintive lament of a peeled and woe-smitten people.

By the rivers of Babylon, there we sat down. Yea! We wept when we remembered Zion. We hanged our harps upon the willows in the midst thereof. For there, they that carried us away captive, required of us a song; and they who wasted us required of us mirth, saying, "Sing us one of the songs of Zion." How can we sing the Lord's song in a strange land? If I forget thee, O Jerusalem, let my right hand forget her cunning. If I do not remember thee, let my tongue cleave to the roof of my mouth.

13. What is the tone of the first paragraph of this passage?
   a. Exasperated
   b. Inclusive
   c. Contemplative
   d. Nonchalant

14. Which word CANNOT be used synonymously with the term *obdurate* as it is conveyed in the text below?

> Who so obdurate and dead to the claims of gratitude, that would not thankfully acknowledge such priceless benefits?

a. Steadfast
b. Stubborn
c. Contented
d. Unwavering

15. What is the central purpose of this text?
a. To demonstrate the author's extensive knowledge of the Bible
b. To address the feelings of exclusion expressed by African Americans after the establishment of the Fourth of July holiday
c. To convince wealthy landowners to adopt new holiday rituals
d. To explain why minorities often relished the notion of segregation in government institutions

16. Which statement serves as evidence of the question above?
a. By the rivers of Babylon . . . down.
b. Fellow citizens . . . today.
c. I can . . . woe-smitten people.
d. The rich inheritance of justice . . . *not by me.*

17. The statement below features an example of which of the following literary devices?

> Oh pity! Your high independence only reveals the immeasurable distance between us.

a. Assonance
b. Parallelism
c. Amplification
d. Hyperbole

18. The speaker's use of biblical references, such as "rivers of Babylon" and the "songs of Zion," helps the reader to do all of the following EXCEPT:
a. Identify with the speaker through the use of common text.
b. Convince the audience that injustices have been committed by referencing another group of people who have been previously affected by slavery.
c. Display the equivocation of the speaker and those that he represents.
d. Appeal to the listener's sense of humanity.

Passage #4

Questions 19-24 are based upon the following passage:

This excerpt is adaptation from Abraham Lincoln's Address Delivered at the Dedication of the Cemetery at Gettysburg, November 19, 1863.

> Four score and seven years ago our fathers brought forth on this continent, a new nation, conceived in liberty, and dedicated to the proposition that all men are created equal.

Now we are engaged in a great civil war, testing whether that nation, or any nation so conceived and so dedicated, can long endure. We are met on a great battlefield of that war. We have come to dedicate a portion of that field, as a final resting place for those who here gave their lives that this nation might live. It is altogether fitting and proper that we should do this.

But, in a larger sense, we cannot dedicate—we cannot consecrate that we cannot hallow—this ground. The brave men, living and dead, who struggled here, have consecrated it, far above our poor power to add or detract. The world will little note, nor long remember what we say here, but it can never forget what they did here. It is for us the living, rather, to be dedicated here to the unfinished work which they who fought here have thus far so nobly advanced. It is rather for us to be here and dedicated to the great task remaining before us—that from these honored dead we take increased devotion to that cause for which they gave the last full measure of devotion—that we here highly resolve that these dead shall not have died in vain—that these this nation, under God, shall have a new birth of freedom—and that government of people, by the people, for the people, shall not perish from the earth.

19. The best description for the phrase *four score and seven years ago* is which of the following?
    a. A unit of measurement
    b. A period of time
    c. A literary movement
    d. A statement of political reform

20. What is the setting of this text?
    a. A battleship off of the coast of France
    b. A desert plain on the Sahara Desert
    c. A battlefield in North America
    d. The residence of Abraham Lincoln

21. Which war is Abraham Lincoln referring to in the following passage?
    Now we are engaged in a great civil war, testing whether that nation, or any nation so conceived and so dedicated, can long endure.

    a. World War I
    b. The War of the Spanish Succession
    c. World War II
    d. The American Civil War

22. What message is the author trying to convey through this address?
    a. The audience should consider the death of the people that fought in the war as an example and perpetuate the ideals of freedom that the soldiers died fighting for.
    b. The audience should honor the dead by establishing an annual memorial service.
    c. The audience should form a militia that would overturn the current political structure.
    d. The audience should forget the lives that were lost and discredit the soldiers.

23. Which rhetorical device is being used in the following passage?

    . . . we here highly resolve that these dead shall not have died in vain—that these this nation, under God, shall have a new birth of freedom—and that government of people, by the people, for the people, shall not perish from the earth.

    a. Antimetabole
    b. Antiphrasis
    c. Anaphora
    d. Epiphora

24. What is the effect of Lincoln's statement in the following passage?

    But, in a larger sense, we cannot dedicate—we cannot consecrate that we cannot hallow—this ground. The brave men, living and dead, who struggled here, have consecrated it, far above our poor power to add or detract.

    a. His comparison emphasizes the great sacrifice of the soldiers who fought in the war.
    b. His comparison serves as a remainder of the inadequacies of his audience.
    c. His comparison serves as a catalyst for guilt and shame among audience members.
    d. His comparison attempts to illuminate the great differences between soldiers and civilians.

Passage #5

Questions 25-30 are based upon the following passage:

This excerpt is adaptation from Charles Dickens' speech in Birmingham in England on December 30, 1853 on behalf of the Birmingham and Midland Institute.

My Good Friends,—When I first imparted to the committee of the projected Institute my particular wish that on one of the evenings of my readings here the main body of my audience should be composed of working men and their families, I was animated by two desires; first, by the wish to have the great pleasure of meeting you face to face at this Christmas time, and accompany you myself through one of my little Christmas books; and second, by the wish to have an opportunity of stating publicly in your presence, and in the presence of the committee, my earnest hope that the Institute will, from the beginning, recognise one great principle—strong in reason and justice—which I believe to be essential to the very life of such an Institution. It is, that the working man shall, from the first unto the last, have a share in the management of an Institution which is designed for his benefit, and which calls itself by his name.

I have no fear here of being misunderstood—of being supposed to mean too much in this. If there ever was a time when any one class could of itself do much for its own good, and for the welfare of society—which I greatly doubt—that time is unquestionably past. It is in the fusion of different classes, without confusion; in the bringing together of employers and employed; in the creating of a better common understanding among those whose interests are identical, who depend upon each other, who are vitally essential to each other, and who never can be in unnatural antagonism without deplorable results, that one of the chief principles of a Mechanics' Institution should consist. In this world a great deal of the bitterness among us arises from an imperfect understanding of one another. Erect in Birmingham a great Educational Institution, properly educational; educational of the feelings as well as of the reason; to which all orders of Birmingham men contribute; in which all orders of Birmingham men meet; wherein all orders of Birmingham men are faithfully represented—and you will erect a Temple of Concord here which will be a model edifice to the whole of England.

Contemplating as I do the existence of the Artisans' Committee, which not long ago considered the establishment of the Institute so sensibly, and supported it so heartily, I earnestly entreat the gentlemen—earnest I know in the good work, and who are now among us,—by all means to avoid the great shortcoming of similar institutions; and in asking the working man for his confidence, to set him the great example and give him theirs in return. You will judge for yourselves if I promise too much for the working man, when I say that he will stand by such an enterprise with the utmost of his patience, his perseverance, sense, and support; that I am sure he will need no charitable aid or condescending patronage; but will readily and cheerfully pay for the advantages which it confers; that he will prepare himself in individual cases where he feels that the adverse circumstances around him have rendered it necessary; in a word, that he will feel his responsibility like an honest man, and will most honestly and manfully discharge it. I now proceed to the pleasant task to which I assure you I have looked forward for a long time.

25. Which word is most closely synonymous with the word *patronage* as it appears in the following statement?

> . . . that I am sure he will need no charitable aid or condescending patronage

a. Auspices
b. Aberration
c. Acerbic
d. Adulation

26. Which term is most closely aligned with the definition of the term *working man* as it is defined in the following passage?

> You will judge for yourselves if I promise too much for the working man, when I say that he will stand by such an enterprise with the utmost of his patience, his perseverance, sense, and support . . .

a. Plebian
b. Viscount
c. Entrepreneur
d. Bourgeois

27. Which of the following statements most closely correlates with the definition of the term *working man* as it is defined in Question 26?

a. A working man is not someone who works for institutions or corporations, but someone who is well versed in the workings of the soul.
b. A working man is someone who is probably not involved in social activities because the physical demand for work is too high.
c. A working man is someone who works for wages among the middle class.
d. The working man has historically taken to the field, to the factory, and now to the screen.

28. Based upon the contextual evidence provided in the passage above, what is the meaning of the term *enterprise* in the third paragraph?
    a. Company
    b. Courage
    c. Game
    d. Cause

29. The speaker addresses his audience as *My Good Friends*—what kind of credibility does this salutation give to the speaker?
    a. The speaker is an employer addressing his employees, so the salutation is a way for the boss to bridge the gap between himself and his employees.
    b. The speaker's salutation is one from an entertainer to his audience and uses the friendly language to connect to his audience before a serious speech.
    c. The salutation gives the serious speech that follows a somber tone, as it is used ironically.
    d. The speech is one from a politician to the public, so the salutation is used to grab the audience's attention.

30. According to the aforementioned passage, what is the speaker's second desire for his time in front of the audience?
    a. To read a Christmas story
    b. For the working man to have a say in his institution which is designed for his benefit.
    c. To have an opportunity to stand in their presence
    d. For the life of the institution to be essential to the audience as a whole

Passage #6

Questions 31-36 are based upon the following passage:

This excerpt is adapted from *Our Vanishing Wildlife,* by William T. Hornaday

> Three years ago, I think there were not many bird-lovers in the United States, who believed it possible to prevent the total extinction of both egrets from our fauna. All the known rookeries accessible to plume-hunters had been totally destroyed. Two years ago, the secret discovery of several small, hidden colonies prompted William Dutcher, President of the National Association of Audubon Societies, and Mr. T. Gilbert Pearson, Secretary, to attempt the protection of those colonies. With a fund contributed for the purpose, wardens were hired and duly commissioned. As previously stated, one of those wardens was shot dead in cold blood by a plume hunter. The task of guarding swamp rookeries from the attacks of money-hungry desperadoes to whom the accursed plumes were worth their weight in gold, is a very chancy proceeding. There is now one warden in Florida who says that "before they get my rookery they will first have to get me."

> Thus far the protective work of the Audubon Association has been successful. Now there are twenty colonies, which contain all told, about 5,000 egrets and about 120,000 herons and ibises which are guarded by the Audubon wardens. One of the most important is on Bird Island, a mile out in Orange Lake, central Florida, and it is ably defended by Oscar E. Baynard. To-day, the plume hunters who do not dare to raid the guarded rookeries are trying to study out the lines of flight of the birds, to and from their feeding-grounds, and shoot them in transit. Their motto is—"Anything to beat the law, and get the plumes." It is there that the state of Florida should take part in the war.

The success of this campaign is attested by the fact that last year a number of egrets were seen in eastern Massachusetts—for the first time in many years. And so to-day the question is, can the wardens continue to hold the plume-hunters at bay?

31. The author's use of first person pronoun in the following text does NOT have which of the following effects?

Three years ago, I think there were not many bird-lovers in the United States, who believed it possible to prevent the total extinction of both egrets from our fauna.

    a. The phrase *I think* acts as a sort of hedging, where the author's tone is less direct and/or absolute.
    b. It allows the reader to more easily connect with the author.
    c. It encourages the reader to empathize with the egrets.
    d. It distances the reader from the text by overemphasizing the story.

32. What purpose does the quote serve at the end of the first paragraph?
    a. The quote shows proof of a hunter threatening one of the wardens.
    b. The quote lightens the mood by illustrating the colloquial language of the region.
    c. The quote provides an example of a warden protecting one of the colonies.
    d. The quote provides much needed comic relief in the form of a joke.

33. What is the meaning of the word *rookeries* in the following text?

To-day, the plume hunters who do not dare to raid the guarded rookeries are trying to study out the lines of flight of the birds, to and from their feeding-grounds, and shoot them in transit.

    a. Houses in a slum area
    b. A place where hunters gather to trade tools
    c. A place where wardens go to trade stories
    d. A colony of breeding birds

34. What is on Bird Island?
    a. Hunters selling plumes
    b. An important bird colony
    c. Bird Island Battle between the hunters and the wardens
    d. An important egret with unique plumes

35. What is the main purpose of the passage?
    a. To persuade the audience to act in preservation of the bird colonies
    b. To show the effect hunting egrets has had on the environment
    c. To argue that the preservation of bird colonies has had a negative impact on the environment.
    d. To demonstrate the success of the protective work of the Audubon Association

36. Why are hunters trying to study the lines of flight of the birds?
    a. To study ornithology, one must know the lines of flight that birds take.
    b. To help wardens preserve the lives of the birds
    c. To have a better opportunity to hunt the birds
    d. To builds their homes under the lines of flight because they believe it brings good luck

Passage #7

Questions 37-42 are based upon the following passage, which is an is adaptation from The Life-Story of Insects, by Geo H. Carpenter:

Insects as a whole are preeminently creatures of the land and the air. This is shown not only by the possession of wings by a vast majority of the class, but by the mode of breathing to which reference has already been made, a system of branching air-tubes carrying atmospheric air with its combustion-supporting oxygen to all the insect's tissues. The air gains access to these tubes through a number of paired air-holes or spiracles, arranged segmentally in series.

It is of great interest to find that, nevertheless, a number of insects spend much of their time under water. This is true of not a few in the perfect winged state, as for example aquatic beetles and water-bugs ('boatmen' and 'scorpions') which have some way of protecting their spiracles when submerged, and, possessing usually the power of flight, can pass on occasion from pond or stream to upper air. But it is advisable in connection with our present subject to dwell especially on some insects that remain continually under water till they are ready to undergo their final moult and attain the winged state, which they pass entirely in the air. The preparatory instars of such insects are aquatic; the adult instar is aerial. All may-flies, dragon-flies, and caddis-flies, many beetles and two-winged flies, and a few moths thus divide their life-story between the water and the air. For the present we confine attention to the Stone-flies, the May-flies, and the Dragon-flies, three well-known orders of insects respectively called by systematists the Plecoptera, the Ephemeroptera and the Odonata.

In the case of many insects that have aquatic larvae, the latter are provided with some arrangement for enabling them to reach atmospheric air through the surface-film of the water. But the larva of a stone-fly, a dragon-fly, or a may-fly is adapted more completely than these for aquatic life; it can, by means of gills of some kind, breathe the air dissolved in water.

37. Which statement best details the central idea in this passage?
   a. It introduces certain insects that transition from water to air.
   b. It delves into entomology, especially where gills are concerned.
   c. It defines what constitutes as insects' breathing.
   d. It invites readers to have a hand in the preservation of insects.

38. Which definition most closely relates to the usage of the word *moult* in the passage?
   a. An adventure of sorts, especially underwater
   b. Mating act between two insects
   c. The act of shedding part or all of the outer shell
   d. Death of an organism that ends in a revival of life

39. What is the purpose of the first paragraph in relation to the second paragraph?
   a. The first paragraph serves as a cause and the second paragraph serves as an effect.
   b. The first paragraph serves as a contrast to the second.
   c. The first paragraph is a description for the argument in the second paragraph.
   d. The first and second paragraphs are merely presented in a sequence.

40. What does the following sentence most nearly mean?
    The preparatory instars of such insects are aquatic; the adult instar is aerial.

    a. The volume of water is necessary to prep the insect for transition rather than the volume of the air.
    b. The abdomen of the insect is designed like a star in the water as well as the air.
    c. The stage of preparation in between molting is acted out in the water, while the last stage is in the air.
    d. These insects breathe first in the water through gills yet continue to use the same organs to breathe in the air.

41. Which of the statements reflect information that one could reasonably infer based on the author's tone?
    a. The author's tone is persuasive and attempts to call the audience to action.
    b. The author's tone is passionate due to excitement over the subject and personal narrative.
    c. The author's tone is informative and exhibits interest in the subject of the study.
    d. The author's tone is somber, depicting some anger at the state of insect larvae.

42. Which statement best describes stoneflies, mayflies, and dragonflies?
    a. They are creatures of the land and the air.
    b. They have a way of protecting their spiracles when submerged.
    c. Their larvae can breathe the air dissolved in water through gills of some kind.
    d. The preparatory instars of these insects are aerial.

Passage #8

Questions 43-47 are based upon the following passage, which is an adaptation from "The 'Hatchery' of the Sun-Fish"--- Scientific American, #711:

I have thought that an example of the intelligence (instinct?) of a class of fish which has come under my observation during my excursions into the Adirondack region of New York State might possibly be of interest to your readers, especially as I am not aware that any one except myself has noticed it, or, at least, has given it publicity.

The female sun-fish (called, I believe, in England, the roach or bream) makes a "hatchery" for her eggs in this wise. Selecting a spot near the banks of the numerous lakes in which this region abounds, and where the water is about 4 inches deep, and still, she builds, with her tail and snout, a circular embankment 3 inches in height and 2 thick. The circle, which is as perfect a one as could be formed with mathematical instruments, is usually a foot and a half in diameter; and at one side of this circular wall an opening is left by the fish of just sufficient width to admit her body.

The mother sun-fish, having now built or provided her "hatchery," deposits her spawn within the circular inclosure, and mounts guard at the entrance until the fry are hatched out and are sufficiently large to take charge of themselves. As the embankment, moreover, is built up to the surface of the water, no enemy can very easily obtain an entrance within the inclosure from the top; while there being only one entrance, the fish is able, with comparative ease, to keep out all intruders.

I have, as I say, noticed this beautiful instinct of the sun-fish for the perpetuity of her species more particularly in the lakes of this region; but doubtless the same habit is common to these fish in other waters.

43. What is the purpose of this passage?
   a. To show the effects of fish hatcheries on the Adirondack region
   b. To persuade the audience to study Ichthyology (fish science)
   c. To depict the sequence of mating among sun-fish
   d. To enlighten the audience on the habits of sun-fish and their hatcheries

44. What does the word *wise* in this passage most closely mean?
   a. Knowledge
   b. Manner
   c. Shrewd
   d. Ignorance

45. What is the definition of the word *fry* as it appears in the following passage?
   The mother sun-fish, having now built or provided her "hatchery," deposits her spawn within the circular inclosure, and mounts guard at the entrance until the fry are hatched out and are sufficiently large to take charge of themselves.

   a. Fish at the stage of development where they are capable of feeding themselves.
   b. Fish eggs that have been fertilized.
   c. A place where larvae is kept out of danger from other predators.
   d. A dish where fish is placed in oil and fried until golden brown.

46. How is the circle that keeps the larvae of the sun-fish made?
   a. It is formed with mathematical instruments.
   b. The sun-fish builds it with her tail and snout.
   c. It is provided to her as a "hatchery" by Mother Nature.
   d. The sun-fish builds it with her larvae.

47. The author included the third paragraph in the following passage to achieve which of the following effects?
   a. To complicate the subject matter
   b. To express a bias
   c. To insert a counterargument
   d. To conclude a sequence and add a final detail

Passage #9

Questions 48-56 are based on the following passage.

In the quest to understand existence, modern philosophers must question if humans can fully comprehend the world. Classical western approaches to philosophy tend to hold that one can understand something, be it an event or object, by standing outside of the phenomena and observing it. It is then by unbiased observation that one can grasp the details of the world. This seems to hold true for many things. Scientists conduct experiments and record their findings, and thus many natural phenomena become comprehendible. However, several of these observations were possible because humans used tools in order to make these discoveries.

This may seem like an extraneous matter. After all, people invented things like microscopes and telescopes in order to enhance their capacity to view cells or the movement of stars. While humans are still capable of seeing things, the question remains if human beings have the capacity to fully observe and see the world in order to understand it. It would not be an impossible stretch to argue that what humans see through a microscope is not the exact thing itself, but a human interpretation of it.

This would seem to be the case in the "Business of the Holes" experiment conducted by Richard Feynman. To study the way electrons behave, Feynman set up a barrier with two holes and a plate. The plate was there to indicate how many times the electrons would pass through the hole(s). Rather than casually observe the electrons acting under normal circumstances, Feynman discovered that electrons behave in two totally different ways depending on whether or not they are observed. The electrons that were observed had passed through either one of the holes or were caught on the plate as particles. However, electrons that weren't observed acted as waves instead of particles and passed through both holes. This indicated that electrons have a dual nature. Electrons seen by the human eye act like particles, while unseen electrons act like waves of energy.

This dual nature of the electrons presents a conundrum. While humans now have a better understanding of electrons, the fact remains that people cannot entirely perceive how electrons behave without the use of instruments. We can only observe one of the mentioned behaviors, which only provides a partial understanding of the entire function of electrons. Therefore, we're forced to ask ourselves whether the world we observe is objective or if it is subjectively perceived by humans. Or, an alternative question: can man understand the world only through machines that will allow them to observe natural phenomena?

Both questions humble man's capacity to grasp the world. However, those ideas don't take into account that many phenomena have been proven by human beings without the use of machines, such as the discovery of gravity. Like all philosophical questions, whether man's reason and observation alone can understand the universe can be approached from many angles.

48. The word *extraneous* in paragraph two can be best interpreted as referring to which one of the following?
    a. Indispensable
    b. Bewildering
    c. Superfluous
    d. Exuberant

49. What is the author's motivation for writing the passage?
    a. Bring to light an alternative view on human perception by examining the role of technology in human understanding.
    b. Educate the reader on the latest astroparticle physics discovery and offer terms that may be unfamiliar to the reader.
    c. Argue that humans are totally blind to the realities of the world by presenting an experiment that proves that electrons are not what they seem on the surface.
    d. Reflect on opposing views of human understanding.

50. Which of the following most closely resembles the way in which paragraph four is structured?
    a. It offers one solution, questions the solution, and then ends with an alternative solution.
    b. It presents an inquiry, explains the detail of that inquiry, and then offers a solution.
    c. It presents a problem, explains the details of that problem, and then ends with more inquiry.
    d. It gives a definition, offers an explanation, and then ends with an inquiry.

51. For the classical approach to understanding to hold true, which of the following must be required?
    a. A telescope.
    b. The person observing must prove their theory beyond a doubt.
    c. Multiple witnesses present.
    d. The person observing must be unbiased.

52. Which best describes how the electrons in the experiment behaved like waves?
    a. The electrons moved up and down like actual waves.
    b. The electrons passed through both holes and then onto the plate.
    c. The electrons converted to photons upon touching the plate.
    d. Electrons were seen passing through one hole or the other.

Writing and Language Test

Aircraft Engineers

The knowledge of an aircraft engineer is acquired through years of education, and special licenses are required. Ideally, an individual will begin his or her preparation for the profession in high school by taking chemistry, physics, trigonometry, and calculus. Such curricula will aid in one's pursuit of a bachelor's degree in aircraft engineering, which requires several physical and life sciences, mathematics, and design courses.

(2) Some of universities provide internship or apprentice opportunities for the students enrolled in aircraft engineer programs. A bachelor's in aircraft engineering is commonly accompanied by a master's degree in advanced engineering or business administration. Such advanced degrees enable an individual to position himself or herself for executive, faculty, and/or research opportunities. (3) These advanced offices oftentimes require a Professional Engineering (PE) license which can be obtained through additional college courses, professional experience, and acceptable scores on the Fundamentals of Engineering (FE) and Professional Engineering (PE) standardized assessments.

Once the job begins, this line of work requires critical thinking, business skills, problem solving, and creativity. This level of (5) expertise (6) allows aircraft engineers to apply mathematical equations and scientific processes to aeronautical and aerospace issues or inventions. (8) For example, aircraft engineers may test, design, and construct flying vessels such as airplanes, space shuttles, and missile weapons. As a result, aircraft engineers are compensated with generous salaries. In fact, in May 2014, the lowest 10 percent of all American aircraft engineers earned less than $60,110 while the highest paid ten-percent of all American aircraft engineers earned $155,240. (9) In May 2015, the United States Bureau of Labor Statistics (BLS) reported that the median annual salary of aircraft engineers was $107, 830. (10) Conversely, (11) employment opportunities for aircraft engineers are projected to decrease by 2 percent by 2024. This decrease may be the result of a decline in the manufacturing industry. Nevertheless, aircraft engineers who know how to utilize modeling and simulation programs, fluid dynamic software, and robotic engineering tools are projected to remain the most employable.

2015 Annual Salary of Aerospace Engineers

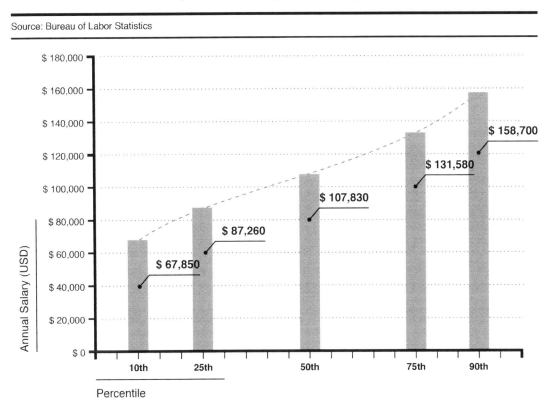

Source: Bureau of Labor Statistics

1. What type of text is utilized in the passage?
    a. Argumentative
    b. Narrative
    c. Biographical
    d. Informative

2.
   a. NO CHANGE
   b. Some of universities provided internship or apprentice opportunities
   c. Some of universities provide internship or apprenticeship opportunities
   d. Some universities provide internship or apprenticeship opportunities

3.
   a. NO CHANGE
   b. These advanced positions oftentimes require acceptable scores on the Fundamentals of Engineering (FE) and Professional Engineering (PE) standardized assessments in order to achieve a Professional Engineering (PE) license. Additional college courses and professional experience help.
   c. These advanced offices oftentimes require acceptable scores on the Fundamentals of Engineering (FE) and Professional Engineering (PE) standardized assessments to gain the Professional Engineering (PE) license which can be obtained through additional college courses, professional experience.
   d. These advanced positions oftentimes require a Professional Engineering (PE) license which is obtained by acceptable scores on the Fundamentals of Engineering (FE) and Professional Engineering (PE) standardized assessments. Further education and professional experience can help prepare for the assessments.

4. "The knowledge of an aircraft engineer is acquired through years of education." Which statement serves to support this claim?
   a. Aircraft engineers are compensated with generous salaries.
   b. Such advanced degrees enable an individual to position himself or herself for executive, faculty, or research opportunities.
   c. Ideally, an individual will begin his or her preparation for the profession in high school by taking chemistry, physics, trigonometry, and calculus.
   d. Aircraft engineers who know how to utilize modeling and simulation programs, fluid dynamic software, and robotic engineering tools will be the most employable.

5. What is the meaning of "expertise" in the marked sentence?
   a. Care
   b. Skill
   c. Work
   d. Composition

6.
   a. NO CHANGE
   b. Inhibits
   c. Requires
   d. Should

7. In the third paragraph, which of the following claims is supported?
   a. This line of work requires critical thinking, business skills, problem solving, and creativity.
   b. Aircraft engineers are compensated with generous salaries.
   c. The knowledge of an aircraft engineer is acquired through years of education.
   d. Those who work hard are rewarded accordingly.

8.
    a. NO CHANGE
    b. Therefore,
    c. However,
    d. Furthermore,

9.
    a. NO CHANGE
    b. May of 2015, the United States Bureau of Labor Statistics (BLS) reported that the median annual salary of aircraft engineers was $107, 830.
    c. In May of 2015 the United States Bureau of Labor Statistics (BLS) reported that the median annual salary of aircraft engineers was $107, 830.
    d. In May, 2015, the United States Bureau of Labor Statistics (BLS) reported that the median annual salary of aircraft engineers was $107, 830.

10.
    a. NO CHANGE
    b. Similarly,
    c. In other words,
    d. Accordingly,

11.
    a. NO CHANGE
    b. Employment opportunities for aircraft engineers will be projected to decrease by 2 percent in 2024.
    c. Employment opportunities for aircraft engineers is projected to decrease by 2 percent in 2024.
    d. Employment opportunities for aircraft engineers were projected to decrease by 2 percent in 2024.

Attacks of September 11th

On September 11th 2001, a group of terrorists hijacked four American airplanes. The terrorists crashed the planes into the World Trade Center in New York City, the Pentagon in Washington D.C., and a field in Pennsylvania. Nearly 3,000 people died during the attacks, which propelled the United States into a "War on Terror".

About the Terrorists

Terrorists commonly use fear and violence to achieve political goals. The nineteen terrorists who orchestrated and implemented the attacks of September 11th were militants associated with al-Qaeda, an Islamic extremist group founded by Osama bin Landen, Abdullah Azzam, and others in the late 1980s. (13) Bin Laden orchestrated the attacks as a response to what he felt was American injustice against Islam and hatred towards Muslims. In his words, "Terrorism against America deserves to be praised."

Islam is the religion of Muslims, who live mainly in South and Southwest Asia and Sub-Saharan Africa. The majority of Muslims practice Islam peacefully. However, fractures in Islam have led to the growth of Islamic extremists who strictly oppose Western influences. They seek to institute stringent Islamic law and destroy those who (15) violate Islamic code.

In November 2002, bin Laden provided the explicit motives for the 9/11 terror attacks. According to this list, America's support of Israel, military presence in Saudi Arabia, and other anti-Muslim actions were the causes.

The Timeline of the Attacks

The morning of September 11 began like any other for most Americans. Then, at 8:45 a.m., a Boeing 767 plane crashed into the north tower of the World Trade Center in New York City. Hundreds were instantly killed. Others were trapped on higher floors. The (17) crash was initially thought to be a freak accident. When a second plane flew directly into the south tower eighteen minutes later, it was determined that America was under attack.

At 9:45 a.m., a third plane slammed into the Pentagon, America's military headquarters in Washington D.C. The jet fuel of this plane caused a major fire and partial building collapse that resulted in nearly 200 deaths. By 10:00 a.m., the south tower of the World Trade Center collapsed. Thirty minutes later, the north tower followed suit.

While this was happening, a fourth plane that departed from New Jersey, United Flight 93, was hijacked. The passengers learned of the attacks that occurred in New York and Washington D.C. and realized that they faced the same fate as the other planes that crashed. The passengers were determined to overpower the terrorists in an effort to prevent the deaths of additional innocent American citizens. Although the passengers were successful in (18) diverging the plane, it crashed in a western Pennsylvania field and killed everyone on board. The plane's final target remains uncertain, but many believe that United Flight 93 was heading for the White House.

Heroes and Rescuers

Close to 3,000 people died in the World Trade Center attacks. This figure includes 343 New York City firefighters and paramedics, 23 New York City police officers, and 37 Port Authority officers. Nevertheless, thousands of men and women in service worked valiantly to evacuate the buildings, save trapped workers, extinguish infernos, uncover victims trapped in fallen rubble, and tend to nearly 10,000 injured individuals.

About 300 rescue dogs played a major role in the after-attack salvages. Working twelve-hour shifts, the dogs scoured the rubble and alerted paramedics when they found signs of life. While doing so, the dogs served as a source of comfort and therapy for the rescue teams.

Initial Impacts on America

The attacks of September 11, 2001 resulted in the immediate suspension of all air travel. No flights could take off from or land on American soil. American airports and airspace closed to all national and international flights. Therefore, over five hundred flights had to turn back or be redirected to other countries. Canada alone received 226 flights and thousands of stranded passengers. Needless to say, as canceled flights are rescheduled, air travel became backed up and chaotic for quite some time.

At the time of the attacks, George W. Bush was the president of the United States. President Bush announced that "We will make no distinction between the terrorists who committed these acts and those who harbor them." The rate of hate crimes against American Muslims spiked, despite President Bush's call for the country to treat them with respect.

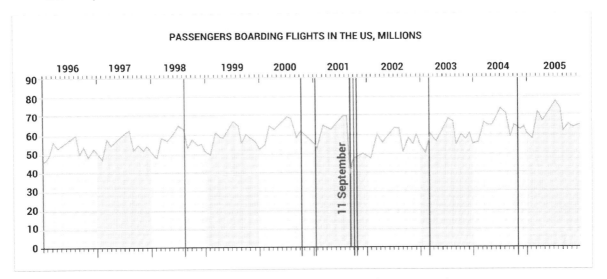

Additionally, relief funds were quickly arranged. The funds were used to support families of the victims, orphaned children, and those with major injuries. In this way, the tragic event brought the citizens together through acts of service towards those directly impacted by the attack.

Long-term Effects of the Attacks

Over the past fifteen years, the attacks of September 11th have transformed the United States' government, travel safety protocols, and international relations. Anti-terrorism legislation became a priority for many countries as law enforcement and intelligence agencies teamed up to find and defeat alleged terrorists.

Present George W. Bush announced a War on Terror. He (21) desired to bring bin Laden and al-Qaeda to justice and prevent future terrorist networks from gaining strength. The War in Afghanistan began in October of 2001 when the United States and British forces bombed al-Qaeda camps. (22) The Taliban, a group of fundamental Muslims who protected Osama bin Laden, was overthrown on December 9, 2001. However, the war continued in order to defeat insurgency campaigns in neighboring countries. Ten years later, the United State Navy SEALS killed Osama bin Laden in Pakistan. During 2014, the United States declared the end of its involvement in the War on Terror in Afghanistan.

Museums and memorials have since been erected to honor and remember the thousands of people who died during the September 11th attacks, including the brave rescue workers who gave their lives in the effort to help others.

12. How does the structure of the text help readers better understand the topic?
    a. By stating that anti-terrorism legislation was a priority for many countries, the reader can determine which laws were made and how they changed the life in the country.
    b. By placing the events in the order that they occurred, readers are better able to understand how the day unfolded.
    c. By using descriptive language, the readers are able to develop detailed images of the events that occurred during September 11, 2001.
    d. None of the above

13.
    a. NO CHANGE
    b. Bin Laden orchestrated the attacks as a response to what he felt was American injustice against Islam, and hatred towards Muslims.
    c. Bin Laden orchestrated the attacks, as a response to what he felt was American injustice against Islam and hatred towards Muslims.
    d. Bin Laden orchestrated the attacks as responding to what he felt was American injustice against Islam and hatred towards Muslims.

14. How could the author best express that most Muslims are peaceful people?
    a. By describing the life of a Muslim after the attacks.
    b. By including an anecdote about a Muslim friend.
    c. By reciting details from religious texts.
    d. By explicitly stating that fact.

15. What word could be used in exchange for "violate"?
    a. Respect
    b. Defile
    c. Deny
    d. Obey

16. What technique does the author use to highlight the impact of United Flight 93?
    a. An image of the crash
    b. An allusion to illustrate what may have occurred had the passengers not taken action
    c. An anecdote about a specific passenger
    d. A point of view consideration, where the author forces the reader to think about how he or she would have responded to such a situation

17. Which of the following would NOT be an appropriate replacement for the underlined portion of the sentence?
    a. First crash was thought to be
    b. Initial crash was thought to be
    c. Thought was that the initial crash
    d. Initial thought was that the crash was

18.
    a. NO CHANGE
    b. Diverting
    c. Converging
    d. Distracting

19. What statement is best supported by the graph included in this passage?
    a. As canceled flights were rescheduled, air travel became backed up and chaotic for quite some time.
    b. Over five hundred flights had to turn back or be redirected to other countries.
    c. Canada alone received 226 flights and thousands of stranded passengers.
    d. The attacks of September 11, 2001 resulted in the immediate suspension of all air travel.

20. What is the purpose of the last paragraph?
    a. It shows that beautiful art can be used to remember a past event.
    b. It demonstrates that Americans will always remember the 9/11 attacks and the lives that were lost.
    c. It explains how America fought back after the attacks.
    d. It provides the author with an opportunity to explain how the location of the towers is used today.

21.
    a. NO CHANGE
    b. Perceived
    c. Intended
    d. Assimilated

22.
    a. NO CHANGE
    b. The Taliban was overthrown on December 9, 2001. They were a group of fundamental Muslims who protected Osama bin Laden. However, the war continued in order to defeat insurgency campaigns in neighboring countries.
    c. The Taliban, a group of fundamental Muslims who protected Osama bin Laden, on December 9, 2001 was overthrown. However, the war continued in order to defeat insurgency campaigns in neighboring countries.
    d. Osama bin Laden's fundamental Muslims who protected him were called the Taliban and overthrown on December 9, 2001. Yet the war continued in order to defeat the insurgency campaigns in neighboring countries.

Fred Hampton

Fred Hampton desired to see lasting social change for African American people through nonviolent means and community recognition. (23) As a result, he became an African American activist during the American Civil Rights Movement and led the Chicago chapter of the Black Panther Party.

Hampton's Education

Hampton was born and raised in Maywood of Chicago, Illinois in 1948. (24) Gifted academically and a natural athlete, he became a stellar baseball player in high school. After graduating from Proviso East High School in 1966, he later went on to study law at Triton Junior College.

While studying at Triton, Hampton joined and became a leader of the National Association for the Advancement of Colored People (NAACP). (25) As a result of his leadership, the NAACP gained more than 500 members. Hampton worked relentlessly to acquire recreational facilities in the neighborhood and improve the educational resources provided to the impoverished black community of Maywood.

The Black Panthers

The Black Panther Party (BPP) was another activist group that formed around the same time as the NAACP. Hampton was quickly attracted to the Black Panther's approach to the fight for equal rights for African Americans. (26) Hampton eventually joined the chapter and relocated to downtown Chicago to be closer to its headquarters.

His (27) charismatic personality, organizational abilities, sheer determination, and rhetorical skills enabled him to quickly rise through the chapter's ranks. (28) Hampton soon became the leader of the Chicago chapter of the BPP where he organized rallies, taught political education classes, and established a free medical clinic. He also took part in the community police supervision project and played an (40) instrumental role in the BPP breakfast program for impoverished African American children.

Hampton's greatest achievement as the leader of the BPP may be his fight against street gang violence in Chicago. In 1969, Hampton held a press conference where he made the gangs agree to a nonaggression pact known as the Rainbow Coalition. As a result of the pact, a multiracial alliance between blacks, Puerto Ricans, and poor youth was developed.

Assassination

As the Black Panther Party's popularity and influence grew, the Federal Bureau of Investigation (FBI) placed the group under constant surveillance. In an attempt to (30) neutralize the party, the FBI launched several harassment campaigns against the BPP, raided its headquarters in Chicago three times, and arrested over one hundred of the group's members. Hampton was shot during such a raid that occurred on the morning of December 4th, 1969.

In 1976, seven years after the event, it was revealed that William O'Neal, Hampton's trusted bodyguard, was an undercover FBI agent. (31) O'Neal provided the FBI with detailed floor plans of the BPP's headquarters, identifying the exact location of Hampton's bed. It was because of these floor plans that the police were able to target and kill Hampton.

The assassination of Hampton fueled outrage amongst the African American community. It was not until years after the assassination that the police admitted wrongdoing. The Chicago City Council now (32) commemorates December 4th as Fred Hampton Day.

23.
  a. NO CHANGE
  b. As a result he became an African American activist
  c. As a result: he became an African American activist
  d. As a result of, he became an African American activist

24. What word could be used in place of the underlined description?
    a. Vacuous
    b. Energetic
    c. Intelligent
    d. Athletic

25. Which of the following statements, if true, would further validate the selected sentence?
    a. Several of these new members went on to earn scholarships.
    b. With this increase in numbers, Hampton was awarded a medal for his contribution to the NAACP.
    c. Many of these new members would go on to hold high positions in the organization, often accrediting Hampton for his encouragement and guidance.
    d. The NAACP has been growing steadily every year.

26. How else could this sentence be re-structured while maintaining the context of the fourth paragraph?
    a. NO CHANGE
    b. Eventually, Hampton joined the chapter and relocated to downtown Chicago to be closer to its headquarters.
    c. Nevertheless, Hampton joined the chapter and relocated to downtown Chicago to be closer to its headquarters.
    d. Hampton then joined the chapter and relocated to downtown Chicago to be closer to its headquarters

27. What word is synonymous with the underlined description?
    a. Egotistical
    b. Obnoxious
    c. Chauvinistic
    d. Charming

28.
    a. NO CHANGE
    b. As the leader of the BPP, Hampton: organized rallies, taught political education classes, and established a free medical clinic.
    c. As the leader of the BPP, Hampton; organized rallies, taught political education classes, and established a free medical clinic.
    d. As the leader of the BPP, Hampton—organized rallies, taught political education classes, and established a medical free clinic.

29. The author develops the idea that Frank Hampton should not have been killed at the hands of the police. Which could best be used to support that claim?
    a. The manner in which the police raided the BPP headquarters.
    b. The eventual admission from the police that they were wrong in killing Hampton.
    c. The description of previous police raids that resulted in the arrest of hundreds BPP members.
    d. All of the above.

30.
   a. NO CHANGE
   b. Accommodate
   c. Assuage
   d. Praise

31. How could this sentence be rewritten without losing its original meaning?
   a. NO CHANGE
   b. O'Neal provided the FBI with detailed floor plans of the BPP's headquarters, which identified the exact location of Hampton's bed.
   c. O'Neal provided the FBI with detailed floor plans and Hampton's bed.
   d. O'Neal identified the exact location of Hampton's bed that provided the FBI with detailed floor plans of the BPP's headquarters.

32. What word could be used in place of the underlined word?
   a. Disregards
   b. Memorializes
   c. Communicates
   d. Denies

33. How would the author likely describe the FBI during the events of the passage?
   a. Corrupt
   b. Confused
   c. Well-intended
   d. Prejudiced

Here Comes the Flood!

A flood occurs when an area of land that is normally dry becomes submerged with water. Floods have affected Earth since the beginning of time and are caused by many different factors. (36) Flooding can occur slowly or within seconds and can submerge small regions or extend over vast areas of land. Their impact on society and the environment can be harmful or helpful.

What Causes Flooding?

Floods may be caused by natural phenomenon, induced by the activities of humans and other animals, or the failure of an infrastructure. Areas located near bodies of water are prone to flooding as are low-lying regions.

Global warming is the result of air pollution that prevents the sun's radiation from being emitted back into space. Instead, the radiation is trapped in Earth and results in global warming. The warming of the Earth has resulted in climate changes. As a result, floods have been occurring with increasing regularity. Some claim that the increased temperatures on Earth may cause the icebergs to melt. They fear that the melting of icebergs will cause the (37) oceans levels to rise and flood coastal regions.

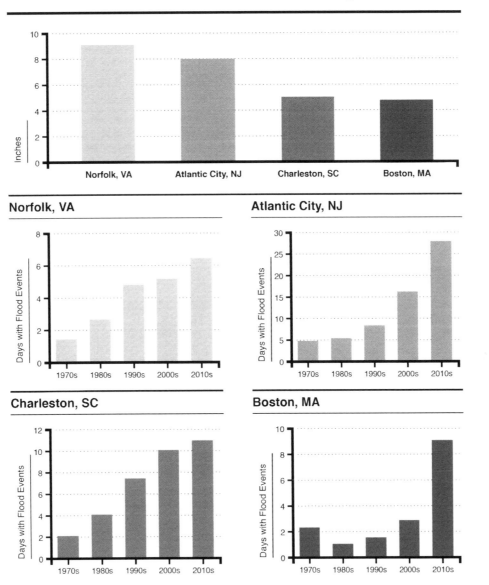

Local Sea Level Rise and Tidal Flooding, 1970-2012

Most commonly, flooding is caused by excessive rain. The ground is not able to absorb all the water produced by a sudden heavy rainfall or rainfall that occurs over a prolonged period of time. Such rainfall may cause the water in rivers and other bodies of water to overflow. The excess water can cause dams to break. Such events can cause flooding of the surrounding riverbanks or coastal regions.

Flash flooding can occur without warning and without rainfall. Flash floods may be caused by a river being blocked by a glacier, avalanche, landslide, logjam, a beaver's obstruction, construction, or dam. Water builds behind such a blockage. Eventually, the mass and force of the built-up water become so extreme that it causes the obstruction to break. Thus, enormous amounts of water rush out towards the surrounding areas.

Areal or urban flooding occurs because the land has become hardened. The hardening of land may result from urbanization or drought. Either way, the hardened land prevents water from seeping into the ground. Instead, the water resides on top of the land.

Finally, flooding may result after severe hurricanes, tsunamis, or tropical cyclones. Local defenses and infrastructures are no matches for the tidal surges and waves caused by these natural phenomena. Such events are bound to result in the flooding of nearby coastal regions or estuaries.

A Floods After-Effects

Flooding can result in severe devastation of nearby areas. Flash floods and tsunamis can result in sweeping waters that travel at destructive speeds. Fast-moving water has the power to demolish all obstacles in its path such as homes, trees, bridges, and buildings. Animals, plants, and humans may all lose their lives during a flood.

Floods can also cause pollution and infection. Sewage may seep from drains or septic tanks and contaminate drinking water or surrounding lands. Similarly, toxins, fuels, debris from annihilated buildings, and other hazardous materials can leave water unusable for consumption. (38) As the water begins to drain, mold may begin to grow. As a result, residents of flooded areas may be left without power, drinkable water, or be exposed to toxins and other diseases.

(39) Although often associated with devastation, not all flooding results in adverse circumstances. For millions of years, peoples have inhabited floodplains of rivers. (41) Examples include the Mississippi Valley of the United States, the Nile River in Egypt, and the Tigris River of the Middle East. The flooding of such rivers (42) caused nutrient-rich silts to be deposited on the floodplains. Thus, after the floods recede, an extremely fertile soil is left behind. This soil is conducive to the agriculture of bountiful crops and has sustained the diets of humans for millennium.

Proactive Measures Against Flooding

Technologies now allow scientists to predict where and when flooding is likely to occur. Such technologies can also be used (43) to project the severity of an anticipated flood. In this way, local inhabitants can be warned and take preventative measures such as boarding up their homes, gathering necessary provisions, and moving themselves and possessions to higher grounds.

The (44) picturesque views of coastal regions and rivers have long enticed people to build near such locations. Due to the costs associated with the repairs needed after the flooding of such residencies, many governments now require inhabitants of flood-prone areas to purchase flood insurance and build flood-resistant structures. Pictures of all items within a building or home should be taken so that proper reimbursement for losses can be made in the event that a flood does occur.

Staying Safe During a Flood

If a forecasted flood does occur, then people should retreat to higher ground such as a mountain, attic, or roof. Flooded waters may be contaminated, contain hidden debris, or travel at high speeds. Therefore, people should not attempt to walk or drive through a flooded area. To prevent electrocution, electrical outlets and downed power lines need to be avoided.

The Flood Dries Up

Regardless of the type or cause of a flood, floods can result in detrimental alterations to nearby lands and serious injuries to nearby inhabitants. By understanding flood cycles, civilizations can learn to take advantage of flood seasons. By taking the proper precautionary measures, people can stay safe when floods occur. Thus, proper knowledge can lead to safety and prosperity during such an adverse natural phenomenon.

34. What information from the graphs could be used to support the claims found in the third paragraph?
    a. Between 1970-1980, Boston experienced a decrease in the number of days with flood events.
    b. Between 1970-1980, Atlantic City, New Jersey did not experience an increase in the number of days with flood events.
    c. Since 1970, the number of days with floods has decreased in major coastal cities across America.
    d. Since 1970, sea levels have risen along the East Coast.

35. One of the headings is entitled "A Floods After-Effects." How should this heading be rewritten?
    a. A Flood's After-Effect
    b. A Flood's After-Effects
    c. A Floods After-Affect
    d. A Flood's After-Affects

36. Which of the following revisions can be made to the sentence that will still maintain the original meaning while making the sentence more concise?
    a. NO CHANGE
    b. Flooding can either be slow or occur within seconds. It doesn't take long to submerge small regions or extend vast areas of land.
    c. Flooding occurs slowly or rapidly submerging vast areas of land.
    d. Vast areas of land can be flooded slowly or within seconds.

37.
    a. NO CHANGE
    b. Ocean levels
    c. Ocean's levels
    d. Levels of the oceans

38. Which choice best maintains the pattern of the first sentence of the paragraph?
     a. NO CHANGE
     b. As the rain subsides and the water begins to drain, mold may begin to grow.
     c. Mold may begin to grow as the water begins to drain.
     d. The water will begin to drain and mold will begin to grow.

39.
     a. NO CHANGE
     b. Although often associated with devastation not all flooding results
     c. Although often associated with devastation. Not all flooding results
     d. While often associated with devastation, not all flooding results

40. What is the author's intent of the final paragraph?
     a. To explain that all bad occurrences eventually come to an end.
     b. To summarize the key points within the passage.
     c. To explain that, with time, all flooded lands will eventually dry.
     d. To relay a final key point about floods.

41. The author is considering deleting this sentence from the tenth paragraph. Should the sentence be kept or deleted?
     a. Kept, because it provides examples of floodplains that have been successfully inhabited by civilizations.
     b. Kept, because it provides an example of how floods can be beneficial.
     c. Deleted, because it blurs the paragraph's focus on the benefits of floods.
     d. Deleted, because it distracts from the overall meaning of the paragraph.

42.
     a. NO CHANGE
     b. Cause
     c. Causing
     d. Causes

43.
     a. NO CHANGE
     b. Projecting
     c. Project
     d. Projected

44. Which term could best replace the underlined word?
     a. Colorful
     b. Drab
     c. Scenic
     d. Candid

162

Math Test

1. If $6t + 4 = 16$, what is t?
    a. 1
    b. 2
    c. 3
    d. 4

2. The variable y is directly proportional to x. If $y = 3$ when $x = 5$, then what is y when $x = 20$?
    a. 10
    b. 12
    c. 14
    d. 16

3. A line passes through the point (1, 2) and crosses the y-axis at $y = 1$. Which of the following is an equation for this line?
    a. $y = 2x$
    b. $y = x + 1$
    c. $x + y = 1$
    d. $y = \frac{x}{2} - 2$

4. There are $4x + 1$ treats in each party favor bag. If a total of $60x + 15$ treats are distributed, how many bags are given out?
    a. 15
    b. 16
    c. 20
    d. 22

5. Apples cost $2 each, while oranges cost $3 each. Maria purchased 10 fruits in total and spent $22. How many apples did she buy?
    a. 5
    b. 6
    c. 7
    d. 8

6. What are the roots of $x^2 + x - 2$?
    a. 1 and -2
    b. -1 and 2
    c. 2 and -2
    d. 9 and 13

7. What is the y-intercept of $y = x^{5/3} + (x - 3)(x + 1)$?
    a. 3.5
    b. 7.6
    c. -3
    d. -15.1

8. $x^4 - 16$ can be simplified to which of the following?
    a. $(x^2 - 4)(x^2 + 4)$
    b. $(x^2 + 4)(x^2 + 4)$
    c. $(x^2 - 4)(x^2 - 4)$
    d. $(x^2 - 2)(x^2 + 4)$

9. $(4x^2y^4)^{\frac{3}{2}}$ can be simplified to which of the following?
    a. $8x^3y^6$
    b. $4x^{\frac{5}{2}}y$
    c. $4xy$
    d. $32x^{\frac{7}{2}}y^{\frac{11}{2}}$

10. If $\sqrt{1 + x} = 4$, what is x?
    a. 10
    b. 15
    c. 20
    d. 25

11. Suppose $\frac{x+2}{x} = 2$. What is x?
    a. -1
    b. 0
    c. 2
    d. 4

12. A ball is thrown from the top of a high hill, so that the height of the ball as a function of time is $h(t) = -16t^2 + 4t + 6$, in feet. What is the maximum height of the ball in feet?
    a. 6
    b. 6.25
    c. 6.5
    d. 6.75

13. A rectangle has a length that is 5 feet longer than three times its width. If the perimeter is 90 feet, what is the length in feet?
    a. 10
    b. 20
    c. 25
    d. 35

14. Five students take a test. The scores of the first four students are 80, 85, 75, and 60. If the median score is 80, which of the following could NOT be the score of the fifth student?
    a. 60
    b. 80
    c. 85
    d. 100

15. In an office, there are 50 workers. A total of 60% of the workers are women, and the chances of a woman wearing a skirt is 50%. If no men wear skirts, how many workers are wearing skirts?

    a. 12

    b. 15

    c. 16

    d. 20

16. Ten students take a test. Five students get a 50. Four students get a 70. If the average score is 55, what was the last student's score?

    a. 20

    b. 40

    c. 50

    d. 60

17. A company invests $50,000 in a building where they can produce saws. If the cost of producing one saw is $40, then which function expresses the amount of money the company pays? The variable y is the money paid and x is the number of saws produced.

    a. $y = 50,000x + 40$

    b. $y + 40 = x - 50,000$

    c. $y = 40x - 50,000$

    d. $y = 40x + 50,000$

18. A six-sided die is rolled. What is the probability that the roll is 1 or 2?

    a. $\frac{1}{6}$

    b. $\frac{1}{4}$

    c. $\frac{1}{3}$

    d. $\frac{1}{2}$

19. A line passes through the origin and through the point (-3, 4). What is the slope of the line?

    a. $-\frac{4}{3}$

    b. $-\frac{3}{4}$

    c. $\frac{4}{3}$

    d. $\frac{3}{4}$

20. A pair of dice is thrown, and the sum of the two scores is calculated. What's the expected value of the roll?

    a. 5

    b. 6

    c. 7

    d. 8

21.

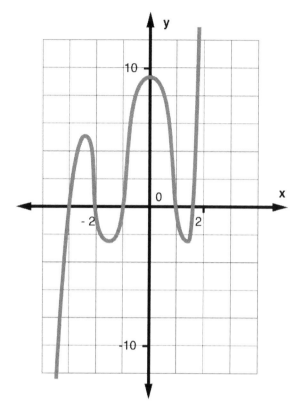

Which of the following functions represents the graph above?

a. $y = x^5 + 3.5x^4 - 2.5x^2 + 1.5x + 9$
b. $y = x^5 - 3.5x^4 + 2.5x^2 - 1.5x - 9$
c. $y = 5x^4 - 2.5x^2 + 1.5x + 9$
d. $y = -5x^4 - 2.5x^2 + 1.5x + 9$

22. Katie works at a clothing company and sold 192 shirts over the weekend. $^1/_3$ of the shirts that were sold were patterned, and the rest were solid. Which mathematical expression would calculate the number of solid shirts Katie sold over the weekend?

a. $192 \times \frac{1}{3}$

b. $192 \div \frac{1}{3}$

c. $192 \times (1 - \frac{1}{3})$

d. $192 \div 3$

23. Which measure for the center of a small sample set is most affected by outliers?

a. Mean
b. Median
c. Mode
d. None of the above

24. Given the value of a given stock at monthly intervals, which graph should be used to best represent the trend of the stock?
   a. Box plot
   b. Line plot
   c. Line graph
   d. Circle graph

25. What is the probability of randomly picking the winner and runner-up from a race of 4 horses and distinguishing which is the winner?
   a. $\dfrac{1}{4}$

   b. $\dfrac{1}{2}$

   c. $\dfrac{1}{16}$

   d. $\dfrac{1}{12}$

26. What is the next number in the following series: $1, 3, 6, 10, 15, 21, \ldots$?
   a. 26
   b. 27
   c. 28
   d. 29

27. A shipping box has a length of 8 inches, a width of 14 inches, and a height of 4 inches. If all three dimensions are doubled, what is the relationship between the volume of the new box and the volume of the original box?
   a. The volume of the new box is double the volume of the original box.
   b. The volume of the new box is four times as large as the volume of the original box.
   c. The volume of the new box is six times as large as the volume of the original box.
   d. The volume of the new box is eight times as large as the volume of the original box.

28. What is the product of the following expression?
$$(3 + 2i)(5 - 4i).$$
   a. $23 - 2i$
   b. $15 - 8i$
   c. $15 - 8i^2$
   d. $15 - 10i$

29.

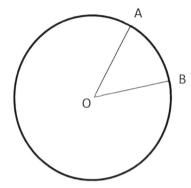

The length of arc $AB = 3\pi$ cm. The length of $\overline{OA} = 12$ cm. What is the degree measure of $\angle AOB$?
    a. 30 degrees
    b. 40 degrees
    c. 45 degrees
    d. 55 degrees

30.

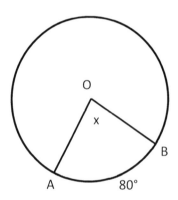

The area of circle O is 49π m. What is the area of the sector formed by $\angle AOB$?
    a. 80π m
    b. 10.9π m
    c. 4.9π m
    d. 10π m

31. The triangle shown below is a right triangle. What's the value of x?

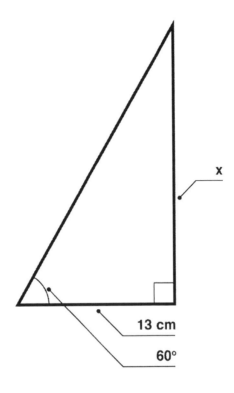

13 cm

60°

x

 a. $x = 1.73$
 b. $x = 0.57$
 c. $x = 13$
 d. $x = 22.49$

32. A ball is drawn at random from a ball pit containing 8 red balls, 7 yellow balls, 6 green balls, and 5 purple balls. What's the probability that the ball drawn is yellow?

 a. $\dfrac{1}{26}$

 b. $\dfrac{19}{26}$

 c. $\dfrac{7}{26}$

 d. 1

33. What's the probability of rolling a 6 at least once in two rolls of a die?

 a. $\dfrac{1}{3}$

 b. $\dfrac{1}{36}$

 c. $\dfrac{1}{6}$

 d. $\dfrac{11}{36}$

34. For a group of 20 men, the median weight is 180 pounds and the range is 30 pounds. If each man gains 10 pounds, which of the following would be true?
    a. The median weight will increase, and the range will remain the same.
    b. The median weight and range will both remain the same.
    c. The median weight will stay the same, and the range will increase.
    d. The median weight and range will both increase.

35. If the ordered pair $(-3, -4)$ is reflected over the x-axis, what's the new ordered pair?
    a. $(-3, -4)$
    b. $(3, -4)$
    c. $(3, 4)$
    d. $(-3, 4)$

36. If the volume of a sphere is 288π cubic meters, what are the radius and surface area of the same sphere?
    a. Radius 6 meters and surface area 144π square meters
    b. Radius 36 meters and surface area 144π square meterc. Radius 6 meters and surface area 12π square meters
    d. Radius 36 meters and surface area 12π square meters

37. Which four-sided shape is always a rectangle?
    a. Rhombus
    b. Square
    c. Parallelogram
    d. Quadrilateral

38. Using trigonometric ratios for a right angle, what is the value of the angle whose opposite side is equal to 25 centimeters and whose hypotenuse is equal to 50 centimeters?
    a. 15°
    b. 30°
    c. 45°
    d. 90°

39. Using trigonometric ratios for a right angle, what is the value of the closest angle whose adjacent side is equal to 7.071 centimeters and whose hypotenuse is equal to 10 centimeters?
    a. 15°
    b. 30°
    c. 45°
    d. 90°

40. Using trigonometric ratios, what is the value of the other angle whose opposite side is equal to 1 in and whose adjacent side is equal to the square root of 3 inches?
    a. 15°
    b. 30°
    c. 45°
    d. 90°

41. What is the function that forms an equivalent graph to $y = \cos(x)$?
   a. $y = \tan(x)$
   b. $y = \csc(x)$
   c. $y = \sin(x + \frac{\pi}{2})$
   d. $y = \sin(x - \frac{\pi}{2})$

42. A solution needs 5 mL of saline for every 8 mL of medicine given. How much saline is needed for 45 mL of medicine?
   a. $\frac{225}{8}$ mL
   b. 72 mL
   c. 28 mL
   d. $\frac{45}{8}$ mL

43. What's the midpoint of a line segment with endpoints $(-1, 2)$ and $(3, -6)$?
   a. $(1, 2)$
   b. $(1, 0)$
   c. $(-1, 2)$
   d. $(1, -2)$

44. A sample data set contains the following values: 1, 3, 5, 7. What's the standard deviation of the set?
   a. 2.58
   b. 4
   c. 6.23
   d. 1.1

No Calculator Questions

45. An equilateral triangle has a perimeter of 18 feet. If a square whose sides have the same length as one side of the triangle is built, what will be the area of the square?
   a. 6 square feet
   b. 36 square feet
   c. 256 square feet
   d. 1000 square feet

46. What is the volume of a sphere, in terms of π, with a radius of 3 inches?
   a. $36\,\pi$ in³
   b. $27\,\pi$ in³
   c. $9\,\pi$ in³
   d. $72\,\pi$ in³

47. What is the length of the other leg of a right triangle with a hypotenuse of 10 inches and a leg of 8 inches?
   a. 6 in
   b. 18 in
   c. 80 in
   d. 13 in

48. A pizzeria owner regularly creates jumbo pizzas, each with a radius of 9 inches. She is mathematically inclined, and wants to know the area of the pizza to purchase the correct boxes and know how much she is feeding her customers. What is the area of the circle, in terms of π, with a radius of 9 inches?

    a. 81π in²

    b. 18π in²

    c. 90π in²

    d. 9π in²

49. How will the following number be written in standard form: $(1 \times 10^4) + (3 \times 10^3) + (7 \times 10^1) + (8 \times 10^0)$

    a. 137

    b. 13,078

    c. 1,378

    d. 8,731

50. What is the simplified form of the expression $tan\theta \ cos\theta$?

    a. $sin\theta$

    b. 1

    c. $csc\theta$

    d. $\dfrac{1}{sec\theta}$

51. What is the value of the sum of $\dfrac{1}{3}$ and $\dfrac{2}{5}$?

    a. $\dfrac{3}{8}$

    b. $\dfrac{11}{15}$

    c. $\dfrac{11}{30}$

    d. $\dfrac{4}{5}$

52. If the cosine of $30° = x$, the sine of what angle also equals x?

    a. 30°

    b. 60°

    c. 90°

    d. 120°

53. If sine of $60° = x$, the cosine of what angle also equals x?

    a. 30°

    b. 60°

    c. 90°

    d. 120°

54.

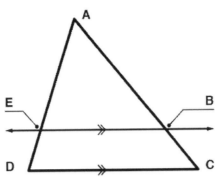

If $\overline{AE} = 4$, $\overline{AB} = 5$, and $\overline{AD} = 5$, what is the length of $\overline{AC}$?

55. $\frac{3}{25} =$

56. 6 is 30% of what number?

174

57. What is the value of the following expression?

$$\sqrt{8^2 + 6^2}$$

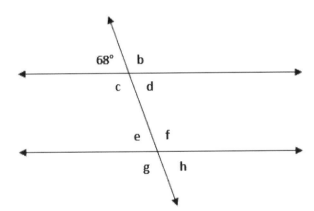

58. What is the measurement of angle f in the following picture? Assume the lines are parallel.

Answer Explanations #3

Reading Test

1. C: Gulliver becomes acquainted with the people and practices of his new surroundings. Choice *C* is the correct answer because it most extensively summarizes the entire passage. While Choices *A* and *B* are reasonable possibilities, they reference portions of Gulliver's experiences, not the whole. Choice *D* is incorrect because Gulliver doesn't express repentance or sorrow in this particular passage.

2. A: Principal refers to *chief* or *primary* within the context of this text. Choice *A* is the answer that most closely aligns with this answer. Choices *B* and *D* make reference to a helper or followers while Choice *C* doesn't meet the description of Gulliver from the passage.

3. C: One can reasonably infer that Gulliver is considerably larger than the children who were playing around him because multiple children could fit into his hand. Choice *B* is incorrect because there is no indication of stress in Gulliver's tone. Choices *A* and *D* aren't the best answer because though Gulliver seems fond of his new acquaintances, he didn't travel there with the intentions of meeting new people or to express a definite love for them in this particular portion of the text.

4. C: The emperor made a *definitive decision* to expose Gulliver to their native customs. In this instance, the word *mind* was not related to a vote, question, or cognitive ability.

5. A: Choice *A* is correct. This assertion does *not* support the fact that games are a commonplace event in this culture because it mentions conduct, not games. Choices *B*, *C*, and *D* are incorrect because these do support the fact that games were a commonplace event.

6. B: Choice *B* is the only option that mentions the correlation between physical ability and leadership positions. Choices *A* and *D* are unrelated to physical strength and leadership abilities. Choice *C* does not make a deduction that would lead to the correct answer—it only comments upon the abilities of common townspeople.

7. D: It emphasizes Mr. Utterson's anguish in failing to identify Hyde's whereabouts. Context clues indicate that Choice *D* is correct because the passage provides great detail of Mr. Utterson's feelings about locating Hyde. Choice *A* does not fit because there is no mention of Mr. Lanyon's mental state. Choice *B* is incorrect; although the text does make mention of bells, Choice *B* is not the *best* answer overall. Choice *C* is incorrect because the passage clearly states that Mr. Utterson was determined, not unsure.

8. A: In the city. The word *city* appears in the passage several times, thus establishing the location for the reader.

9. B: It scares children. The passage states that the Juggernaut causes the children to scream. Choices *A* and *D* don't apply because the text doesn't mention either of these instances specifically. Choice *C* is incorrect because there is nothing in the text that mentions space travel.

10. B: To constantly visit. The mention of *morning*, *noon*, and *night* make it clear that the word *haunt* refers to frequent appearances at various locations. Choice *A* doesn't work because the text makes no mention of levitating. Choices *C* and *D* are not correct because the text makes mention of Mr. Utterson's anguish and disheartenment because of his failure to find Hyde but does not make mention of Mr. Utterson's feelings negatively affecting anyone else.

11. D: This is an example of alliteration. Choice *D* is the correct answer because of the repetition of the *L*-words. Hyperbole is an exaggeration, so Choice *A* doesn't work. No comparison is being made, so no simile or metaphor is being used, thus eliminating Choices *B* and *C*.

12. D: The speaker intends to continue to look for Hyde. Choices *A* and *B* are not possible answers because the text doesn't refer to any name changes or an identity crisis, despite Mr. Utterson's extreme obsession with finding Hyde. The text also makes no mention of a mistaken identity when referring to Hyde, so Choice *C* is also incorrect.

13. A: The tone is exasperated. While contemplative is an option because of the inquisitive nature of the text, Choice *A* is correct because the speaker is annoyed by the thought of being included when he felt that the fellow members of his race were being excluded. The speaker is not nonchalant, nor accepting of the circumstances which he describes.

14. C: Choice *C*, *contented*, is the only word that has different meaning. Furthermore, the speaker expresses objection and disdain throughout the entire text.

15. B: To address the feelings of exclusion expressed by African Americans after the establishment of the Fourth of July holiday. While the speaker makes biblical references, it is not the main focus of the passage, thus eliminating Choice *A* as an answer. The passage also makes no mention of wealthy landowners and doesn't speak of any positive response to the historical events, so Choices *C* and *D* are not correct.

16. D: Choice *D* is the correct answer because it clearly makes reference to justice being denied.

17. D: Hyperbole. Choices *A* and *B* are unrelated. Assonance is the repetition of sounds and commonly occurs in poetry. Parallelism refers to two statements that correlate in some manner. Choice *C* is incorrect because amplification normally refers to clarification of meaning by broadening the sentence structure, while hyperbole refers to a phrase or statement that is being exaggerated.

18. C: Display the equivocation of the speaker and those that he represents. Choice *C* is correct because the speaker is clear about his intention and stance throughout the text. Choice *A* could be true, but the words "common text" is arguable. Choice *B* is also partially true, as another group of people affected by slavery are being referenced. However, the speaker is not trying to convince the audience that injustices have been committed, as it is already understood there have been injustices committed. Choice *D* is also close to the correct answer, but it is not the *best* answer choice possible.

19. B: A period of time. It is apparent that Lincoln is referring to a period of time within the context of the passage because of how the sentence is structured with the word *ago*.

20. C: Lincoln's reference to *the brave men, living and dead, who struggled here,* proves that he is referring to a battlefield. Choices *A* and *B* are incorrect, as a *civil war* is mentioned and not a war with France or a war in the Sahara Desert. Choice *D* is incorrect because it does not make sense to consecrate a President's ground instead of a battlefield ground for soldiers who died during the American Civil War.

21. D: Abraham Lincoln is the former president of the United States, and he references a "civil war" during his address.

22. A: The audience should consider the death of the people that fought in the war as an example and perpetuate the ideals of freedom that the soldiers died fighting for. Lincoln doesn't address any of the topics outlined in Choices *B*, *C*, or *D*. Therefore, Choice *A* is the correct answer.

23. D: Choice *D* is the correct answer because of the repetition of the word *people* at the end of the passage. Choice *A*, *antimetabole*, is the repetition of words in a succession. Choice *B*, *antiphrasis*, is a form of denial of an assertion in a text. Choice *C*, *anaphora*, is the repetition that occurs at the beginning of sentences.

24. A: Choice *A* is correct because Lincoln's intention was to memorialize the soldiers who had fallen as a result of war as well as celebrate those who had put their lives in danger for the sake of their country. Choices *B* and *D* are incorrect because Lincoln's speech was supposed to foster a sense of pride among the members of the audience while connecting them to the soldiers' experiences.

25. A: The word *patronage* most nearly means *auspices*, which means *protection* or *support*. Choice *B*, *aberration*, means *deformity* and does not make sense within the context of the sentence. Choice *C*, *acerbic*, means *bitter* and also does not make sense in the sentence. Choice *D*, *adulation*, is a positive word meaning *praise*, and thus does not fit with the word *condescending* in the sentence.

26. D: *Working man* is most closely aligned with Choice *D*, *bourgeois*. In the context of the speech, the word *bourgeois* means *working* or *middle class*. Choice *A*, *plebian*, does suggest *common people*; however, this is a term that is specific to ancient Rome. Choice *B*, *viscount*, is a European title used to describe a specific degree of nobility. Choice *C*, *entrepreneur*, is a person who operates their own business.

27. C: In the context of the speech, the term *working man* most closely correlates with Choice *C*, *working man is someone who works for wages among the middle class*. Choice *A* is not mentioned in the passage and is off-topic. Choice *B* may be true in some cases, but it does not reflect the sentiment described for the term *working man* in the passage. Choice *D* may also be arguably true. However, it is not given as a definition but as *acts* of the working man, and the topics of *field*, *factory*, and *screen* are not mentioned in the passage.

28. D: *Enterprise* most closely means *cause*. Choices *A*, *B*, and *C* are all related to the term *enterprise*. However, Dickens speaks of a *cause* here, not a company, courage, or a game. *He will stand by such an enterprise* is a call to stand by a cause to enable the working man to have a certain autonomy over his own economic standing. The very first paragraph ends with the statement that the working man *shall . . . have a share in the management of an institution which is designed for his benefit*.

29. B: The speaker's salutation is one from an entertainer to his audience and uses the friendly language to connect to his audience before a serious speech. Recall in the first paragraph that the speaker is there to "accompany [the audience] . . . through one of my little Christmas books," making him an author there to entertain the crowd with his own writing. The speech preceding the reading is the passage itself, and, as the tone indicates, a serious speech addressing the "working man." Although the passage speaks of employers and employees, the speaker himself is not an employer of the audience, so Choice *A* is incorrect. Choice *C* is also incorrect, as the salutation is not used ironically, but sincerely, as the speech addresses the wellbeing of the crowd. Choice *D* is incorrect because the speech is not given by a politician, but by a writer.

30. B: For the working man to have a say in his institution which is designed for his benefit. Choice *A* is incorrect because that is the speaker's *first* desire, not his second. Choices *C* and *D* are tricky because the language of both of these is mentioned after the word *second*. However, the speaker doesn't get to the second wish until the next sentence. Choices *C* and *D* are merely prepositions preparing for the statement of the main clause, Choice *B*.

31. D: The use of "I" could have all of the effects for the reader; it could serve to have a "hedging" effect, allow the reader to connect with the author in a more personal way, and cause the reader to empathize more with the egrets. However, it doesn't distance the reader from the text, thus eliminating Choice *D*.

32. C: The quote provides an example of a warden protecting one of the colonies. Choice *A* is incorrect because the speaker of the quote is a warden, not a hunter. Choice B is incorrect because the quote does not lighten the mood but shows the danger of the situation between the wardens and the hunters. Choice *D* is incorrect because there is no humor found in the quote.

33. D: A *rookery* is a colony of breeding birds. Although *rookery* could mean Choice *A*, houses in a slum area, it does not make sense in this context. Choices *B* and *C* are both incorrect, as this is not a place for hunters to trade tools or for wardens to trade stories.

34. B: An important bird colony. The previous sentence is describing "twenty colonies" of birds, so what follows should be a bird colony. Choice *A* may be true, but we have no evidence of this in the text. Choice *C* does touch on the tension between the hunters and wardens, but there is no official "Bird Island Battle" mentioned in the text. Choice *D* does not exist in the text.

35. D: To demonstrate the success of the protective work of the Audubon Association. The text mentions several different times how and why the association has been successful and gives examples to back this fact. Choice *A* is incorrect because although the article, in some instances, calls certain people to act, it is not the purpose of the entire passage. There is no way to tell if Choices *B* and *C* are correct, as they are not mentioned in the text.

36. C: To have a better opportunity to hunt the birds. Choice *A* might be true in a general sense, but it is not relevant to the context of the text. Choice *B* is incorrect because the hunters are not studying lines of flight to help wardens, but to hunt birds. Choice *D* is incorrect because nothing in the text mentions that hunters are trying to build homes underneath lines of flight of birds for good luck.

37. A: It introduces certain insects that transition from water to air. Choice *B* is incorrect because although the passage talks about gills, it is not the central idea of the passage. Choices *C* and *D* are incorrect because the passage does not "define" or "invite," but only serves as an introduction to stoneflies, dragonflies, and mayflies and their transition from water to air.

38. C: The act of shedding part or all of the outer shell. Choices *A*, *B*, and *D* are incorrect.

39. B: The first paragraph serves as a contrast to the second. Notice how the first paragraph goes into detail describing how insects are able to breathe air. The second paragraph acts as a contrast to the first by stating "[i]t is of great interest to find that, nevertheless, a number of insects spend much of their time under water." Watch for transition words such as "nevertheless" to help find what type of passage you're dealing with.

40: C: The stage of preparation in between molting is acted out in the water, while the last stage is in the air. Choices *A, B,* and *D* are all incorrect. *Instars* is the phase between two periods of molting, and the text explains when these transitions occur.

41. C: The author's tone is informative and exhibits interest in the subject of the study. Overall, the author presents us with information on the subject. One moment where personal interest is depicted is when the author states, "It is of great interest to find that, nevertheless, a number of insects spend much of their time under water."

42. C: Their larva can breathe the air dissolved in water through gills of some kind. This is stated in the last paragraph. Choice *A* is incorrect because the text mentions this in a general way at the beginning of the passage concerning "insects as a whole." Choice *B* is incorrect because this is stated of beetles and water-bugs, and not the insects in question. Choice *D* is incorrect because this is the opposite of what the text says of instars.

43. D: To enlighten the audience on the habits of sun-fish and their hatcheries. Choice *A* is incorrect because although the Adirondack region is mentioned in the text, there is no cause or effect relationships between the region and fish hatcheries depicted here. Choice *B* is incorrect because the text does not have an agenda, but rather is meant to inform the audience. Finally, Choice *C* is incorrect because the text says nothing of how sun-fish mate.

44. B: The word *wise* in this passage most closely means *manner*. Choices *A* and *C* are synonyms of *wise*; however, they are not relevant in the context of the text. Choice *D*, *ignorance*, is opposite of the word *wise*, and is therefore incorrect.

45. A: Fish at the stage of development where they are capable of feeding themselves. Even if the word *fry* isn't immediately known to the reader, the context gives a hint when it says "until the fry are hatched out and are sufficiently large to take charge of themselves."

46. B: The sun-fish builds it with her tail and snout. The text explains this in the second paragraph: "she builds, with her tail and snout, a circular embankment 3 inches in height and 2 thick." Choice *A* is used in the text as a simile.

47. D: To conclude a sequence and add a final detail. The concluding sequence is expressed in the phrase "[t]he mother sun-fish, having now built or provided her 'hatchery.'" The final detail is the way in which the sun-fish guards the "inclosure." Choices *A, B,* and *C* are incorrect.

48. C: *Extraneous* most nearly means *superfluous*, or *trivial*. Choice *A*, *indispensable*, is incorrect because it means the opposite of *extraneous*. Choice *B, bewildering*, means *confusing* and is not relevant to the context of the sentence. Finally, Choice *D* is wrong because although the prefix of the word is the same, *ex-*, the word *exuberant* means *elated* or *enthusiastic*, and is irrelevant to the context of the sentence.

49. A: Bring to light an alternative view on human perception by examining the role of technology in human understanding. This is a challenging question because the author's purpose is somewhat open-ended. The author concludes by stating that the questions regarding human perception and observation can be approached from many angles. Thus, they do not seem to be attempting to prove one thing or another. Choice B is incorrect because we cannot know for certain whether the electron experiment is the latest discovery in astroparticle physics because no date is given. Choice C is a broad generalization that does not reflect accurately on the writer's views. While the author does appear to reflect on opposing views of human understanding (Choice D), the best answer is Choice A.

50. C: It presents a problem, explains the details of that problem, and then ends with more inquiry. The beginning of this paragraph literally "presents a conundrum," explains the problem of partial understanding, and then ends with more questions, or inquiry. There is no solution offered in this paragraph, making Choices *A* and *B* incorrect. Choice *D* is incorrect because the paragraph does not begin with a definition.

51. D: Looking back in the text, the author describes that classical philosophy holds that understanding can be reached by careful observation. This will not work if they are overly invested or biased in their pursuit. Choices *A* and *C* are in no way related and are completely unnecessary. A specific theory is not necessary to understanding, according to classical philosophy mentioned by the author. Again, the key to understanding is observing the phenomena outside of it, without biased or predisposition. Thus, Choice *B* is wrong.

52. B: The electrons passed through both holes and then onto the plate. Choices *A* and *C* are wrong because such movement is not mentioned at all in the text. In the passage the author says that electrons that were physically observed appeared to pass through one hole or another. Remember, the electrons that were observed doing this were described as acting like particles. Therefore, Choice D is wrong. Recall that the plate actually recorded electrons passing through both holes simultaneously and hitting the plate This behavior, the electron activity that wasn't seen by humans, was characteristic of waves. Thus, Choice *B* is the right answer.

Writing and Language Test

1. D: This passage is informative (*D*) because it is nonfiction and factual. The passage's intent is not to state an opinion, discuss an individual's life, or tell a story. Thus, the passage is not argumentative (*A*), biographical (*C*), or narrative (*B*).

2. D: To begin, *of* is not required here. *Apprenticeship* is also more appropriate in this context than *apprentice opportunities*, *apprentice* describes an individual in an apprenticeship, not an apprenticeship itself. Both of these changes are needed, making (*D*) the correct answer.

3. D: To begin, the selected sentence is a run-on, and displays confusing information. Thus, the sentence does need revision, making (*A*) wrong. The main objective of the selected section of the passage is to communicate that many positions (*positions* is a more suitable term than *offices*, as well) require a PE license, which is gained by scoring well on the FE and PE assessments. This must be the primary focus of the revision. It is necessary to break the sentence into two, to avoid a run-on. Choice *B* fixes the run-on aspect, but the sentence is indirect and awkward in construction. It takes too long to establish the importance of the PE license. Choice *C* is wrong for the same reason and it is a run on. Choice *D* is correct because it breaks the section into coherent sentences and emphasizes the main point the author is trying to communicate: the PE license is required for some higher positions, it's obtained by scoring well on the two standardized assessments, and college and experience can be used to prepare for the assessments in order to gain the certification.

4. C: Any time a writer wants to validate a claim, he or she ought to provide factual information that proves or supports that claim: "beginning his or her preparation for the profession in high school" supports the claim that aircraft engineers undergo years of education. For this reason, Choice *C* is the correct response. However, completing such courses in high school does not guarantee that aircraft engineers will earn generous salaries (*A*), become employed in executive positions (*B*), or stay employed (*D*).

5. B: Choice *B* is correct because "skill" is defined as having certain aptitude for a given task. (*C*) is incorrect because "work" does not directly denote "critical thinking, business skills, problem solving, and creativity." (A) is incorrect because the word "care" doesn't fit into the context of the passage, and (D), "composition," is incorrect because nothing in this statement points to the way in which something is structured.

6. C: *Allows* is inappropriate because it does not stress what those in the position of aircraft engineers actually need to be able to do. *Requires* is the only alternative that fits because it actually describes necessary skills of the job.

7. B: The third paragraph discusses reports made by the United States Bureau of Labor Statistics (BLS) in regards to the median, upper 10 percent, and lower 10 percent annual salaries of aircraft engineers in 2015. Therefore, this paragraph is used to support the claim that aircraft engineers are compensated with generous salaries (B). The paragraph has nothing to do with an aircraft engineer's skill set (A), education (C), or incentive program (D).

8. A: The correct response is (A) because this statement's intent is to give examples as to how aircraft engineers apply mathematical equations and scientific processes towards aeronautical and aerospace issues and/or inventions. The answer is not "therefore" (B) or "furthermore" (D) because no causality is being made between ideas. Two items are neither being compared nor contrasted, so "however" (C) is also not the correct answer.

9. A: No change is required. The comma is properly placed after the introductory phrase "In May of 2015." Choice *B* is missing the word "in." Choice *C* does not separate the introductory phrase from the rest of the sentence. Choice *D* places an extra, and unnecessary, comma prior to 2015.

10. A: The word "conversely" best demonstrates the opposite sentiments in this passage. Choice *B* is incorrect because it denotes agreement with the previous statement. Choice C is incorrect because the sentiment is not restated but opposed. Choice *D* is incorrect because the previous statement is not a cause for the sentence in question.

11. A: Choice *A* is the correct answer because the projections are taking place in the present, even though they are making reference to a future date.

12. B: The passage contains clearly labeled subheadings. These subheadings inform the reader what will be addressed in upcoming paragraphs. Choice *A* is incorrect because the anti-terrorism laws of other countries were never addressed in the passage. The text is written in an informative manner; overly descriptive language is not utilized. Therefore, Choice *C* is incorrect. Choice *D* is incorrect because as mentioned, the structure of the text does help in the manner described in Choice *B*.

13. A: No change is needed. Choices *B* and *C* utilize incorrect comma placements. Choice *D* utilizes an incorrect verb tense (responding).

14. D: The third paragraph states "The majority of Muslims practice Islam peacefully". Therefore, the author explicitly states that most Muslims are peaceful peoples (D). Choices *B*, *C*, and *A* are not included in the passage and are incorrect.

15. B: The term "violate" implies a lack of respect or compliance. "Defile" means to degrade or show no respect. Therefore, (B) is the correct answer. Choice *A* is incorrect because "respect" is the opposite of violate. To "deny" is to refuse, so (C) is not the answer because the weight of the word "deny" is not as heavy as the word "violate." To "obey" is to follow orders, so (D) is not the answer.

16. B: An allusion is a direct or indirect literary reference or figure of speech towards a person, place, or event. By referencing the diversion of the airplanes to alternate locations, the author uses an allusion (Choice *B*) to highlight the impact of United Flight 93. Although a graph depicting the decline in the number of aircraft passengers is provided, an image is not. Therefore, Choice *A* is not the answer. The passage does not tell the story from a single passenger's point of view. Thus, Choice *C* and Choice *D* are not the answers.

17. C: All of the choices except (*C*) go with the flow of the original underlined portion of the sentence and communicate the same idea. Choice *C*, however, does not take into account the rest of the sentence and therefore, becomes awkward and incorrect.

18. B: Although "diverging" means to separate from the main route and go in a different direction, it is used awkwardly and unconventionally in this sentence. Therefore, Choice *A* is not the answer. Choice *B* is the correct answer because it implies that the passengers distracted the terrorists, which caused a change in the plane's direction. "Converging" (*C*) is incorrect because it implies that the plane met another in a central location. Although the passengers may have distracted the terrorists, they did not distract the plane. Therefore, Choice *D* is incorrect.

19. D: The graph shows the number of people (in millions) boarding United States' flights between 1996-2005. The graph includes a vertical red line that indicates the dip in the number people that boarded U.S. flights on September 11, 2001. Therefore, the graph illustrates the effects of suspending air travel immediately after the attacks (*D*). The graph does not show where the flights were redirected (*B*), the number of passengers that other countries received as a result of the redirected air travel (*C*), or the resulting flight schedule implications (Choice *A*).

20. B: The last paragraph explains that museums and monuments have been erected to honor those who died as a result of the attacks and those who risked their lives to save the injured. Thus, the paragraph serves to explain the lasting impact on America and honor those impacted by the event (*B*). The design of the museums and monuments are not described, so Choice *A* is incorrect. Choice *C* is incorrect because America's War on Terror was not discussed in the last paragraph. Choice *D* is incorrect, because although the previous location of the towers was converted into a park, this was not mentioned in the passage.

21. C: *Intended means planned or meant to. Intended is a far better choice than desired, because it would communicate goals and strategy more than simply saying that Bush desired to do something.* Desired communicates wishing or direct motive. Choices B and D have irrelevant meanings and wouldn't serve the sentence at all.

22. A: While (*B*) isn't necessarily wrong, it lacks the direct nature that the original sentence has. Also, by breaking up the sentences like this, the reader becomes confused because the connection between the Taliban's defeat and ongoing war is now separated by a second sentence that is not necessary. Choice *C* corrects this problem but the fluidity of the sentence is marred because of the awkward construction of the first sentence. Choice *D* begins well, but lacks the use of *was* before overthrown, which discombobulates the sentence. While *yet* provides an adequate transition for the next sentence, the term *however* is more appropriate. Thus, the original structure of the two sentences is correct, making Choice *A*, NO CHANGE, the correct answer.

23. A: The comma after *result* is necessary for the sentence structure, making it an imperative component. The original sentence is correct, making Choice *A* correct. For the reason just listed, Choice *B* is incorrect because it lacks the crucial comma that introduces a new idea. Choice *C* is incorrect because a colon is unnecessary, and Choice D is wrong because the addition of "of" is both unnecessary and incorrect when applied to the rest of the sentence.

24. C: To be "gifted" is to be talented. "Academically" refers to education. Therefore, Fred Hampton was intellectually talented, or intelligent (C). Choice B is incorrect because it refers to a level of energy or activity. Choice A is incorrect because "vacuous" means the opposite of being gifted academically. Choice D is incorrect because it refers to one's physical build and/or abilities.

25. C: The goal for this question is to select a sentence that not only affirms, or backs up, the selected statement, but could also appear after it and flows with the rest of the piece. Choice A is irrelevant to the sentence; just because new members earned scholarships this doesn't necessarily mean that this was testament of Hampton's leadership or that this actually benefitted the NAACP. Choice B is very compelling. If Hampton got an award for the increase in numbers, this could bolster the idea that he was the direct cause of the rise in numbers and that he was of great value to the organization. However, it does not say directly that he was the cause of the increase and that this was extremely beneficial to the NAACP. Let's keep looking. Choice C is a much better choice than Choice B. Choice C has the new members directly accrediting Hampton for his leadership; the fact that such new members went on to hold high positions is also testament to Hampton's leadership. Thus, Choice C is correct. Choice D does nothing for the underlined section.

26. B: Choice B moves the word "eventually" to the beginning of the sentences. By using the term as an introductory word, continuity from one sentence to another is created. Meanwhile, the syntax is not lost. Choice A is incorrect because the sentence requires a proper transition. Choice C is incorrect because the sentence does not contain surprising or contrasting information, as is indicated by the introductory word "nevertheless." Choice D is incorrect -because the term "then" implies that Hampton's relocation to the BPP's headquarters in Chicago occurred shortly or immediately after leading the NAACP.

27. D: An individual with a charismatic personality is charming and appealing to others. Therefore, Choice D is the correct answer. Choice A is incorrect because someone with an egotistical personality is conceited or self-serving. Choice B is incorrect because "obnoxious" is the opposite of charismatic. Choice C is incorrect because someone with a chauvinistic personality is aggressive or prejudiced towards one's purpose, desire, or sex.

28. A: No change is needed: Choice A. The list of events accomplished by Hampton is short enough that each item in the list can be separated by a comma. Choice B is incorrect. Although a colon can be used to introduce a list of items, it is not a conventional choice for separating items within a series. Semicolons are used to separate at least three items in a series that have an internal comma. Semicolons can also be used to separate clauses in a sentence that contain internal commas intended for clarification purposes. Neither of the two latter uses of semicolons is required in the example sentence. Therefore, Choice C is incorrect. Choice D is incorrect because a dash is not a conventional choice for punctuating items in a series.

29. D: Claims can be supported with evidence or supporting details found within the text. Choice D is correct because Choices A, B, and C are all either directly stated or alluded to within the passage.

30. A: The term *neutralize* means to counteract, or render ineffective, which is exactly what the FBI is wanting to do. Accommodate means to be helpful or lend aid, which is the opposite of *neutralize*. Therefore (B) is wrong. *Assuage* means to ease, while *praise* means to express warm feeling, so they are in no way close to the needed context. Therefore, *neutralize* is the best option, making Choice A, NO CHANGE, the correct answer.

31. B: The order of the original sentence suggests that the floor plans that were provided to the FBI by O'Neal enabled the FBI to identify the exact location of Hampton's bed. This syntax is maintained in Choice B. Therefore, Choice B is correct, which makes Choice A incorrect. Choice C is incorrect because the sentence's word order conveys the meaning that O'Neal provided the FBI with Hampton's bed as well as the floor plans. Choice D is incorrect because it implies that it was the location of the bed that provided the FBI with the headquarters' floor plans.

32. B: "Commemorates" means to honor, celebrate, or memorialize a person or event. Therefore, Choice B is correct. Choice A is incorrect because "disregards" is the opposite of "commemorates." Choice C is incorrect because to communicate means to converse or to speak. Choice D is incorrect because to "deny" means to reject, negate, refuse, or rebuff.

33. D: From the context of the passage, it is clear that the author does not think well of the FBI and their investigation of Hampton and the Black Panthers. Choices B and C can be easily eliminated. "Well intended" is positive, which is not a characteristic that he would probably attribute to the FBI in the passage. Nor would he think they were "confused" but deliberate in their methods.. Choice A, "corrupt", is very compelling; he'd likely agree with this, but Choice D, "prejudiced" is better. The FBI may not have been corrupt but there certainly seemed to have particular dislike/distrust for the Black Panthers. Thus, Choice D, "prejudiced", is correct.

34. D: All of the cities included in the graphs are along the East Coast of the United States. All of the bars on the graphs show an increase in sea level or the number of days with flood events since 1970. Therefore, the author chose to include the graphs to support the claim that sea levels have risen along the East Coast since 1970, choice D. Choice A and Choice B are incorrect because the bars above 1970 on Boston's graph and Atlantic City's graph are shorter than the graphs' bars above 1980. Therefore, between 1970-1980, both cities experienced an increase in the number of days with flood events. Choice C is incorrect because the bars increase in height on all of the cities' graphs, showing an increase in the number of days with floods along the entire East coast.

35. B: Although "affect" and "effect" sound the same, they have different meanings. "Affect" is used as a verb. It is defined as the influence of a person, place, or event on another. "Effect" is used as a noun. It is defined as the result of an event. Therefore, the latter ought to be used in the heading. For this reason, Choices C and D are incorrect. Because the effect is a result of the flood, a possessive apostrophe is needed for the singular noun "flood." For this reason, Choice A is incorrect and Choice B is correct.

36. D: Again, the objective for questions like this is to determine if a revision is possible within the choices and if it can adhere to the specific criteria of the question; in this case, we want the sentence to maintain the original meaning while being more concise, or shorter. Choice B can be eliminated. The meaning of the original sentence is split into two distinct sentences. The second of the two sentences is also incorrectly constructed. Choice C is very intriguing but there is a jumble of verbs present in: "Flooding occurs slowly or rapidly submerging" that it makes the sentence awkward and difficult to understand without the use of a comma after *rapidly*, making it a poor construction. Choice C is wrong. Choice D is certainly more concise and it is correctly phrased; it communicates the meaning message that flooding can overtake great lengths of land either slowly or very fast. The use of "Vast areas of land" infers that smaller regions or small areas can flood just as well. Thus, Choice D is a good revision that maintains the meaning of the original sentence while being concise and more direct. This rules out Choice *A* in the process.

37. B: In this sentence, the word *ocean* does not require an *s* after it to make it plural because "ocean levels" is plural. Therefore (A) and (C) are incorrect. Because the passage is referring to multiple – if not all ocean levels – *ocean* does not require an apostrophe (*'s*) because that would indicate that only one ocean is the focus, which is not the case. Choice *D* does not fit well into the sentence and, once again, we see that *ocean* has an *s* after it. This leaves Choice *B*, which correctly completes the sentence and maintains the intended meaning.

38. C: Choice *C* is the best answer because it most closely maintains the sentence pattern of the first sentence of the paragraph, which begins with a noun and passive verb phrase. Choice *A* and *C* are incorrect. Choice *B* is incorrect because it does not maintain the sentence pattern of the first sentence of the paragraph. Instead, Choice *B* shifts the placement of the modifying prepositional phrase to the beginning of the sentence. Choice *D* is incorrect because it does not maintain the sentence pattern established by the first sentence of the paragraph. Instead, Choice *D* is an attempt to combine two independent clauses.

39. A: Choice *C* can be eliminated because creating a new sentence with *not* is grammatically incorrect and it throws off the rest of the sentence. Choice *B* is wrong because a comma is definitely needed after *devastation* in the sentence. Choice *D* is also incorrect because "while" is a poor substitute for "although". *Although* in this context is meant to show contradiction with the idea that floods are associated with devastation. Therefore, none of these choices would be suitable revisions because the original was correct: NO CHANGE, Choice *A,* is the correct answer.

40. B: Choice *B* is the correct answer because the final paragraph summarizes key points from each subsection of the text. Therefore, the final paragraph serves as the conclusion. A concluding paragraph is often found at the end of a text. It serves to remind the reader of the main points of a text. Choice *A* is incorrect because the last paragraph does not just mention adverse effects of floods. For example, the paragraph states "By understanding flood cycles, civilizations can learn to take advantage of flood seasons." Choice *C* is incorrect; although the subheading mentions the drying of floods, the phenomena is not mentioned in the paragraph. Finally, Choice *D* is incorrect because no new information is presented in the last paragraph of the passage.

41. A: Idea and claims are best expressed and supported within a text through examples, evidence, and descriptions. Choice *A* is correct because it provides examples of rivers that support the tenth paragraph's claim that "not all flooding results in adverse circumstances." Choice *B* is incorrect because the sentence does not explain how floods are beneficial. Therefore, Choices *C* and *D* are incorrect.

42. D: In the sentence, *caused* is an incorrect tense, making (A) wrong. Choice *B* is incorrect because this used as a noun, we need *cause* in verb form. Choices *C* and *D* are very compelling. *Causing* (C) is a verb and it is in the present continuous tense, which appears to agree with the verb flooding, but it is incorrectly used. This leaves (D), *causes*, which does fit because it is in the indefinite present tense. Fitting each choice into the sentence and reading it in your mind will also reveal that (D), *causes*, correctly completes the sentence. Apply this method to all the questions when possible.

43. A: To *project* means to anticipate or forecast. This goes very well with the sentence because it describes how new technology is trying to estimate flood activity in order to prevent damage and save lives. "Project" in this case needs to be assisted by "to" in order to function in the sentence. Therefore, Choice *A* is correct. Choices *B* and *D* are the incorrect tenses. Choice *C* is also wrong because it lacks *to*.

44. C: *Picturesque* is an adjective used for an attractive, scenic, or otherwise striking image. Thus, Choice C is correct. Choice A is incorrect because although "colorful" can be included in a picturesque view, it does not encompass the full meaning of the word. Choice B is incorrect because "drab" is the opposite of "picturesque." Choice D is incorrect because "candid" is defined as being frank, open, truthful, or honest.

Math Test

1. B: First, subtract 4 from each side. This yields $6t = 12$. Now, divide both sides by 6 to obtain $t = 2$.

2. B: To be directly proportional means that $y = mx$. If x is changed from 5 to 20, the value of x is multiplied by 4. Applying the same rule to the y-value, also multiply the value of y by 4. Therefore, $y = 12$.

3. B: From the slope-intercept form, $y = mx + b$, it is known that b is the y-intercept, which is 1. Compute the slope as $\frac{2-1}{1-0} = 1$, so the equation should be $y = x + 1$.

4. A: Each bag contributes $4x + 1$ treats. The total treats will be in the form $4nx + n$ where n is the total number of bags. The total is in the form $60x + 15$, from which it is known $n = 15$.

5. D: Let a be the number of apples and o the number of oranges. Then, the total cost is $2a + 3o = 22$, while it also known that $a + o = 10$. Using the knowledge of systems of equations, cancel the o variables by multiplying the second equation by -3. This makes the equation $-3a - 3o = -30$. Adding this to the first equation, the o values cancel to get $-a = -8$, which simplifies to $a = 8$.

6. A: Finding the roots means finding the values of x when y is zero. The quadratic formula could be used, but in this case it is possible to factor by hand, since the numbers -1 and 2 add to 1 and multiply to -2. So, factor $x^2 + x - 2 = (x - 1)(x + 2) = 0$, then set each factor equal to zero. Solving for each value gives the values $x = 1$ and $x = -2$.

7. C: To find the y-intercept, substitute zero for x, which gives us $y = 0^{5/3} + (0 - 3)(0 + 1) = 0 + (-3)(1) = -3$.

8. A: This has the form $t^2 - y^2$, with $t = x^2$ and $y = 4$. It's also known that $t^2 - y^2 = (t + y)(t - y)$, and substituting the values for t and y into the right-hand side gives $(x^2 - 4)(x^2 + 4)$.

9. A: Simplify this to:

$$(4x^2 y^4)^{\frac{3}{2}} = 4^{\frac{3}{2}}(x^2)^{\frac{3}{2}}(y^4)^{\frac{3}{2}}$$

Now, $4^{\frac{3}{2}} = (\sqrt{4})^3 = 2^3 = 8$. For the other, recall that the exponents must be multiplied, so this yields:

$$8x^{2 \cdot \frac{3}{2}} y^{4 \cdot \frac{3}{2}} = 8x^3 y^6$$

10. B: Start by squaring both sides to get $1 + x = 16$. Then subtract 1 from both sides to get $x = 15$.

11. C: Multiply both sides by x to get $x + 2 = 2x$, which simplifies to $-x = -2$, or $x = 2$.

12. B: The independent variable's coordinate at the vertex of a parabola (which is the highest point, when the coefficient of the squared independent variable is negative) is given by $x = -\frac{b}{2a}$. Substitute and solve for x to get $x = -\frac{4}{2(-16)} = \frac{1}{8}$. Using this value of x, the maximum height of the ball (y), can be calculated. Substituting x into the equation yields $h(t) = -16\frac{1}{8}^2 + 4\frac{1}{8} + 6 = 6.25$.

13. D: Denote the width as w and the length as l. Then, $l = 3w + 5$. The perimeter is $2w + 2l = 90$. Substituting the first expression for l into the second equation yields $2(3w + 5) + 2w = 90$, or $8w = 80$, so $l = 10$. Putting this into the first equation, it yields $l = 3(10) + 5 = 35$.

14. A: Lining up the given scores provides the following list: 60, 75, 80, 85, and one unknown. Because the median needs to be 80, it means 80 must be the middle data point out of these five. Therefore, the unknown data point must be the fourth or fifth data point, meaning it must be greater than or equal to 80. The only answer that fails to meet this condition is 60.

15. B: If 60% of 50 workers are women, then there are 30 women working in the office. If half of them are wearing skirts, then that means 15 women wear skirts. Since none of the men wear skirts, this means there are 15 people wearing skirts.

16. A: Let the unknown score be x. The average will be $\frac{5 \cdot 50 + 4 \cdot 70 + x}{10} = \frac{530 + x}{10} = 55$. Multiply both sides by 10 to get $530 + x = 550$, or $x = 20$.

17. D: For manufacturing costs, there is a linear relationship between the cost to the company and the number produced, with a y-intercept given by the base cost of acquiring the means of production, and a slope given by the cost to produce one unit. In this case, that base cost is $50,000, while the cost per unit is $40. So, $y = 40x + 50,000$.

18. C: A die has an equal chance for each outcome. Since it has six sides, each outcome has a probability of $\frac{1}{6}$. The chance of a 1 or a 2 is therefore $\frac{1}{6} + \frac{1}{6} = \frac{1}{3}$.

19. A: The slope is given by $m = \frac{y_2 - y_1}{x_2 - x_1} = \frac{0 - 4}{0 - (-3)} = -\frac{4}{3}$.

20. C: The expected value is equal to the total sum of each product of individual score and probability. There are 36 possible rolls. The probability of rolling a 2 is $\frac{1}{36}$. The probability of rolling a 3 is $\frac{2}{36}$. The probability of rolling a 4 is $\frac{3}{36}$. The probability of rolling a 5 is $\frac{4}{36}$. The probability of rolling a 6 is $\frac{5}{36}$. The probability of rolling a 7 is $\frac{6}{36}$. The probability of rolling an 8 is $\frac{5}{36}$. The probability of rolling a 9 is $\frac{4}{36}$. The probability of rolling a 10 is $\frac{3}{36}$. The probability of rolling an 11 is $\frac{2}{36}$. Finally, the probability of rolling a 12 is $\frac{1}{36}$.

Each possible outcome is multiplied by the probability of it occurring. Like this:

$$2 \times \frac{1}{36} = a$$

$$3 \times \frac{2}{36} = b$$

$$4 \times \frac{3}{36} = c$$

And so forth.

Then all of those results are added together:

$$a + b + c \ldots = expected\ value$$

In this case, it equals 7.

21. A: The graph contains four turning points (where the curve changes from rising to falling or vice versa). This indicates that the degree of the function (highest exponent for the variable) is 5, eliminating Choices *C* and *D*. The y-intercepts of the functions can be determined by substituting 0 for x and finding the value of y. The function for Choice *A* has a y-intercept of 9, and the function for Choice *B* has a y-intercept of −9. Therefore, Choice *B* is eliminated.

22. C: $\frac{1}{3}$ of the shirts sold were patterned. Therefore, $1 - \frac{1}{3} = \frac{2}{3}$ of the shirts sold were solid. Anytime "of" a quantity appears in a word problem, multiplication should be used. Therefore, $192 \times \frac{2}{3} = \frac{192 \times 2}{3} = \frac{384}{3} = 128$ solid shirts were sold. The entire expression is $192 \times \left(1 - \frac{1}{3}\right)$.

23. A: Mean. An outlier is a data value that is either far above or far below the majority of values in a sample set. The mean is the average of all the values in the set. In a small sample set, a very high or very low number could drastically change the average of the data points. Outliers will have no more of an effect on the median (the middle value when arranged from lowest to highest) than any other value above or below the median. If the same outlier does not repeat, outliers will have no effect on the mode (value that repeats most often).

24. C: Line graph. The scenario involves data consisting of two variables, month, and stock value. Box plots display data consisting of values for one variable. Therefore, a box plot is not an appropriate choice. Both line plots and circle graphs are used to display frequencies within categorical data. Neither can be used for the given scenario. Line graphs display two numerical variables on a coordinate grid and show trends among the variables.

25. D: $\frac{1}{12}$. The probability of picking the winner of the race is $\frac{1}{4}$ $\left(\frac{number\ of\ favorable\ outcomes}{number\ of\ total\ outcomes}\right)$. Assuming the winner was picked on the first selection, three horses remain from which to choose the runner-up (these are dependent events). Therefore, the probability of picking the runner-up is $\frac{1}{3}$. To determine the probability of multiple events, the probability of each event is multiplied: $\frac{1}{4} \times \frac{1}{3} = \frac{1}{12}$.

26. C: Each number in the sequence is adding one more than the difference between the previous two. For example, $10 - 6 = 4, 4 + 1 = 5$. Therefore, the next number after 10 is $10 + 5 = 15$. Going forward, $21 - 15 = 6, 6 + 1 = 7$. The next number is $21 + 7 = 28$. Therefore, the difference between numbers is the set of whole numbers starting at 2: 2, 3, 4, 5, 6, 7....

27. D: The formula for finding the volume of a rectangular prism is $V = l \times w \times h$ where l is the length, w is the width, and h is the height. The volume of the original box is calculated: $V = 8 \times 14 \times 4 = 448 \text{ in}^3$. The volume of the new box is calculated: $V = 16 \times 28 \times 8 = 3584 \text{ in}^3$. The volume of the new box divided by the volume of the old box equals 8.

28. A: The notation i stands for an imaginary number. The value of i is equal to $\sqrt{-1}$. When performing calculations with imaginary numbers, treat i as a variable, and simplify when possible. Multiplying the binomials by the FOIL method produces $15 - 12i + 10i - 8i^2$. Combining like terms yields $15 - 2i - 8i^2$. Since $i = \sqrt{-1}$, $i^2 = (\sqrt{-1})^2 = -1$. Therefore, substitute -1 for i^2: $15 - 2i - 8(-1)$. Simplifying results in $15 - 2i + 8 \rightarrow 23 - 2i$.

29. C: The formula to find arc length is $s = \theta r$ where s is the arc length, θ is the radian measure of the central angle, and r is the radius of the circle. Substituting the given information produces $3\pi \text{ cm} = \theta 12 \text{ cm}$. Solving for θ yields $\theta = \frac{\pi}{4}$. To convert from radian to degrees, multiply the radian measure by $\frac{180}{\pi}$: $\frac{\pi}{4} \times \frac{180}{\pi} = 45^\circ$.

30. B: Given the area of the circle, the radius can be found using the formula $A = \pi r^2$. In this case, $49\pi = \pi r^2$, which yields $r = 7$ m. A central angle is equal to the degree measure of the arc it inscribes; therefore, $\angle x = 80^\circ$. The area of a sector can be found using the formula $A = \frac{\theta}{360^\circ} \times \pi r^2$. In this case, $A = \frac{80^\circ}{360^\circ} \times \pi(7)r^2 = 10.9\pi$ m.

31. D: SOHCAHTOA is used to find the missing side length. Because the angle and adjacent side are known, $\tan 60 = \frac{x}{13}$. Making sure to evaluate tangent with an argument in degrees, this equation gives $x = 13 \tan 60 = 13 \cdot 1.73 = 22.49$.

32. C: The sample space is made up of $8 + 7 + 6 + 5 = 26$ balls. The probability of pulling each individual ball is $\frac{1}{26}$. Since there are 7 yellow balls, the probability of pulling a yellow ball is $\frac{7}{26}$.

33. D: The addition rule is necessary to determine the probability because a 6 can be rolled on either roll of the die. The rule used is $P(A \text{ or } B) = P(A) + P(B) - P(A \text{ and } B)$. The probability of a 6 being individually rolled is $\frac{1}{6}$ and the probability of a 6 being rolled twice is $\frac{1}{6} \times \frac{1}{6} = \frac{1}{36}$. Therefore, the probability that a 6 is rolled at least once is $\frac{1}{6} + \frac{1}{6} - \frac{1}{36} = \frac{11}{36}$.

34. A: If each man gains 10 pounds, every original data point will increase by 10 pounds. Therefore, the man with the original median will still have the median value, but that value will increase by 10. The smallest value and largest value will also increase by 10 and, therefore, the difference between the two won't change. The range does not change in value and, thus, remains the same.

35. D: When an ordered pair is reflected over an axis, the sign of one of the coordinates must change. When it's reflected over the x-axis, the sign of the y coordinate must change. The x value remains the same. Therefore, the new ordered pair is $(-3, 4)$.

36. A: Because the volume of the given sphere is 288π cubic meters, this gives $^4/_3\,\pi r^3 = 288\pi$. This equation is solved for r to obtain a radius of 6 meters. The formula for surface area is $4\pi r^2$ so $SA = 4\pi 6^2 = 144\pi$ square meters.

37. B: A rectangle is a specific type of parallelogram. It has 4 right angles. A square is a rhombus that has 4 right angles. Therefore, a square is always a rectangle because it has two sets of parallel lines and 4 right angles.

38. B: The sine of 30° is equal to ½. Choice *A* is not the correct answer because the sine of 15° is .2588. Choice *C* is not the answer because the sine of 45° is .707. Choice *D* is not the answer because the sine of 90 degrees is 1.

39. C: The cosine of 45° is equal to .7071. Choice *A* is not the correct answer because the cosine of 15° is .9659. Choice *B* is not the correct answer because the cosine of 30° is .8660. Choice *D* is not correct because the cosine of 90° is 0.

40. B: The tangent of 30° is 1 over the square root of 3. Choice *A* is not the correct answer because the tangent of 15° is .2679. Choice *C* is not the correct answer because the tangent of 45° is 1. Choice *D* is not the correct answer because the tangent of 90° is undefined.

41. C: Graphing the function $y = \cos(x)$ shows that the curve starts at $(0, 1)$, has an amplitude of 2, and a period of 2π. This same curve can be constructed using the sine graph, by shifting the graph to the left $\frac{\pi}{2}$ units. This equation is in the form $y = \sin(x + \frac{\pi}{2})$.

42. A: Every 8 ml of medicine requires 5 mL. The 45 mL first needs to be split into portions of 8 mL. This results in $\frac{45}{8}$ portions. Each portion requires 5 mL. Therefore, $\frac{45}{8} \times 5 = \frac{45*5}{8} = \frac{225}{8}$ mL is necessary.

43. D: The midpoint formula should be used.
$$M = \left(\frac{x_1 + x_2}{2}, \frac{y_1 + y_2}{2}\right) = \left(\frac{-1 + 3}{2}, \frac{2 + (-6)}{2}\right) = (1, -2)$$

44. A: First, the sample mean must be calculated. $\bar{x} = \frac{1}{4}(1 + 3 + 5 + 7) = 4$. The standard deviation of the data set is $\sigma = \sqrt{\frac{\Sigma(x - \bar{x})^2}{n-1}}$, and $n = 4$ represents the number of data points. Therefore:

$$\sigma = \sqrt{\frac{1}{3}[(1 - 4)^2 + (3 - 4)^2 + (5 - 4)^2 + (7 - 4)^2]}$$

$$\sqrt{\frac{1}{3}(9 + 1 + 1 + 9)} = 2.58$$

45. B: An equilateral triangle has three sides of equal length, so if the total perimeter is 18 feet, each side must be 6 feet long. A square with sides of 6 feet will have an area of $6^2 = 36$ square feet.

46. A: The formula for the volume of a sphere is $\frac{4}{3}\pi r^3$, and $\frac{4}{3} \times \pi \times 3^3$ is 36 π in³. Choice *B* is not the correct answer because that is only 3^3. Choice *C* is not the correct answer because that is 3^2, and Choice *D* is not the correct answer because that is 36×2.

47. A: This answer is correct because $100 - 64$ is 36, and taking the square root of 36 is 6. Choice B is not the correct answer because that is $10 + 8$. Choice C is not the correct answer because that is 8×10. Choice D is also not the correct answer because there is no reason to arrive at that number.

48. A: The formula for the area of the circle is πr^2 and 9 squared is 81. Choice B is not the correct answer because that is 2×9. Choice C is not the correct answer because that is 9×10. Choice D is not the correct answer because that is simply the value of the radius.

49. B: 13,078. The power of 10 by which a digit is multiplied corresponds with the number of zeros following the digit when expressing its value in standard form. Therefore, $(1 \times 10^4) + (3 \times 10^3) + (7 \times 10^1) + (8 \times 10^0) = 10,000 + 3,000 + 70 + 8 = 13,078$.

50. A: Using the trigonometric identity $\tan(\theta) = \frac{\sin(\theta)}{\cos(\theta)}$, the expression becomes $\frac{\sin\theta}{\cos\theta}\cos\theta$. The factors that are the same on the top and bottom cancel out, leaving the simplified expression $\sin\theta$.

51. B: $\frac{11}{15}$. Fractions must have like denominators to be added. The least common multiple of the denominators 3 and 5 is found. The LCM is 15, so both fractions should be changed to equivalent fractions with a denominator of 15. To determine the numerator of the new fraction, the old numerator is multiplied by the same number by which the old denominator is multiplied to obtain the new denominator. For the fraction $\frac{1}{3}$, 3 multiplied by 5 will produce 15. Therefore, the numerator is multiplied by 5 to produce the new numerator $\left(\frac{1\times5}{3\times5} = \frac{5}{15}\right)$. For the fraction $\frac{2}{5}$, multiplying both the numerator and denominator by 3 produces $\frac{6}{15}$. When fractions have like denominators, they are added by adding the numerators and keeping the denominator the same: $\frac{5}{15} + \frac{6}{15} = \frac{11}{15}$.

52. B: $90° - 30° = 60°$. Choice A is not the correct answer because that is simply the original angle given. Choice C is not the correct answer since that is the angle you subtract from. Choice D is not the correct answer because that is $90° + 30°$.

53. A: $90° - 60° = 30°$. Choice B is not the correct answer because this is simply the original angle given. Choice C is not the correct answer since that is the angle you subtract from. Choice D is not the correct answer because that is $90° + 30°$.

54.

If a line is parallel to a side of a triangle and intersects the other two sides of the triangle, it separates the sides into corresponding segments of proportional lengths. To solve, set up a proportion: $\frac{AE}{AD} = \frac{AB}{AC} \rightarrow$ $\frac{4}{5} = \frac{5}{x}$. Cross multiplying yields $4x = 25 \rightarrow x = 6.25$.

55.

The fraction is converted so that the denominator is 100 by multiplying the numerator and denominator by 4, to get $\frac{3}{25} = \frac{12}{100}$. Dividing a number by 100 just moves the decimal point two places to the left, with a result of 0.12.

56.

30% is $\frac{3}{10}$. The number itself must be $\frac{10}{3}$ of 6, or $\frac{10}{3} \times 6 = 10 \times 2 = 20$.

57.

8 squared is 64, and 6 squared is 36. These should be added together to get $64 + 36 = 100$. Then, the last step is to find the square root of 100 which is 10.

58.

Because the 68-degree angle and angle b sum to 180 degrees, the measurement of angle b is 112 degrees. From the Parallel Postulate, angle b is equal to angle f. Therefore, angle f measures 112 degrees.

Dear PSAT Test Taker,

We would like to start by thanking you for purchasing this practice test book for your PSAT exam. We hope that we exceeded your expectations.

We strive to make our practice questions as similar as possible to what you will encounter on test day. With that being said, if you found something that you feel was not up to your standards, please send us an email and let us know.

We would also like to let you know about other books in our catalog that may interest you.

SAT

This can be found on Amazon: amazon.com/dp/1628455217

PSAT Study Guide

amazon.com/dp/1628455020

ACT

amazon.com/dp/1628454709

ACCUPLACER

amazon.com/dp/162845492X

AP Biology

amazon.com/dp/1628454989

CLEP College Composition

amazon.com/dp/1628454199

We have study guides in a wide variety of fields. If the one you are looking for isn't listed above, then try searching for it on Amazon or send us an email.

Thanks Again and Happy Testing!
Product Development Team
info@studyguideteam.com

Interested in buying more than 10 copies of our product? Contact us about bulk discounts:

bulkorders@studyguideteam.com

FREE Test Taking Tips DVD Offer

To help us better serve you, we have developed a Test Taking Tips DVD that we would like to give you for FREE. **This DVD covers world-class test taking tips that you can use to be even more successful when you are taking your test.**

All that we ask is that you email us your feedback about your study guide. Please let us know what you thought about it – whether that is good, bad or indifferent.

To get your **FREE Test Taking Tips DVD**, email freedvd@studyguideteam.com with "FREE DVD" in the subject line and the following information in the body of the email:

    a. The title of your study guide.

    b. Your product rating on a scale of 1-5, with 5 being the highest rating.

    c. Your feedback about the study guide. What did you think of it?

    d. Your full name and shipping address to send your free DVD.

If you have any questions or concerns, please don't hesitate to contact us at freedvd@studyguideteam.com.

Thanks again!

90008144R10115

Made in the USA
San Bernardino, CA
05 October 2018